THE PLANT-BASED COOKBOOK FOR BEGINNERS

2000-Days of Inspiring, Affordable, and Tasty Recipes and a 30-Day Smart Meal Plan to Build Healthy Habits on Your Table

JOSEPHINE HARMON

TABLE OF CONTENTS

INTRODUCTION

There are numerous benefits of a vegan diet, such as reducing the risk of heart disease and diabetes, lowering cholesterol levels and blood pressure, promoting weight loss, improving digestion, boosting energy levels and cognitive function, and increasing your strength and endurance.

But there's one huge advantage derived from a vegan diet: it reduces the amount of meat you eat. Meat is not only harmful to our health, but the production of meat is also an environmental hazard. Eating plant-based foods can reduce your carbon footprint significantly — even a small change to your diet can make a huge difference:

Every year, an individual whom adheres to a plant-based diet is responsible for sparing the lives of one animal, 1,100 gallons of water, 45 pounds of CO_2 equivalent, 15 square feet of land, and 15 square feet of forest.

This leads us to the conclusion that the best decision we can make is to cut out meat from our diet and replace it with plant-based foods. Living a healthy lifestyle begins with eating healthy foods, but when you eat animal products, you're potentially throwing away a lot of nutritious food by serving it up on your plate. It's time to shift our perception of what we consider food and start eating good foods instead.

There are many definitions of what constitutes "plant-based." Most people agree that plant-based foods do not contain animal products, but there is some disagreement about whether processed foods are allowed. However, on the whole, the focus of plant-based eating is vegetables and other plants.

The following is how to live a healthier lifestyle by eliminating meat from your diet and choosing to eat only plants instead!

- You will save money on groceries because a plant-based diet doesn't require many expensive items like eggs or dairy milk.
- You will lose weight because a plant-based diet causes you to burn fat rather than carbs.
- You will save the environment from being consumed by animals because a plant-based diet prevents you from consuming a large amount of meat, dairy, and eggs.
- You will become healthier because your body needs more nutrients from plants than it does from animal products.
- Your mental health will improve because avoiding animal products and the hormones, antibiotics, chemicals, and preservatives in them can help with mental health issues like anxiety and depression
- Your family's health will improve because you can teach your children better eating habits that are better for their organs.
- You won't be hurting animals because the animals on factory farms are kept in extremely inhumane conditions. They are treated like machines rather than living beings, so you will be doing them a favor by leaving them off your plate.
- You will promote kindness for animals by refusing to consume animal products and therefore promoting the kindness for animals that you would not be promoting if you still ate meat.
- Your risk of developing cardiovascular disease, diabetes, and possibly cancer can drop significantly if you stop eating meat. These diseases may sound scary at first, but they can be treated. If caught early enough, they even have a chance of being reversed.
- You will become a more effective leader because you have more knowledge than someone who eats meat. For example, you can talk to people about which foods are good for your body.

If you're new to the plant-based lifestyle, you may be overwhelmed by the number of cookbooks on the market. We've compiled a list of beginner-friendly recipes in order to simplify things for you! This way, whether you're looking for a protein-packed breakfast or simple snacks, we've got something that will suit your needs.

CHAPTER 1:

WHAT IS A PLANT-BASED DIET

The term "plant-based" is commonly used to differentiate vegetarian and vegan diets from other types of vegetarian diets that include eggs or dairy products. Many people adopt the plant-based diet for environmental reasons or because they have specific chronic illnesses that can be improved with this type of diet. Some common health benefits associated with a plant-based diet include weight loss, lowered cholesterol levels, and decreased blood sugar levels.

A vegan diet also excludes other animal products such as honey and beeswax. "Vegan" is derived from the word "vegetarian."

"Plant-based" does not mean that a person's diet must be devoid of any animal products such as meat or seafood. Many people simply prefer not to eat any meat and wish to consume dairy and/or eggs while consuming only vegetables, fruit, and legumes. Eggs and dairy can often be found on the menus at many restaurants, so a plant-based diet is more than just not eating meat.

The Difference Between Plant-Based and Vegan

A plant-based diet is any diet plan centered about plants. However, a vegan diet completely excludes animal products like meat, eggs, and dairy from their daily intake.

However, a vegan diet can be more advantageous as it may also provide protein in beans and peas — which are also rich in micronutrients like iron or calcium.

Both plant-based and vegan diets are low in cholesterol and saturated fats, making them heart-healthy options. They also help limit the intake of refined sugars and can improve blood sugar levels — which may help with weight management. Vegan diets exclude all animal products but still allow for sweets, refined flours, and other foods that contain toxins. Vegetarian diets typically allow dairy products and sweets, refined flours, white bread, and other man-made foods that are full of artificial ingredients that may harm health. Think of the whole-food, plant-based diet as the cleanest vegan diet possible.

CHAPTER 2:

LIST OF THE MOST COMMON VEGETARIAN PRACTICES

Fruitarian

A fruitarian is someone who lives on a diet composed primarily or exclusively of fruits, nuts, and seeds. They might eat vegetables but not in as great quantities as other types of vegetarians, depending on the intensity of their fruitarian lifestyle. Many fruitarians follow a completely vegan diet, eating no animal byproducts, including meat and dairy products. However, there is no standardization in these terms. Like vegans, the fruitarian will not consume any form of meat or dairy, but the vast majority of these people consume eggs and honey. There are also more moderate and less strict fruitarians who may eat small amounts of eggs and/or honey.

Vegan

What does it mean to be vegan? A vegan is someone who chooses not to consume (or use) any animal products whatsoever; this includes any meat (including poultry), dairy products, eggs or honey — even if they are organic or local. Vegans generally avoid products that have been tested on animals, even products that are labeled as vegetarian. There is so much to learn about the vegan lifestyle. Not only is it a diet that does not harm animals, but it's also one that excludes all animal products — meat, dairy, and eggs. There are many types of veganism with varying degrees of strictness, but they're all relatively similar in their environmental impact and ethical values.

Lacto-Vegetarian

A Lacto-vegetarian is someone who's not a vegetarian but still eats dairy and eggs. They sometimes also eat meat that comes from animals that were raised on farms by humans. What does be dairy and egg-free have to do with cooking?

Well, since they aren't vegetarians, this often means lacto-vegetarians are more than willing to experiment with different types of meat or animal products. That makes them ideal for people who want to try veganism as well as people who enjoy the freedom of doing foods like bacon without feeling guilty about it.

Being a Lacto-vegetarian can also make it much easier to be vegan. Many lacto-vegetarians and vegans have found they can use eggs, cheese, and dairy substitutes to replicate many foods that would normally contain meat. That way, they can enjoy some of the same foods while not really needing to deal with tasting or eating meat.

Lacto-Ovo-Vegetarian

You'll be incorporating plenty of fruits, veggies, whole grains, nuts and seeds, but cheese and eggs are also included in this well-balanced food plan.

That means it's perfect for people who are used to eating animal protein but don't want to give up their favorite foods. It's also a great diet if you're an advocate for healthy eating but need to cut down on animal protein consumption.

Peach-Vegetarian

A strict vegan will exclude all animal by-products such as eggs, dairy, and honey. A vegetarian will exclude red meat and poultry but not fish or eggs. A peach-vegetarian would eliminate red meat, poultry, dairy, and fish from their diet but still consume eggs and honey.

The term 'peach' reflects the idea that people who have chosen this type of diet might pursue a more pleasurable vegetarian lifestyle because they are open to eating foods that many vegetarians find off-limits — namely fruits such as peaches. The word 'vegetarian' refers to this lifestyle, not the food that a person eats.

Partially-Vegetarian

A partially vegetarian diet hinges on the level of consumption of animal flesh. Some people adopt this type of diet to reduce their intake of animal protein while maintaining a non-vegan lifestyle for other reasons or as a transitional step to veganism. People who follow a partially-vegetarian diet include pescatarians, lacto-ovo-vegetarians, and lacto-vegetarians. Each of these categories is based on the level of animal consumption that the individual engages in. The decision to adopt a partially-vegetarian diet is usually made for health reasons such as lower cholesterol levels or weight loss.

In fact, over 2/3 of grown-ups in the US are either vegetarians or have reduced their meat consumption. Nowadays, vegetarianism is not just for weight loss; it has become a way to change your life and make a powerful statement about sustainability. That being said, most people don't know how to maintain this lifestyle without causing themselves serious dietary deprivation.

The Vegetarian Resource Group states that anyone who is vegetarian and works out daily should consume a minimum of 2000 calories a day. With that said, if you're eating meatless meals five days a week, that leaves you with 2200 calories to add to your diet every day. If you are following the [Fruitarian Diet], which is essentially all fruit, 100% of those calories should come from fruits/vegetables. In addition, according to the Fruitarian Diet website, a fruitarian's caloric needs can be met by eating about 150-250 grams of fruit each day.

While this diet plan is one of the more restrictive ones featured on this site, it can be done with little to no exercise. However, depending on your current weight and training regimen, you may have to carefully watch how many calories you consume just in fruit.

If you're already on a strict vegan or vegetarian diet and want to try becoming fully fruitarian, you should slowly transition into the diet over several weeks. However, if you don't feel comfortable eating a completely raw diet (most people don't), cooked foods such as stews and smoothies are allowed on this diet as long as they are derived primarily from fruit.

CHAPTER 3:

WHAT A PLANT-BASED DIET DOES TO OUR BODIES

The benefits of a plant-based diet are abundantly clear, and it is something more people should consider incorporating into their lives.

Benefits for doing this type of diet:

- Reduced total fat and energy intake
- Blood pressure is generally lower
- Reduced risk of heart disease
- Lower digestive problems

- Reduced risk of certain cancers
- Reduced risk of kidney disease
- Good mental health

A plant-based diet can be better for your mental health by reducing the risk of depression, anxiety, and other mood disorders. It can also help you live longer by minimizing the risk of developing certain chronic diseases.

This diet also helps reduce your intake of saturated fats and cholesterol and hormones, which can all help lower blood pressure. You also consume more protective vitamins, minerals, antioxidants, and phytochemicals that help your body fight chronic disease. This can help you avoid the need for medication or surgery in the future.

Having a plant-based diet during pregnancy has been linked to reducing the risks of certain chronic ailments, such as heart disease in the mother later in life, increasing birth weights, and decreasing the risk of preterm labor.

The diet should include: fruits, vegetables, nuts, seeds, avocado, olive oil, and non-GMO grains.

Eating an unprocessed food diet predominantly from whole plant-based foods like fruits and vegetables can help reduce your risk of autoimmune illnesses such as Hashimoto's disease or rheumatoid arthritis.

A plant-based diet can also reduce your risk of developing certain types of tumors, such as prostate cancer or breast cancer.

Plant foods also contain a lot of fiber, which can help your digestion. Soluble fiber helps lower cholesterol, and insoluble fiber can help you feel full between meals to potentially suppress your appetite.

On the other hand, foods derived from animals tend to be heavy in both fat and cholesterol, which can increase the likelihood that a person will get heart disease. They additionally contain a relatively less amount of dietary fiber and meals derived from plants.

Vegetarian diets can range from lacto-ovo vegetarianism (eating dairy products and eggs) to veganism (excluding all animal products).

This type of diet is also helpful for people who are diabetic because it has been shown to lower their insulin levels as well as help them lose weight. They also have an easier time controlling their diabetes by eating a balanced meal that can help them avoid spikes in blood sugar, a common problem with traditional diabetic diets. The high fiber and plant foods also help to stabilize blood sugar levels.

You still need to have a healthy lifestyle by exercising regularly, staying hydrated, avoiding refined sugars and processed foods, and managing stress.

A plant-based diet can also be incorporated into other eating patterns, such as the Paleolithic (or caveman) diet as long as you include mostly plants in your diet, but other types of diets may differ depending on what nutrients you are looking for. You may have heard of the Mediterranean Diet or the Diabetes Diet, which incorporates whole grains and vegetables and omega-3 fatty acids. You can also eat a vegan diet if you prefer daily meals prepared from raw, living, vegan foods. When adopting a plant-based regime, you have the opportunity to include more fruits and vegetables into your daily diet and, at the same time, remove meat, dairy products, eggs, fish and seafood. It also helps to increase your lifespan by slashing the risk of developing certain diseases.

Some Tips to Help You Start a Plant-Based Diet

It's not about just giving up meat, but rather making a lifestyle change that will improve your health and the environment. These are just suggestions that you can use in your own way. Instead of becoming more plant-based overnight, take it slowly and enjoy the fruits of your labor!

- Start with one meal per day first. Start with a smaller amount of meat or other animal products, then build up as desired.
- Experiment with all the available plant-based meals. Try a good variety of grains, fruits, vegetables, legumes, or chickpeas that are low in fat content.
- Find recipes online or in books at the library. You can find many veggie recipes online by just searching on Google!
- Look for ingredients that you recognize and can pronounce.
- Buy fresh seasonal fruits and vegetables. Although they may cost a bit more, they're better for you because they absorb more nutrients from the ground. Your body will thank you with fewer stomach aches!

CHAPTER 4:

RULES TO FOLLOW AND THINGS TO KNOW ABOUT THE PLANT-BASED DIET

The word diet is often a trigger for those that are looking to lose or maintain their weight by limiting certain elements in their diets. These individuals often find it helpful to understand what they should and should not be putting in their bodies. Gluten-free diets and other such dietary regimens are also basically plant-based. Some foods are animal products from livestock like cows or poultry or human products like eggs (and sometimes dairy). The health benefits of this type of diet include reduced risk for heart disease and cancer along with lowered cholesterol levels. It is a more environmentally sound diet to follow, and it is also generally a diet that, once adhered to for a period of time, can prove to be permanent.

While there are many different guidelines for following this type of diet, we will find some common features in all, which include:

- Eating a well-balanced and varied diet consisting only of plant products in order to receive adequate nutrition.
- Avoiding all processed meats, including bologna, sausage, bacon, etc., and all fast foods that often contain animal products or high levels of salt. This includes foods such as donuts and cakes that generally aren't made with animal products but do have high-fat content and very little nutritional value.
- Eating whole plant foods instead of processed foods.   This means brown rice instead of white rice, whole wheat bread instead of white bread, fruits and vegetables containing more fiber as well as fewer calories.
- Including fresh fruits and vegetables in your daily diet in order to receive your required nutrients.

Many people notice that losing weight proves to be easier on a plant-based diet. This means that while those following other diets might have to count calories or restrict portions, those adhering to a plant-based diet generally don't have to and can still lose weight.

Following a plant-based diet offers numerous health benefits as well as being good for the environment. Eating organic is encouraged when possible, and it is important not only to eat locally grown foods but also to do so seasonally.

In addition, it is essential to give special attention to how animals are raised, including free-ranging, humanely slaughtered, and processed in a way that should be as healthful for them as possible. It is also helpful to think about what you will do if the meat or dairy products you were used to eating were suddenly banned (which has happened with some products in the past). Planning for this can allow most people to continue living their lives without any major adjustments.

Do your own research, ask questions and be sure to take a good vitamin B12 supplement if you don't eat any animal products.

You can do this by finding out what foods contain B12, calcium and iron so that you can substitute these items in your diet with plant-based sources.

CHAPTER 5:

TIPS ON HOW TO CHOOSE, TREAT AND ENHANCE INGREDIENTS BASED ON THEIR FUNCTIONAL BUT ALSO NUTRITIONAL CHARACTERISTICS

Tips

1. Choose organic ingredients rather than those that have been grown with pesticides and other chemicals. They are usually more expensive, but it's worth it when you think about the health of your family and yourself.
2. Enhance the flavor of foods with herbs such as parsley, celery leaves, cilantro or basil; fresh garlic; rosemary; bay leaves; fresh ginger root or hot peppers (if desired). For meats, make sure to use lots of salt and pepper.
3. Increase the nutritional value of foods by adding a good source of vitamins and minerals such as nuts, seeds, dried fruits, legumes, or oils. For example: almonds (mainly calcium) and sesame seeds (mainly iron). Also, take care with your choices. Try avoiding food products containing added sugars since they will only make you fat.
4. Processed foods are usually high in sodium, and the same thing happens to salt when it is added to food. Therefore, try to limit processed foods such as canned vegetables, ready-made sauces, breads, or pastries. On the other hand, fresh vegetables are easier to digest, so you will probably benefit from them more often.
5. You should try to consume seasonal foods. It not only makes them more affordable, but you will probably benefit from their flavor and nutritional content.
6. Cook with homemade broth rather than adding salt.
7. Foods can be treated after cooking to enhance their flavor, such as: sautéing; reposado (i.e., ripening) or curing; marinating or pickling.
8. If the recipe calls for a small amount of any ingredient, try adding it at the very end so that a rich aroma won't escape.
9. Try substituting foods with similar textures and flavor.
10. Use fresh ingredients rather than canned or frozen ones.
11. Try to vary your cooking style and recipes for a healthier approach based on seasonal availability.
12. Try new recipes.
13. Take care while preparing food because it might be easy to cut yourself when you are in the process of chopping or slicing ingredients.
14. Add something crunchy to salad recipes such as romaine lettuce or cabbage and raw veggies like carrots, celery, cucumber and jicama.
15. Choose lean meats but don't forget the fat content since it has been shown that fat is the most effective energy source for the brain when exercising. Therefore, make sure that the meat is cooked at a higher temperature and keep an eye on the cooking time to avoid undercooking.
16. If the recipe you are making calls for cooking food in oil, keep in mind that oils have different fat contents. You can use vegetable oil when frying and olive oil for baking and roasting.
17. Choose fruits and vegetables with similar nutritional qualities such as a dark color (vegetables) or high-water content (fruits), especially if they are in season.

18. Use your imagination to combine foods for different textures and tastes, such as herbs with various nuts; olive oil with vegetables; apples, carrots, or pears with meats or cheeses.
19. Try to avoid fried food recipes because they contain a lot of bad fats and use small amounts if you have no other choice.
20. When possible, make sure that the water used for boiling vegetables (e.g., potatoes) is replaced with homemade broth since it has more flavor and nutrients than plain water.
21. Make sure to distinguish between different types of salt: table salt; sea salt; kosher salt; mineral salts and flavored salts, and don't forget that sodium is added to commercial products.
22. Choose lean cuts of meat such as chicken breast, turkey or pork loin, cut off excess fat when possible, and try different preparation methods such as roasting or grilling so that the meat will stay juicy while maintaining its flavor.
23. Cook with a variety of cooking methods (i.e., roasting, frying, boiling and grilling).
24. Use the right tools for the job, such as a good sharp knife (check out your local kitchen store), and don't forget to use heat resistant gloves when using hot oil on the stove.
25. Try not to overcook food since it will result in a dry product and it will be harder to digest.

Precautions to Avoid Nutritional Deficiencies with a Plant-based Diet

1. You can be at risk for vitamin B12 deficiency: If you're not taking B12 supplementation, eat more seaweed, beans, tofu or tempeh.
2. Not getting enough protein can lead to muscle loss: Eat more beans, whole grains, soy products or nuts and seeds. If you're not eating enough calories to gain weight, try eating between two and three servings of whole grains per day.
3. Iron deficiency: If you don't like spinach or other iron-rich foods, eat more beans, lentils, soybeans, tofu or whole grains.
4. Zinc deficiency: Eat beans and grains for dinner at least several nights a week.
5. Calcium deficiency: Eat more tofu or soy products and leafy green vegetables (like kale).
6. Omega-3 fatty acid deficiency: Eat one to two tablespoons of ground flaxseeds per day in addition to your regular diet. You could also eat walnuts, chia seeds or canola oil for healthy fats as well.

CHAPTER 6:

VEGETABLE SOURCES OF VITAMINS AND MINERALS

Vegetables are an important component of a healthy diet and are the most affordable way to get your daily recommended number of essential vitamins and minerals.

The most well-known vegetables for their nutritional value are dark leafy greens, such as spinach and kale. Carrots, corn, asparagus, avocados, and sweet potatoes also contain a variety of nutrients.

Animal proteins, such as meat and dairy products, or fish, can contain high levels of vitamins A and D. However, fiber—found in legumes—may contain up to 10 times the amount of vitamin E found in animal foods.

Dairy products, especially milk and cheese, account for the greatest portion of total calcium intake in the US population (79% of daily calcium added in food). Other sources include tofu (a good source of calcium), enriched soymilk (a good source), almonds (a great source), and fortified cereal products like orange juice or soy milk (very good sources).

It's not surprising that dark greens, such as kale and spinach, are good sources of iron—as are dried beans, lentils, and chickpeas.

Potassium is primarily found in fruit and vegetables, such as bananas, prunes, dried apricots, and oranges, but it can also be found in some mineral-rich whole grains.

Two widely-underused sources of vitamin A are carrots and sweet potatoes. The beta-carotene found in these orange vegetables is converted to vitamin A in the body, so they're great for good vision.

Foods that provide dietary fiber, vitamins, and minerals are vital to health. Many of these foods are available in grocery stores across the country. But there are other options in areas where a variety of fresh fruits and vegetables may not be available or affordable.

In addition to eating fresh produce, people can purchase frozen or canned vegetables. Frozen vegetables can be just as nutritious as fresh ones—and canned, or "crisper pack" vegetables are a great last resort—because they can be kept for up to one year without losing much of their nutritional value. Finally, people who live in remote areas that lack access to grocery stores may benefit from the USDA's food distribution program, which helps low-income families receive boxes each month with food items that meet the daily recommended amounts of nutrients.

Have a discussion with your primary care provider regarding your eating habits as a whole, and figure out which ways you can assist yourself in remaining healthy by supplying your body with the nutrients and minerals it requires. It's cheaper than ever before to do so; there simply aren't that many things to worry about.

Essential Vitamins and Minerals for Those Who Follow This Diet

Many people who follow a plant-based diet are concerned about getting enough vitamins and minerals from their food. This is because many of the most significant sources of these nutrients, such as meat, fish, poultry, and dairy products, are off-limits to them. But don't stress! Plenty of high-quality vegetables can make up for these missing nutrients in your diet. Here is a list of the most essential vegan-friendly sources of various vitamins and minerals.

Meat Eaters Plant-eaters

1. Vitamin A

- Beta carotene: Broccoli, carrots, cantaloupe, sweet potatoes, kale, spinach.
- Vitamin A: Carrots and dark green leafy vegetables (e.g., broccoli and kale)
- Recommended daily intake for women: 900 mcg RAE. Recommended daily intake for men: 800 mcg RAE. Percent of recommended daily intake in one cup of cooked carrots: 105%
- Percent of recommended daily intake in one cup of cooked spinach: 54%

2. Vitamin B12 (cobalamin)

- Protein from fortified soy products can be used by the body to synthesize B12. No supplemental B12 is required for vegans.
- However, if you consume a lot of foods that do not naturally contain added B12, and that do not have a good source of B12 (such as grains) and are eating a diet that is low in animal products, it's recommended to include foods fortified with B12 in your vegan meal plans.
- Recommended daily intake: 2 mcg for men; 1.5 mcg for women. Percent of recommended daily intake in one cup of cooked kale: 97% (source).

3. Vitamin D

- Vitamin D: The body produces vit D through cholesterol elements obtained from diets derived from animals when it is exposed to sunlight. Recommended daily intake for women: 600 IU RAE. Recommended daily intake for men: 600 IU RAE [CURRENT RECOMMENDATIONS]. In an ideal world, adults would receive regular sun exposure. This is not likely to happen while living in modern society, though many people have tried.
- The majority of vitamin D comes from foods that naturally contain fat-soluble vitamin D (such as fatty fish and oily fish). In regards to vegan diets, it is recommended to use a vitamin D supplement if you do not get regular sun exposure. This is because vitamin D3 from titrated sunlight would not yield enough vitamin D for sufficient oral intake.
- Recommended daily intake: 600 IU RAE. Percent of recommended daily intake in one cup of cooked kale: 97%

4. Vitamin E

- The richest sources of vitamin E come from nuts and seeds: almonds, cashews, sunflower seeds, pumpkin seeds, and walnuts. Recommended daily intake for women: 40 IU RAE · Recommended daily intake for men: 35 IU RAE. Percent of recommended daily intake in one cup of cooked kale: 9%

5. Vitamin K

- Vitamin K is found in leafy greens such as spinach and collards. Recommended daily intake for women: 120 mcg EU. Recommended daily intake for men: 90 mcg EU [RDA + ARA]

CHAPTER 7:

SUPERFOODS

To be clear, most superfoods are already vegan, but some are particularly high in nutrient content. The following are the top vegan superfoods available today. These should be incorporated into your diet every chance you get. These are 10 of the best superfoods that you will find at your local grocery store.

Dark Leafy Greens

These superfoods should be incorporated into your daily meal plan. They are not only a great digestive aid due to their high-fiber content, but they're also dense sources of vitamins C and K, zinc, calcium, magnesium, iron, and folate. They have a high antioxidant profile that assists the body in removing harmful free radicals.

Berries

These nature's little antioxidants are also the most delicious and delicate fruits we know. Berries host an array of benefits to the body, and each one has its special powers:

- Strawberries contain more vitamin C than oranges! They are antioxidant-rich and provide us with fiber, potassium, anthocyanins, and folate. Strawberries reduce the risk of cancer, are supportive in the control of diabetes, and are great anti-inflammatories.
- They contain manganese and vitamins C and K, are supportive of cognitive function and mental health.
- Raspberries are rich in vitamin C, selenium, and phosphorus.
- Research shows they are beneficial in controlling blood sugar in people with diabetes. They are a great source of quercetin known to slow the onset and growth of cancer cells.
- Blackberries are incredibly high in antioxidants and fiber and are loaded with phytochemicals that fight cancer. They are also packed with vitamin C and K.

Nuts and Seeds

They are incredibly nutrient-dense and contain excellent levels of fats, protein, complex carbs, and fiber. They are loaded with vitamins and minerals which are easily absorbed and fun to eat, while at the same time help to protect our bodies against disease. Every nut and seed have their special traits:

- Pine nuts have an excess amount of manganese.
- Brazil nuts are the leading source of selenium.
- Pistachios are well known for their lutein content that supports eye health.
- Almonds and sunflower seeds are great sources of vitamin E.
- Cashews have more iron than any other food in this category.
- Pumpkin seeds are one of the best possible sources of zinc.

Olive Oil

A staple of the Mediterranean diet for a reason, this oil is rich in antioxidants and monounsaturated fats that support cardiovascular health, prevent strokes and feed your hair and skin like nothing else. Despite being fat, it supports healthy weight maintenance.

Mushrooms

The best vegan meat source; it is low in calories while being high in protein and fiber. They're a great source of vitamins B, vitamin D, potassium, and selenium. High in antioxidants, support healthy gut bacteria, and are beneficial in weight loss.

THE PLANT-BASED COOKBOOK FOR BEGINNERS

Seaweed

Used in medicine for centuries, seaweed has antiviral properties and has recently been tested positively in killing certain cancer cells. Seaweed benefits cholesterol levels and is rich in antioxidants proven to lower the instance of heart disease. Seaweed is incredibly rich in vitamin A, C, D, E, and K, and B vitamins. It's brimming with iron and iodine, essential for thyroid function, and has decent amounts of calcium, copper, potassium, and magnesium.

Garlic

Garlic is a powerful medicinal ally to have on hand. It is rich in vitamins B6 and C, but most importantly, it boosts immune function, lowers blood pressure, improves cholesterol levels, and supports cardiovascular health. Fresh garlic is brimming with antioxidants that have a potent effect on overall health.

Avocado

Avocado is a great source of MUFAs (Mono-Unsaturated Fatty Acids), a huge factor in cardiovascular function. They support vitamin and mineral absorption, healthy skin, hair, and eyes, improved digestive function, and contain 20 vitamins and minerals. Avocados provide anti-inflammatory activity and are loaded with soluble fiber.

Turmeric

Highly anti-inflammatory and has potent anti-cancer properties. It has been shown to provide pain relief in arthritic conditions and supports liver health due to its high antioxidant levels. Turmeric can be hard to absorb; however, taking it with black pepper improves its absorptivity.

Chia Seeds

They are antioxidant-rich and packed with protein, calcium, iron, and soluble fiber. Due to this, they are recommended to reduce cardiovascular disease, diabetes, and obesity. They are healing to the digestive tract, contribute to feelings of fullness so support weight loss, help lower cholesterol, and best of all, when mixed with water, they make a great egg substitute.

CHAPTER 8:

SELF-PRODUCTION

Self-production food for plants is when the plant grows in your own garden or on your property. You then harvest the produce yourself, taking care to leave some behind for planting the next year. A few plants that fall under this category are tomatoes, green beans, peas, peppers, eggplant and okra.

A plant-based diet excludes any animal products like meat, dairy, or eggs from our diet and instead focuses on vegetable options like beans and grains with some fruits mixed in.

In order to explain what self-production foods are and make this easy to understand, I will be dividing the list into three groupings - fruits, vegetables, and legumes. (I will also show where you can find this type of product on the market.)

Fruits

The main fruit you will find in self-production veggies is tomato. Tomatoes are grown in a garden setting, but they are also commercially available at many different places, including farmers markets, grocery stores and even on dedicated farms. Tomatoes can be bought fresh from a hydroponic greenhouse or from your local grocery store.

Another fruit that can be grown in a garden is green beans. Green beans can be grown in pots or directly from seeds. You can also buy green beans from your local grocery store or farmers' market. The market will probably have different types of beans, including bush and pole type green beans, to choose from.

Grain-based veggies like lettuce, spinach, and kale are all typically grown in the garden. Grab a plant that you find growing on your property and harvest them at the peak of its season. You will most likely find these leafy greens at your local farmers' market or grocery store too.

Vegetables

Peppers are also typically garden plants, but some can be found in a hydroponic greenhouse. They have many varieties that are grown on the market, including bell peppers, jalapeno, poblano, Serrano, etc.

Eggplant is another plant that can be grown on your property. You can find eggplant at most grocery stores and farmers' markets, even though you will find more varieties at the farmers market compared to the stores. Some of these varieties include white eggplant, baby eggplant, and Asian eggplant, just to name a few.

Moi (pronounced "moy") is a type of vegetable usually grown in a hydroponic greenhouse and not directly from seeds. They are typically orange in color and look similar to bell peppers. They can also be found at your local farmers' market or grocery store, but they are more expensive than bell peppers since they are hydroponic produce. Okra is also a plant that can be grown in the garden. They are an edible green vegetable that has a mucilaginous texture. You can find okra at your local grocery store and farmers' market.

CHAPTER 9:

REASONS WHY PEOPLE CHOOSE THIS LIFESTYLE

While you may hear a lot about the latest diet fads, some of which come and go, the dietary decisions you make could have a significant bearing on how well you take care of your body. When people choose to adopt a plant-based diet lifestyle they are considering both their physical and emotional well-being. The benefits of this type of diet are numerous, including:

- Lower levels of saturated fat
- Reduced risk for heart disease and diabetes
- More fiber than most other diets offer — leading to lower levels of cholesterol

What's more? This lifestyle is also easy on the environment. Choosing to eat a plant-based diet means you get more of your nutrients from natural sources, which also minimizes food waste.

If you're considering a plant-based diet, here are some of the most important things to keep in mind as you transition:

1. Get educated about your new lifestyle. Learn what types of foods you can eat – and which to avoid – so that you don't unknowingly derail your new way of eating.
2. Plan by stocking your kitchen with familiar staples like beans, lentils, leafy greens and veggies.
3. Exercise. Regular exercise is crucial to eating a healthy plant-based diet! Healthy foods tend to be calorie-dense, so if you eat a vegan diet, you will need to replace your regular calorie intake with calorie-dense foods that are rich in fiber (such as vegetables and fruits) or fat (nuts and seeds).
4. Prepare meals in advance, so you don't become overtired from too much shopping, cooking and eating.
5. Try to bring plant-based food into your social life. Many restaurants and cafes have vegan options. Ask them to make a specific dish with no meat or dairy. You might be surprised at how many places they can accommodate you!
6. Remember that it takes time for your body to adjust and reach a point of balance and there should be a period of adjustment in which you go through some mild discomfort so that you can get used to the foods you want to consume.
7. As part of your transition, be sure to eat regularly (at least three meals a day).
8. Keep a food journal so that you keep track of your progress as you go along.
9. Eat a healthy diet of whole foods, such as fruits, vegetables, beans, lentils and whole grains, so that you can be assured of getting the right amount of nutrients on a daily basis.

CHAPTER 10:

WHY WFPB?

The WFPB is a diet that promotes whole foods, plant-based foods, and healthy oils. This diet prohibits processed foods and any animal products. Keeping this in mind, this section will explore how WFPB diets lead to weight loss while improving one's health.

"Do you want to live longer? Do you want to lose weight? Do you want to relieve stress from chronic disease and pain?" Yes! Of course, take the appropriate steps by going vegan with the WFPB diet. In doing so, your body will function at a higher level than ever before as it does not have all of those heavy toxic chemicals found in processed food on its radar screen anymore.

"Let's take a look at the facts. What happens after people go on WFPB diets? Weight loss is constant and sustainable. And there is more than one way to lose weight. You can lose weight by being sedentary or exercising a lot less than you now do. Getting rid of bad habits also helps with weight loss and it would be wise to remove as many foods from your diet as possible."

The truth is that everyone wants to be slim and healthy, but it might not be as easy as some of us would like it to be. For some, it's all of the processed foods they frequently consume. For others, it could be the lack of exercise they do on a regular basis. We can also blame the poor diets they might have been eating.

People are getting heavier and this is a trend that has been happening for decades but continues to gain momentum. Obesity is on the rise and it doesn't look like it will stop any time soon. And so, we come to the WFPB diet, which is touted as the "ultimate" weight loss diet by many in the vegan community.

WFPB diets have been used over the last century by natural health practitioners. The most important aspect of the WFPB diet is to eliminate processed foods and animal products from our diet. No meat, no dairy, no eggs, no fast food only whole plant-based foods which must be organic whenever possible.

The WFPB diet is not new and it has been around for quite some time. In fact, it has lots of different names and labels attached to it, which include: vegan, raw vegan, fruitarian, raw food diet or even living foods. The WFPB diet is different from other diets in that it is based on whole plant foods, not whole plants and not plants, plus added animal products.

What's the WFPB Diet?

The WFPB or Whole Food Plant-Based diet is a vegan, vegetarian or raw food diet that consists of eating a wide variety of fruits, vegetables, nuts, seeds and sprouted whole grains. It is high in fiber and low in fat (some consider it zero fat), making this an ideal weight loss program. The WFPB diet has been around for over 100 years and has helped thousands of people lose excess weight, improve their health's and increase their energy levels.

The Vegan Diet

In the vegan world or the vegetarian world, there are two types of diets. The first one is a raw vegan plant-based diet that includes fruits, vegetables, whole grains and nuts, and unprocessed oils. The second type is called the WFPB diet. This diet consists of eating only plants, no animal products, and no processed foods like food containing added chemicals and oils that are not natural to produce or grow in nature.

Living Foods Diet

The living foods diet was created by Drs. Ann Wigmore and Viktoras Kulvinskas based on the belief that foods should be eaten in their raw state with no oil or heat used in their preparation. Foods like raw fruits, vegetables, sprouts and freshly ground seeds should be a part of our daily diet. Raw foods are believed to contain all of the nutrients that our bodies need for perfect health.

Raw Food Diet

The raw food diet is derived from both the living food diet and the vegan lifestyle. In order to adhere to this type of diet, we should consume 80% of our meals uncooked, while eating an extra 20% cooked foods (low heat). Some raw foodists choose to eat 100% uncooked foods; others choose just a portion of this diet. The main feature about the raw food diet is the fact that it is 100% natural and contains no chemicals or toxins.

The WFPB Diet (Vegan Diet)

The WFPB diet is a vegan diet. We follow this type of lifestyle by eating only plants, no animal products and no processed foods like food that contains added chemicals and oils that are not natural to produce or grown in nature.

Ethical Motivation

Do you know much about plant-based diets? This type of diet is typically vegetarian and excludes certain animal products, such as meat, dairy, and eggs. You might have heard that this is a healthy alternative to the standard Western diet. And, that's true for a lot of people who are committed to this way of eating for various reasons.

But, is it really healthy? Where does your motivation come from? And, how does it depend on the product you eat and the person who accepts a plant-based diet?

The results showed that the main reason why people switched was to improve their health. And a plant-based diet is something that they want to keep for a long time. On the other hand, non-ethical motivations such as the taste or convenience of the product did not major in their choice. Interestingly, the importance of taste and convenience on maintaining preferred choices depended on the product. For meat products, the taste seemed to be important when choosing foods to buy, and the convenient lack of animal products was considered important while shopping for other food.

Most non-ethical motivations were related to environmental concerns, which were highly dependent on the product too. With food containing animal products (meat and dairy), they saw the impact of their consumption as significant, while with plant products, it was not so important.

In conclusion, plant-based diets are ethical in most cases.

Health Motivation

Defining a healthy eating pattern as one that is predominantly plant-based without animal products, the Academy of Nutrition and Dietetics endorses a diet high in fruit, vegetables, whole grains, legumes (beans), nuts/seeds/dried fruit, soy products like tofu or tempeh, while limiting animal products.

"A plant-based diet is necessarily higher in carbohydrate than a non-plant-based diet, and vegan diets are higher in carbohydrate than diets including meat. But the type of carbohydrate can make a difference for chronic health concerns such as heart disease," says Mary Flynn Nolan, PhD, RDN, LDN. "Lower glycemic index plant-based foods are typically higher in fiber content and lower in digestible carbohydrates."

A lower concentration of glucose, along with a decreased intake of saturated fat, has been associated with better weight management when compared to diets that include animal products.

Why 2000-day recipes?

I have carefully selected recipes because I intend to offer the reader the opportunity to prepare meals with ever-changing flavors. Since a diet or eating pattern might be boring in the long run, I want to reassure the reader that thanks to the recipes in this book, they will have delicious and ever-changing dishes for a very long time....at least 2000 days!

CHAPTER 11:

BREAKFAST RECIPES

Cauliflower Oatmeal

Preparation Time: 15 minutes.
Cooking Time: 15 minutes.
Servings: 2
Ingredients:
- 1 cup cauliflower rice
- ½ cup unsweetened almond milk
- ½ teaspoon cinnamon
- 1 tablespoon honey
- ½ tablespoon peanut butter
- 1 strawberry, sliced

Directions:
1. Mix milk with cauliflower rice, honey and cinnamon in a saucepan.
2. Bring the combination that contains the rice to boiling, and afterwards reduce the temperature to a low setting.
3. Cook the mix for 10 mins on a simmer.
4. After the oatmeal has been given the chance to cool down serve it using a strawberry on top.
5. Serve.

Serving Suggestion: Serve the oatmeal with a glass of avocado smoothie.
Variation Tip: Add more berries to the oatmeal.
Nutrition: Calories: 234; Fat: 4.7 g; Sodium: 1 mg; Carbs: 18 g; Fiber: 7 g; Sugar: 3.3 g; Proteins: 6 g.

Pumpkin Oatmeal

Preparation Time: 15 minutes.
Cooking Time: 45 minutes.
Servings: 4
Ingredients:
- 2½ cups rolled oats
- 3 tablespoons chia seeds
- 1 teaspoon baking powder
- 1 teaspoon cinnamon
- ½ teaspoon cardamom
- ½ teaspoon salt
- 1 ¾ cups almond milk
- 1 (15-ounce) can pumpkin
- 1/3 cup maple syrup
- 1 tablespoon pure vanilla extract

Directions:
1. Put the microwave on to heat at 350 degrees Fahrenheit. Wrap parchment paper around the bottom and sides of an eight by eight-inch baking sheet. In a container, combine the oats, salt, cardamom, cinnamon, baking powder, and chia seeds. Stir occasionally.
2. Now, give the remaining oatmeal components a good swirl and combine them together till they are completely homogenous. Broil this batter for forty-five mins after spreading it in the plate used for cooking. The oatmeal should be allowed to chill before being served.

Serving Suggestion: Serve the oatmeal with a glass of green smoothie.
Variation Tip: Drizzle roasted pumpkin seeds over the oatmeal.
Nutrition: Calories: 284; Fat: 7.9 g; Sodium: 704 mg; Carbs: 31 g; Fiber: 3.6 g; Sugar: 6 g; Proteins: 8 g.

Berry Cobbler

Preparation Time: 15 minutes.
Cooking Time: 30 minutes.
Servings: 4
Ingredients:

- 1 cup fresh blueberries
- 1 cup fresh blackberries
- 1 cup fresh raspberries
- 1 cup of water
- 3 tablespoons tapioca starch
- ½ teaspoon cinnamon
- ¼ cup coconut sugar
- Cobbler topping
- 1 cup rolled oats
- 2/3 cup whole wheat flour
- ¼ cup coconut sugar
- 1 tablespoon flaxseeds
- 1 tablespoon hemp seeds
- 1 tablespoon chia seeds
- 3 tablespoons coconut oil, melted
- 1/3 cup almond milk
- ¼ teaspoon pure vanilla extract
- ¼ teaspoon cinnamon
- ¾ teaspoon baking powder
- 1 pinch of pink salt

Directions:

1. Preheat your oven to 375º F.
2. Mix all the berries filling ingredients in a pan and cook on a simmer until it thickens.
3. Remove the filling from the heat and spread it in a greased baking dish.
4. Mix oats with coconut sugar with cinnamon, hemp shells, chia seeds, flour, flaxseeds, salt and baking powder within a big container.
5. Stir in vanilla, milk and coconut oil, then mix well. Spread this batter on top of the filling.
6. Bake the cobbler for 30 minutes at 375º F. Allow it to cool and serve.

Serving Suggestion: Serve the cobbler with a glass of blueberry smoothie.
Variation Tip: Replace blueberries with strawberries for change of taste.
Nutrition: Calories: 317; Fat: 13 g; Sodium: 114 mg; Carbs: 31 g; Fiber: 1 g; Sugar: 10 g; Proteins: 11 g.

Protein Bars

Preparation Time: 10 minutes.
Cooking Time: 20 minutes.
Servings: 6
Ingredients:

- 1½ cup quick-cooking oats
- ½ cup almond meal
- ½ cup flaxseed meal
- 2 teaspoons cinnamon
- ½ teaspoon salt
- 4 tablespoons vegan protein powder
- 1 teaspoon pure vanilla extract
- 2 bananas, ripe and mashed
- ½ cup applesauce
- ¼ cup creamy peanut butter
- 2 tablespoons honey

Directions:

1. Preheat your oven to 350º F. Layer an 8x8 square baking dish with cooking spray.
2. Mix all the ingredients in a large bowl.
3. Spread this mixture in the prepared pan.
4. Bake the batter for 20 mins in the oven.
5. Allow the mixture to cool, then slice.
6. Serve.

Serving Suggestion: Serve the bars with a glass of peanut butter smoothie.
Variation Tip: Drizzle chocolate syrup over the bars.
Nutrition: Calories: 248; Fat: 12 g; Sodium: 321 mg; Carbs: 26 g; Fiber: 4 g; Sugar: 8 g; Proteins: 7 g.

French Toast

Preparation Time: 5 minutes
Cooking Time: 12 minutes
Servings: 4
Ingredients:

- 4 slices of bread, whole-grain
- ½ cup rolled oats
- ½ cup pecans
- 1 tablespoon ground flax seed
- ½ teaspoon ground cinnamon
- 1/3 cup almond milk
- Maple syrup for serving
- Olive oil spray

Directions:

1. Switch on the air fryer, insert the fryer basket, shut it with the lid, set the frying temperature 350° F, and preheat for 5 minutes.
2. Meanwhile, prepare the topping. Place oats in a food processor; add flax seeds, pecans, and cinnamon it and pulse for 2 minutes until the mixture resembles breadcrumbs.
3. Tip the mixture in a shallow dish; take another shallow dish and pour milk into it.
4. Add bread slices, one at a time, and then let them soak for 15 seconds. Don't let it be mushy.
5. Open the preheated fryer, place prepared bread slices in it in a single layer. Spray with olive oil, close the lid and cook for 6 minutes until golden brown, turning and spraying with oil halfway.
6. When done, the air fryer will beep. Then open the lid and transfer the toast to a dish. Processed coating is sprinkled on the surface before being wrapped in tinfoil to maintain heat.
7. Complete the similar procedure with the rest of the toast. Sprinkle with remaining topping, and serve straight away.

Nutrition: Calories: 102.2; Fat: 3.4 g; Carbs: 28.2 g; Proteins: 6.2 g; Fiber: 3.6 g.

Hemp Breakfast Cookies

Preparation Time: 10 minutes.
Cooking Time: 15 minutes.
Servings: 6
Ingredients:

- 3 cups almond flour
- 1 cup dried dates, pitted
- ½ cup hemp seeds
- 1 cup almond milk

Directions:

1. Mix almond milk with hemp seeds and dates in a bowl and leave for 1hour.
2. Using a blender, combine the remaining ingredients, including the milk combination, using the almond flour till you get a flour that is homogeneous.
3. Preheat your oven to 350° F.
4. Create 9 individual cookies from the flour by first dividing it into 9 equal parts.

5. The above biscuits should be placed on a baking pan that has been covered using baking parchment.
6. Bake the cookies within the microwave for fifteen mins, turning them over after they have reached the midway mark in their baking time.
7. Serve.

Serving Suggestion: Serve the cookies with a glass of blueberry smoothie.
Variation Tip: Drizzle chocolate syrup over the cookies.
Nutrition: Calories: 217; Fat: 25 g; Sodium: 132 mg; Carbs: 29 g; Fiber: 3.9 g; Sugar: 3 g; Proteins: 8.9 g.

Zucchini Oatmeal

Preparation Time: 15 minutes.
Cooking Time: 4 minutes.
Servings: 4
Ingredients:

- 2 cups rolled oats
- 6 tablespoons pea protein
- 2 teaspoons cinnamon
- 1 teaspoon nutmeg
- 2 ¼ cups almond milk
- 1 cup zucchini, grated
- ¼ cup maple syrup
- 1 teaspoon vanilla extract

Toppings:

- Banana
- Nuts
- Seeds
- Sugar-free chocolate chips
- 1 teaspoon coconut oil, melted

Directions:

1. Cook oats with coconut oil in an Instant Pot for 2 minutes on Sauté mode.
2. After stirring in the remaining components, seal the pot and make sure that the cover is tight.
3. Cook for 2 minutes on high pressure.
4. When it is finished, let out the remaining tension and replace the cover.
5. After the oatmeal has had chance to relax, sprinkle it using whichever fixings take your fancy.
6. Serve.

Serving Suggestion: Serve the oatmeal with a glass of pumpkin smoothie.
Variation Tip: Drizzle chocolate syrup over the oatmeal.

Nutrition: Calories: 232; Fat: 12 g; Sodium: 202 mg; Carbs: 26 g; Fiber: 4 g; Sugar: 8 g; Proteins: 7.3 g.

Broccoli Oatmeal

Preparation Time: 15 minutes.
Cooking Time: 15 minutes.
Servings: 2
Ingredients:

- 1 cup broccoli
- ½ cup unsweetened almond milk
- ½ teaspoon cinnamon
- 1 tablespoon honey
- ½ tablespoon peanut butter
- 1 strawberry, sliced

Directions:

1. In a pan, combine broccoli, honey, and cinnamon with milk. Blend well.
2. Bring the mix that contains the rice to a boil, and afterwards reduce the temperature to a low setting.
3. Next, boil the mix for ten mins while it is still in the pot.
4. After the oatmeal has had a chance to settle, serve it using a strawberry on top.
5. Serve.

Serving Suggestion: Serve the oatmeal with a glass of avocado smoothie.
Variation Tip: Add more berries to the oatmeal.
Nutrition: Calories: 234; Fat: 4.7 g; Sodium: 1 mg; Carbs: 18 g; Fiber: 7 g; Sugar: 3.3 g; Proteins: 6 g.

Peanut Butter Muffins

Preparation Time: 15 minutes.
Cooking Time: 27 minutes.
Servings: 6
Ingredients:

- ¾ cup oat flour
- ¼ cup coconut sugar
- 2 tablespoons pea protein powder
- 1 tablespoon baking powder
- 2 teaspoons baking soda
- 3 large bananas, mashed
- ½ cup peanut butter
- 2 tablespoons flaxseed
- ½ cup water
- ½ cup almond milk
- 1 teaspoon vanilla extract

Directions:

1. Prior to putting anything heat the microwave to 350-degree Fahrenheit and layer two muffin trays with cupcake liners.
2. Soak flaxseed with ½ cup of water in a bowl for 5 minutes.
3. Mix mashed banana with milk, peanut butter and flaxseed mixture within a big container.
4. Now, whisk it with the rest of the muffin ingredients and mix well evenly.
5. Bake the muffins for twenty-seven mins after dividing the prepped mixture among the available slots within the muffin tin.
6. After they have had time to settle, the muffins can be served.

Serving Suggestion: Serve the muffins with a glass of blueberry smoothie.
Variation Tip: Drizzle chocolate syrup over the muffins.
Nutrition: Calories: 297; Fat: 15 g; Sodium: 548 mg; Carbs: 35 g; Fiber: 4 g; Sugar: 1 g; Proteins: 9 g.

Chocolate Zucchini Bread

Preparation Time: 15 minutes.
Cooking Time: 55 minutes.
Servings: 6
Ingredients:

- 1 ¼ cup whole wheat flour
- ¾ cup coconut sugar
- ½ cup raw cacao powder
- 3 teaspoons baking powder
- 2 teaspoons baking soda
- 1 cup zucchini, shredded
- ½ cup almond milk
- 1/3 cup unsweetened applesauce
- 1/3 cup coconut oil, melted
- 2 teaspoons vanilla extract
- 2/3 cup sugar-free chocolate chip

Directions:

1. Prepare a loaf pot with baking parchment that is nine inches wide and prepare the microwave to 350 degrees Fahrenheit.
2. The chopped zucchini should be thoroughly dried before being reserved.
3. Inside a container, combine the dough with the baking soda, baking powder, cocoa powder, and coconut sugar. Stir occasionally.
4. Stir it with vanilla, applesauce, milk, and peanut butter, then mix until smooth.

5. Fold in sugar-free chocolate chips and zucchini shreds.
6. Spread this batter in the set loaf pan.
7. Bake this bread for 55 mins in the oven.
8. Allow the bread to cool, then slice.
9. Serve.

Serving Suggestion: Serve the bread with a glass of strawberry smoothie.
Variation Tip: Drizzle chocolate syrup over the bread.
Nutrition: Calories: 218; Fat: 22 g; Sodium: 350 mg; Carbs: 22 g; Fiber: 0.7 g; Sugar: 1 g; Proteins: 2.3 g.

Corn Muffins

Preparation Time: 15 minutes.
Cooking Time: 20 minutes.
Servings: 6
Ingredients:
- 1½ tablespoons ground flaxseed
- 1 cup almond milk
- ½ cup applesauce
- ½ cup pure maple syrup
- 1 cup corn meal
- 1 cup oat flour
- 1 teaspoon baking soda
- 1 teaspoon baking powder
- ½ teaspoon salt
- 1 cup corn kernels

Directions:
1. Preheat your oven to 375º F.
2. In a big dish, combine the flaxseed and almond milk, allowing the mixture to sit for five mins.
3. Maple syrup and apple sauce should be combined with it, after which it should be thoroughly combined.
4. After adding the salt, baking powder, baking soda, oat flour, and cornmeal, combine the ingredients together till they are completely homogeneous.
5. Add corn kernels and mix evenly.
6. Cook the corn muffins for twenty mins at 400 degrees Fahrenheit, dividing the mixture evenly among twelve muffin cups.
7. Allow the muffins to cool and serve.

Serving Suggestion: Serve the muffins with a glass of blueberry smoothie.
Variation Tip: Drizzle chocolate syrup over the muffins.
Nutrition: Calories: 257; Fat: 12 g; Sodium: 48 mg; Carbs: 32 g; Fiber: 2 g; Sugar: 0 g; Proteins: 14 g.

Quinoa Black Beans Breakfast Bowl

Preparation Time: 15 minutes
Cooking Time: 25 minutes
Servings: 1
Ingredients:
- 1/4 cup brown quinoa, rinsed well
- Salt to taste
- 1 tablespoon plant-based yogurt
- ½ lime, juiced
- 1 tablespoon chopped fresh cilantro
- 1 (5 oz) can black beans, weary and rinsed
- 1 tablespoon tomato salsa
- ¼ small avocado, pitted, peeled, and sliced
- 1 radish, shredded
- 1/4 tablespoons pepitas (pumpkin seeds)

Directions:
1. Boil the quinoa within a moderate pot using two water cups that have been seasoned using a pinch of salt at moderate flame for fifteen mins, or till the fluid is absorbed.
2. Spoon the quinoa into serving bowls and fluff with a fork.
3. Combine the yoghurt, lime juice, cilantro, and salt within a compact container and stir until combined. A portion of this combination should be placed on each serving of quinoa, and then it should be topped by beans, salsa, avocado, radishes, and pepitas.
4. Serve immediately.

Nutrition: Calories: 131; Fats: 3.5 g; Carbs: 20 g; Proteins: 6.5 g.

Corn Griddle Cakes with Tofu Mayonnaise

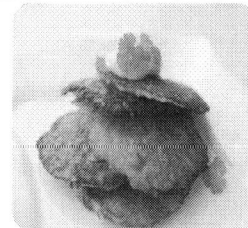

Preparation Time: 15 minutes
Cooking Time: 35 minutes
Servings: 1
Ingredients:
- 1 tbsp flax seed powder + 3 tbsps. water
- 1 cup water or as needed
- 1 cup yellow cornmeal
- 1 teaspoon salt
- 1 teaspoon baking powder
- 1 tablespoon olive oil for frying
- 1 cup tofu mayonnaise for serving

Directions:

1. In a container of suitable size, combine the ground flax seeds well with water, and then set aside for five mins to enable the mixture to solidify into a flax egg.
2. After incorporating the water, stir in the cornmeal, salt, and baking powder till a soupy consistency is achieved while retaining the desired thickness.
3. A pancake pot should be heated with a 1/4 of the olive oil, and then a 1/4 of the batter should be poured into the pot. Heat for three mins, or till the bottom is golden brown and the mixture has formed. After turning the cake over, continue cooking it till both sides are firm and golden brown.
4. Place the cake on a serving dish, then use the residual oil and batter to create 3 more cakes.
5. Top the cakes with some tofu mayonnaise before serving.

Nutrition: Calories: 896; Fats: 50.7 g; Carbs: 91.6 g; Proteins: 17.3 g.

Savory Breakfast Salad

Preparation Time: 15 to 30 minutes
Cooking Time: 20 minutes
Servings: 1
Ingredients:
For the sweet potatoes:
- 2 smalls sweet potatoes
- 1 pinch salt and pepper
- 1 tablespoon coconut oil

For the Dressing:
- 3 tablespoons lemon juice
- 1 pinch salt and pepper
- 1 tablespoon extra-virgin olive oil

For the Salad:
- 4 cups mixed greens

For Serving:
- 4 tablespoons hummus
- 1 cup blueberries
- 1 medium ripe avocado
- Fresh chopped parsley
- 2 tablespoons hemp seeds

Directions:
1. Take a large skillet and apply gentle heat.
2. Add sweet potatoes, coat them with salt and pepper, and pour some oil. Cook till sweet potatoes turn brown.
3. Take a bowl and mix lemon juice, salt, and pepper. Add salad, sweet potatoes, and the serving together. Mix well, dress and serve.

Nutrition: Calories: 523; Carbs: 57.6 g; Proteins: 7.5 g; Fats: 37.6 g.

Almond Plum Oats Overnight

Preparation Time: 15 to 30 minutes
Cooking Time: 10 minutes
Servings: 1
Ingredients:
- "60 g rolled oats:"
- 3 plums, ripe and chopped
- 300 ml almond milk
- 1 tablespoon chia seeds:
- A pinch nutmeg
- A few drops of vanilla extract
- 1 tablespoon whole almonds, roughly chopped

Directions:
1. In a container, combine oats, nutmeg, vanilla essence, almond milk, and chia seeds, then thoroughly combine the ingredients.
2. Add in cubed plums and cover and place in the fridge for one night. Mix the oats well the next morning and add into the serving bowl.
3. Serve with your favorite toppings.

Nutrition: Calories: 248; Carbs: 24.7 g; Proteins: 9.5 g; Fats: 10.8 g.

High Protein Toast

Preparation Time: 30 minutes
Cooking Time: 15 minutes
Servings: 1
Ingredients:
- 1 white bean, drained and rinsed
- ½ cup cashew cream
- 1 ½ tablespoon miso paste
- 1 teaspoon toasted sesame oil
- 1 tablespoon sesame seeds
- 1 spring onion, finely sliced
- Lemon: 1 half for the juice and half wedged to serve
- 4 slices rye bread, toasted

Directions:
1. In a bowl, add sesame oil, white beans, miso, cashew cream, and lemon juice and mash using a potato masher. Make a spread.
2. Spread it on a toast and top with spring onions and sesame seeds. Serve with lemon wedges.

Nutrition: Calories: 332; Carbs: 44.5 g; Proteins: 14.5 g; Fats: 9.25 g.

Hummus Carrot Sandwich

Preparation Time: 30 minutes
Cooking Time: 25 minutes
Servings: 1
Ingredients:

- 1 cup can chickpeas, drain and rinsed
- 1 small tomato, sliced
- 1 cucumber, sliced
- 1 avocado, sliced
- 1 teaspoon cumin
- 1 cup carrot, diced
- 1 teaspoon maple syrup
- 3 tablespoons tahini
- 1 garlic clove
- 2 tablespoons lemon
- 2 tablespoons extra-virgin olive oil
- Salt as per your need
- 4 bread slices

Directions:

1. Add carrot to the boiling hot water and boil for 15 minutes. Blend boiled carrots, maple syrup, cumin, chickpeas, tahini, olive oil, salt, and garlic together.
2. Add in lemon juice and mix.
3. Add to the serving bowl, and you can refrigerate for up to 5 days. In between two bread slices, spread hummus and place 2-3 slices of cucumber, avocado, and tomato and serve.

Nutrition: Calories: 490; Carbs: 53.15 g; Proteins: 14.1 g; Fats: 27 g.

Overnight Oats

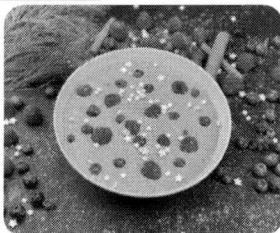

Preparation Time: 30 minutes
Cooking Time: 15 minutes
Servings: 1
Ingredients:

- A pinch cinnamon
- 200 ml almond milk
- 120 g porridge oats
- 1 tablespoon maple syrup
- 1 tablespoon pumpkin seeds
- 1 tablespoon chia seeds

Directions:

1. Put all of the components into the container and mix them together thoroughly. After covering the container, put it inside the refrigerator for overnight. Pour more milk in the morning.
2. Serve with your favorite toppings.

Nutrition: Calories: 298; Carbs: 32.3 g; Proteins: 10.2 g; Fats: 12.7 g.

Avocado Miso Chickpeas Toast

Preparation Time: 30 minutes
Cooking Time: 15 minutes
Servings: 1
Ingredients:

- 400 g chickpeas, drained and rinsed
- 1 medium avocado
- 1 teaspoon toasted sesame oil
- 1 ½ tablespoon white miso paste
- 1 tablespoon sesame seeds
- 1 spring onion, finely sliced
- 1 lemon, half for the juice and half wedged to serve
- 4 rye bread slices toasted

Directions:

1. Inside a container, include sesame oil, chickpeas, miso, and lemon juice and mash using a potato masher.
2. Roughly crush avocado in another bowl using a fork. Add the avocado to the chickpeas and make a spread. Spread it on a toast and top with spring onion and sesame seeds. Serve with lemon wedges.

Nutrition: Calories: 456; Carbs: 33.3 g; Proteins: 14.6 g; Fat: 26.6 g.

Banana Malt Bread

Preparation Time: 30 minutes
Cooking Time: 1 hour and 20 minutes
Servings: 1
Ingredients:

- 120 ml hot strong black tea
- 150 g malt extract + extra for brushing
- 2 bananas, ripe mashed
- 100 g sultanas
- 120 g pitted dates, chopped
- 250 g plain flour
- 50 g soft dark brown sugar
- 2 teaspoons baking powder

Directions:

1. Preheat the oven to 140° C (284°F).
2. Line the loaf tin with the baking paper.

3. Brew tea and include sultanas and dates in it. Take a small pan and heat the malt extract, and gradually add sugar to it. Stir continuously and let it cool.
4. Flour, salt, and baking powder should be added to a container, and then sugar extracts, fruit, bananas, and tea should be sprinkled over.
5. Mix the batter well and add to the loaf tin.
6. Bake the mixture for one hour
7. Brush the bread with extra malt extract and let it cool down before removing it from the tin.
8. When done, wrap in a foil; it can be consumed for a week.

Nutrition: Calories: 194; Carbs: 43.3 g; Proteins: 3.4 g; Fat: 0.3 g.

Banana Vegan Bread

Preparation Time: 30 minutes
Cooking Time: 1 hour and 15 minutes
Servings: 1
Ingredients:
- 3 large bananas, overripe mashed
- 200 g all-purpose flour
- 50 ml unsweetened non-dairy milk
- ½ teaspoon white vinegar
- 10 g ground flaxseed
- ¼ teaspoon ground cinnamon
- 140 g granulated sugar
- ¼ teaspoon vanilla
- ¼ teaspoon baking powder
- ¼ teaspoon baking soda
- ¼ teaspoon salt
- 3 tablespoons canola oil
- ½ cup chopped walnuts

Directions:
1. Prepare the loaf pan by linking it to waxed paper and preheating the microwave to 350 degrees Fahrenheit. Bananas should be mashed with a spatula.
2. Take a large bowl, and add in mash bananas, canola oil, oat milk, sugar, vinegar, vanilla, and ground flax seed.
3. In addition, stir in the baking powder, cinnamon, flour, and salt using the whip. Braise the bread for fifty mins after adding the mixture to the loaf pan. Take it out of the pot, and then give it ten mins to rest. After it has totally cooled, cut it.

Nutrition: Calories: 240; Carbs: 40.3 g; Proteins: 2.8 g; Fat: 8.2 g.

Berry Compote Pancakes

Preparation Time: 30 minutes
Cooking Time: 30 minutes
Servings: 1
Ingredients:
- 200 g mixed frozen berries
- 140 g plain flour
- 140 ml unsweetened almond milk
- 1 tablespoon icing sugar
- 1 tablespoon lemon juice
- 2 teaspoons baking powder
- A dash of vanilla extract
- A pinch salt
- 2 tablespoons caster sugar
- ½ tablespoon vegetable oil

Directions:
1. Take a small pan and add berries, lemon juice, and icing sugar. Cook the mixture for 10 minutes to give it a saucy texture and set it aside. Take a bowl and add caster sugar, flour, baking powder, and salt. Mix well.
2. After adding the almond milk and vanilla, ensure that everything is thoroughly combined to form a mixture. Take a non-stick pan, and heat 2 teaspoons of oil in it, and spread it over the whole surface.
3. Put a quarter cup of the mixture in the pan and cook it for three to four mins per side. Accompany the dish using compote.

Nutrition: Calories: 463; Carbs: 92 g; Proteins: 9.4 g; Fat: 5.2 g.

Southwest Breakfast Bowl

Preparation Time: 30 minutes
Cooking Time: 15 minutes
Servings: 1
Ingredients:
- 1 cup mushrooms, sliced
- ½ cup chopped cilantro
- 1 teaspoon chili powder
- 1/2 red pepper, diced
- 1 cup zucchini, diced
- 1/2 cup green onion, chopped

- 1/2 cup onion
- 1 vegan sausage, sliced
- 1 teaspoon garlic powder
- 1 teaspoon paprika
- 1/2 teaspoons cumin
- Salt and pepper as per your taste
- Avocado for topping

Directions:
1. Put everything in a bowl and apply medium heat until vegetables turn brown.
2. Add some pepper and salt as you like and serve with your favorite toppings

Nutrition: Calories: 361; Carbs: 31.6 g; Proteins: 33.8 g; Fat: 12.2 g.

Buckwheat Crepes

Preparation Time: 30 minutes
Cooking Time: 25 minutes
Servings: 1
Ingredients:
- 1 cup raw buckwheat flour
- 1 and 3/4 cups light coconut milk
- 1/8 teaspoons ground cinnamon
- 3/4 tablespoons flaxseeds
- 1 tablespoon melted coconut oil
- A pinch of sea salt
- Any sweetener as per your taste

Directions:
1. Take a bowl and add flaxseed, coconut milk, salt, avocado, and cinnamon.
2. Mix them all well and fold in the flour.
3. Now take a nonstick pan and pour oil; provide medium heat.
4. Add a big spoon of the mixture.
5. Cook till it appears bubbly, then flip side. Perform the task until all crepes are prepared. For enhancing the taste, add the sweetener of your liking.

Nutrition: Calories: 71; Carbs: 8 g; Proteins: 1 g; Fat: 3 g.

Chickpeas Spread Sourdough Toast

Preparation Time: 30 minutes
Cooking Time: 15 minutes
Servings: 1
Ingredients:
- 1 cup chickpeas, rinsed and drained
- 1 cup pumpkin puree
- ½ cup vegan yogurt
- Salt as per your need
- 2 slices sourdough, toasted

Directions:

1. A potato crusher should be used to crush the chickpeas and pumpkin puree that have been placed in a container. Include some salt and afterwards stir in the yoghurt.
2. Spread it on a toast and serve.

Nutrition: Calories: 187; Carbs: 33.7 g; Proteins: 8.45 g; Fat: 2.5 g.

Chickpeas with Harissa

Preparation Time: 30 minutes
Cooking Time: 20 minutes
Servings: 1
Ingredients:
- 1 cup can chickpeas, rinse and drained
- 1 small onion, diced
- 1 cup cucumber, diced
- 1 cup tomato, diced
- Salt as per your taste
- 2 tablespoons lemon juice
- 2 teaspoons harissa
- 1 tablespoon olive oil
- 2 tablespoons flat-leaf parsley, chopped

Directions:
1. Add lemon juice, harissa, and olive oil inside a container and stir.
2. Incorporate onion, cucumber, chickpeas, and salt.
3. Add parsley from the top and serve.

Nutrition: Calories: 398; Carbs: 55.6 g; Proteins: 17.8 g; Fat: 11.8 g.

Quinoa and Rice Stuffed Peppers (Oven-Baked)

Preparation Time: 30 minutes
Cooking Time: 35 minutes
Servings: 1
Ingredients:
- 3/4 cup long-grain rice
- 2 bell peppers (any color)
- 1 tablespoon olive oil
- 1 onion diced
- 1 clove chopped garlic
- 1 can (11 oz) crushed tomatoes
- 1 teaspoon cumin
- 1 teaspoon coriander
- 2 tablespoon ground walnuts
- 1 cup cooked quinoa
- 1 tablespoon chopped parsley

- Salt and ground black pepper to taste

Directions:
1. Preheat your oven to 200° C or 400° F.
2. Boil rice and drain in a colander.
3. Take out the excess pith and seeds from the peppers, remove the top stem bit of the pepper, and then wash the peppers.
4. In a large sizzling saucepan, warm the oil, gradually fry the garlic and onion till they are tender.
5. Include tomatoes, cumin, ground almonds, salt, pepper, and coriander; stir well and simmer for 2 mins, mixing repetitively.
6. Eradicate from the flame and include the rice, quinoa, and parsley; stir well.
7. Taste and adjust salt and pepper.
8. After you have filled the peppers using the mix, put them in a baking sheet using the chopped part facing upwards and sprinkle a small bit of oil over them.
9. Bake for 15 minutes.
10. Serve warm.

Nutrition: Calories: 335; Fibers: 10 g; Carbs: 35 g; Proteins: 21 g; Fat: 14 g.

Eggplant Sandwich

Preparation Time: 30 minutes
Cooking Time: 30 minutes
Servings: 1
Ingredients:

- 1 eggplant, sliced
- 2 teaspoons parsley, dried
- Salt and black pepper to the taste
- 1/2 cup vegan breadcrumbs
- 1/2 teaspoons Italian seasoning
- 1/2 teaspoons garlic powder
- 1/2 teaspoons onion powder
- 2 tablespoons almond milk
- 4 vegan bread slices
- Cooking spray
- 1/2 cup avocado mayo
- 3/4 cup tomato sauce
- A handful basil, chopped

Directions:
1. Salt and pepper should be sprinkled on eggplant pieces before they are put down for a half an hour and afterwards thoroughly dried.
2. In a bowl, mix parsley with breadcrumbs, Italian flavor, onion and garlic powder, salt and black pepper. Stir.
3. In another bowl, mix milk with vegan mayo and also stir well.
4. Brush eggplant slices with mayo mix. Dip them in breadcrumbs mix and place them on a lined baking sheet. Spray with cooking oil, introduce baking sheet in your air fryer's basket and cook them at 400° F for 15 minutes, flipping them halfway.
5. Brush each bread slice with olive oil and arrange 2 of them on a working surface.
6. Add baked eggplant slices, spread tomato sauce and basil. Top with the other bread slices, greased side down.
7. Divide between plates and serve.

Nutrition: Calories: 324; Fat: 16 g; Fibers: 4 g; Carbs: 19 g; Proteins: 12 g.

Corn with Tofu

Preparation Time: 10 minutes
Cooking Time: 15 minutes
Servings: 1
Ingredients:

- 1 cups corn
- Salt and black pepper to the taste
- 1/2 tablespoon olive oil
- Juice of 1 lime
- 1 teaspoon smoked paprika
- 1/2 cup soft tofu, crumbled

Directions:
1. In your air fryer, mix oil with corn, salt, pepper, lime juice and paprika. Toss well, cover and cook at 400° F for 15 minutes.
2. Divide between plates. Sprinkle tofu crumbles all over, and serve hot.

Nutrition: Calories: 160; Fat: 2 g; Fibers: 2 g; Carbs: 12 g; Proteins: 4 g.

CHAPTER 12:

SOUPS AND SALADS

Nettle Soup with Rice

Preparation Time: 30 minutes
Cooking Time: 40 minutes
Servings: 1
Ingredients:

- 1 tablespoon of olive oil
- 1 onion finely chopped
- 1 cloves garlic finely chopped
- Salt and freshly ground black pepper
- 1 medium potato cut into cubes
- 1/4 cup of rice
- 1 tablespoon arrowroot
- 1 cups vegetable broth
- 1 cups of water
- 1 bunch of young nettle leaves packed
- 1/2 cup fresh parsley finely chopped
- 1 teaspoon cumin

Directions:

1. Heat olive oil in a large pot.
2. Sauté onion and garlic using a touch of salt till softened.
3. Include potato, rice, as well as arrowroot; sauté for 2 to 3 minutes.
4. Pour broth and water and stir well.
5. Sauté at moderate flame for almost twenty mins.
6. Include young nettle leaves, parsley, and cumin; stir and cook for five-seven mins.
7. Allocate the soup to a blender then blend until combined well.
8. Taste and adjust salt and pepper.
9. Serve hot.

Nutrition: Calories: 125; Carbs: 24 g; Proteins: 4 g; Fat: 2 g; Sodium: 318 mg.

Instant Savory Gigante Beans

Preparation Time: 30 minutes
Cooking Time: 55 minutes
Servings: 1

Ingredients:

- 1/4 lb. Gigante Beans soaked overnight
- 1/4 cup olive oil
- 1 onion sliced
- 2 cloves garlic crushed or minced
- 1 red bell pepper (cut into 1/2-inch bits)
- 1 carrot, sliced
- 1/2 tsp salt and ground black pepper
- 1 tomato peeled, grated
- 1 tablespoon celery (chopped)
- 1 tablespoon tomato paste (or ketchup)
- 3/4 teaspoon sweet paprika
- 1 teaspoon oregano
- 1 cup vegetable broth

Directions:

1. Soak Gigante beans overnight.
2. Press the SAUTÉ button on your Instant Pot and heat the oil.
3. Sauté onion, garlic, sweet pepper, carrots with a pinch of salt for 3-4 minutes; stir occasionally.
4. Put the Gigante beans that have been washed inside the Immediate Pan alongside the rest of the components, and give everything a good swirl.
5. Lock lid into place and set on the MANUAL setting for 25 minutes.
6. When the beep sounds, quickly release the pressure by pressing Cancel and twisting the steam handle to the Venting position.
7. Taste and adjust seasonings.
8. Serve warm or cold.
9. Keep refrigerated.

Nutrition: Calories: 279; Carbs: 27 g; Proteins: 16 g; Fat: 13 g; Sodium: 679 mg.

Arugula with Fruits and Nuts

Preparation Time: 10 minutes.
Cooking Time: 8 minutes.
Servings: 1
Ingredients:

- ½ cup arugula
- ½ peach
- ½ red onion
- ¼ cup blueberries
- 5 walnuts, chopped
- 1 tablespoon extra-virgin olive oil
- 2 tablespoons red wine vinegar

- 1 spring of fresh basil

Directions:
1. Halve the peach and remove the seed. Heat a grill pan and grill it briefly on both sides. Cut the red onion into thin half-rings.
1. Roughly chop the pecans.
2. Heat a pan and roast the pecans in it until they are fragrant.
3. Place the arugula on a plate and spread peaches, red onions, blueberries, and roasted pecans over it.
4. Place the entire components for the filling inside a mixing bowl, and blend them together until they form a uniform consistency.
5. Drizzle the dressing over the salad.

Nutrition: Calories: 160; Fat: 7 g; Carbohydrates: 25 g; Proteins: 3 g.

Broccoli Salad

Preparation Time: 25 minutes.
Cooking Time: 10 minutes.
Servings: 2
Ingredients:

- 1 head of broccoli
- 1/2 red onion
- 2 carrots, grated
- 1/4 cup red grapes
- 2 1/2 tablespoons coconut yogurt
- 1 tablespoon water
- 1 teaspoon mustard
- 1 pinch salt

Directions:
1. Cut the broccoli into florets and cook for 8 minutes. Cut the red onion into thin half-rings. Halve the grapes. Mix coconut yogurt, water and mustard with a pinch of salt to make the dressing.
2. To terminate the food preparation, remove the broccoli and then wash it in water that is extremely chilly.
3. Inside a container, combine the chopped broccoli using the chopped carrot, onion, and red grapes.
4. Serve the dressing separately on the side.

Nutrition: Calories: 230; Fat: 18 g; Carbohydrates: 35 g; Proteins: 10 g.

Brunoise Salad

Preparation Time: 10 minutes.
Cooking Time: 0 minutes.
Servings: 2
Ingredients:

- 1 tomato
- 1 zucchini
- ½ red bell pepper
- ½ yellow bell pepper
- ½ red onion
- 3 springs fresh parsley
- ½ lemon

- 2 tablespoons olive oil
- Salt and pepper to taste

Directions:
1. Finely dice tomato, peppers, zucchini and red onion to get a brunoise. Mix all the cubes in a bowl. Chop parsley and mix in the salad. Squeeze the lemon over the salad and add the olive oil.
2. Season with salt and pepper.

Nutrition: Calories: 84; Carbohydrates: 3 g; Fat: 4 g; Proteins: 0 g.

Brussels Sprouts and Ricotta Salad

Preparation Time: 15 minutes.
Cooking Time: 0 minutes.
Servings: 2
Ingredients:

- 1 (½) cup Brussels sprouts, thinly sliced
- 1 green apple cut "à la julienne"
- ½ red onion
- 8 walnuts, chopped
- 1 teaspoon extra-virgin olive oil
- 1 tablespoon lemon juice
- 1 tablespoon orange juice
- 4 ounces ricotta cheese

Directions:
1. Place the red onion inside a cup, then pour boiling water onto it to coat it completely. After letting it sit for ten mins, wipe it and dry it off using some kitchen towel. Slice Brussels sprouts as thin as you can, cut the apple à la julienne (sticks).
2. Mix Brussels sprouts, onion and apple, and season them with oil, salt, pepper, lemon juice and orange juice. Spread it on a serving plate.
3. Spread a small spoonful of ricotta cheese over Brussels sprouts mixture and top with chopped walnuts.

Nutrition: Calories: 353; Fat: 4.8 g; Carbohydrates: 28.1 g; Proteins: 28.3 g.

Celery and Raisins Snack Salad

Preparation Time: 10 minutes.
Cooking Time: 0 minutes.
Servings: 4
Ingredients:

- ½ cup raisins
- 4 cups celery, sliced
- ¼ cup parsley, chopped
- ½ cup walnuts, chopped
- Juice of ½ lemon
- 2 tablespoons olive oil
- Salt and black pepper to taste

Directions:
1. In a salad bowl, mix celery with raisins, walnuts, parsley, lemon juice, oil, salt and black pepper; toss.
2. Divide into small cups and serve as a snack.

Nutrition: Calories: 120; Fat: 1 g; Carbohydrates: 6 g; Proteins: 5 g.

Dijon Celery Salad

Preparation Time: 10 minutes.
Cooking Time: 0 minutes.
Servings: 4
Ingredients:
- 1/2 cup lemon juice
- 1/3 cup Dijon mustard
- 2/3 cup olive oil
- Black pepper to taste
- 2 apples, cored, peeled and cubed
- 1 bunch celery roughly chopped
- 3/4 cup walnuts, chopped

Directions:
1. Inside a salad container, mix celery and its leaves with apple pieces and walnuts.
2. Add black pepper, lemon juice, mustard as well as olive oil. Paddle well and include to your salad. Toss, divide into small cups and serve.

Nutrition: Calories: 125; Fat: 2 g; Carbohydrates: 7 g; Proteins: 7 g.

Fresh Endive Salad

Preparation Time: 10 minutes.
Cooking Time: 0 minutes.
Servings: 1
Ingredients:
- 1/2 red endive
- 1 orange
- 1 tomato
- 1/2 cucumber
- 1/2 red onion
- Olive oil and fresh lemon juice to taste

Directions:
1. To prepare endive, first remove the leaves and the tough stem. Peel the orange and cut the pulp into wedges.
2. Cut the tomato and cucumber into small pieces. Cut the red onion into thin half-rings.
3. Place the endive boats on a plate; spread the orange wedges, tomato, cucumber and red onion over the boats. Drizzle some olive oil and fresh lemon juice and serve.

Nutrition: Calories: 112; Fat: 11 g; Carbohydrates: 2 g; Proteins: 0 g.

Fresh Salad with Orange Dressing

Preparation Time: 10 minutes.
Cooking Time: 0 minutes.
Servings: 2
Ingredients:
- ½ cup lettuce
- 1 yellow bell pepper
- 1 red pepper
- 4 ounces carrot, grated
- 10 almonds
- 4 tablespoons extra-virgin olive oil
- ½ cup orange juice
- 1 tablespoon apple cider vinegar

Directions:
1. Clean the peppers and cut them into long, thin strips. Tear off the lettuce leaves and cut them into smaller pieces.
2. Combine the salad using the peppers as well as the carrots in a bowl. Roughly chop the almonds and sprinkle them over the salad.
3. In a container, thoroughly combine the entire components that will make up the topping. Prior to serving, sprinkle the dressing over the lettuce.

Nutrition: Calories: 150; Fat: 10 g; Carbohydrates: 11 g; Proteins: 2 g.

Greek Salad Skewers

Preparation Time: 10 minutes.
Cooking Time: 0 minutes.
Servings: 2
Ingredients:
- 8 big black olives
- 8 cherry tomatoes
- 1 yellow pepper, cut into eight squares
- 1/2 red onion, split into eight wedges
- 1 cucumber, cut into eight pieces
- 4 ounces feta, cut into eight cubes
- 1 tablespoon extra-virgin olive oil
- Juice of 1/2 lemon
- 1 teaspoon balsamic vinegar
- 1/2 teaspoons garlic, crushed

Directions:
1. Put the salad ingredients on the skewers following this order: cherry tomato, yellow pepper, red onion, cucumber, feta, and black olive.
2. Repeat for each skewer and put on a serving plate.
3. As a dressing, put within a container: olive oil, a tweak of salt and pepper, lemon juice, balsamic vinegar and crushed garlic. Whisk well and drizzle on the skewers.

Nutrition: Calories: 236; Fat: 21 g; Carbohydrates: 14 g; Proteins: 7 g.

Moroccan Leeks Snack Salad

Preparation Time: 10 minutes
Cooking Time: 0 minutes
Servings: 4
Ingredients:

- 1 bunch radishes, sliced
- 3 cups leeks, chopped
- 1 (½) cup olive, pitted and sliced
- A pinch of turmeric powder
- 1 cup parsley, chopped
- 2 tablespoons extra-virgin olive oil
- Black pepper to taste

Directions:

1. In a bowl, mix radishes with leeks, olives and parsley.
2. Add black pepper, oil and turmeric. Toss to coat and serve.

Nutrition: Calories: 135; Fat: 1 g; Carbohydrates: 18 g; Proteins: 9 g.

Beans Snack Salad

Preparation Time: 10 minutes
Cooking Time: 0 minutes
Servings: 6
Ingredients:

- 2 cups tomatoes, chopped
- 2 cups cucumber, chopped
- 2 cups beans, sprouted
- 2 cups clover sprouts
- 1 tablespoon cumin, ground
- 1 cup dill, chopped
- 4 tablespoons lemon juice
- 1 avocado, pitted and roughly chopped
- 1 cucumber, roughly chopped

Directions:

1. In a salad bowl, mix tomatoes with 2 cups of cucumber, clover and sprouts.
2. In your mixer, mix cumin with dill, lemon juice, 1 cucumber and 1 avocado. Blend well and add this to your salad. Toss well and serve.

Nutrition: Calories: 120; Fat: 3 g; Carbohydrates: 10 g; Proteins: 6 g.

Rainbow Salad

Preparation Time: 10 minutes
Cooking Time: 0 minutes
Servings: 1
Ingredients:

- 1 cup lettuce
- 1/2-piece avocado
- 1 egg
- 1/4 green pepper and a pinch of salt
- 1/4 red bell pepper
- 2 tomatoes
- 1/2 red onion
- 1/2 carrot, grated
- 2 tablespoons olive oil
- 2 tablespoons red wine vinegar

Directions:

1. Boil the egg until done (6 minutes for soft boiled, 8 minutes for hard-boiled). Cool it under running water, peel it and cut it into slices.
2. First, scrape the seeds out of the peppers, then slice the peppers lengthwise into small slices.
3. Cut the tomatoes into small cubes and the red onion into thin half-rings.
4. Cut the avocado into thin slices.
5. The lettuce should be placed on a platter, and the various veggies should be arranged in colorful lines.
6. Drizzle the vegetables with olive oil as well as red wine vinegar. Season with salt and pepper.

Nutrition: Calories: 40; Fat: 1 g; Carbohydrates: 5 g; Proteins: 2 g.

Roasted Butternut and Chickpeas Salad

Preparation Time: 10 minutes
Cooking Time: 30 minutes
Servings: 4
Ingredients:

- 1 cup chickpeas, drained
- 1-pound butternut squash
- 2 cups kale
- 2 tablespoons olive oil
- ½ lemon, juiced
- 2 cloves of garlic
- 2 green apples
- ½ teaspoon honey
- A pinch of salt and pepper

Directions:

1. Heat the oven to 400° F.
2. Slice the squash into medium cubes. Put them in a baking tray an add drained chickpeas, garlic, 1 tablespoon oil, salt and pepper. Mix and cook for 25 minutes.
3. Mix the kale using the dressing: salt, pepper, lemon, olive oil and honey so that while the squash is cooking, it becomes softer and more pleasant to eat.
4. When squash and chickpeas are done, put them aside for 10 minutes. In the meantime, chop the apples and mix them with kale.
5. Add squash and chickpeas on the surface and aid warm.

Nutrition: Calories: 353; Fat: 4.8 g; Carbohydrates: 28.1 g; Proteins: 28.3 g.

Salad with Cranberries and Apple

Preparation Time: 50 minutes
Cooking Time: 0 minutes
Servings: 2
Ingredients:

- 1/2 cup arugula

- 1/2 apple
- 2 tablespoons cranberries
- 1/2 red onion
- 1/2 red bell pepper
- 10 walnuts
- 1 teaspoon mustard yellow
- 1 teaspoon honey
- 3 tablespoons extra-virgin olive oil
- 2 slices of bacon, chopped
- 1 teaspoon lemon juice
- A pinch of salt and pepper

Directions:
1. Cut half the red onion into thin rings. Cut the bell pepper into small cubes and the apple into four pieces; remove the core.
2. Then cut into thin wedges. Drizzle some lemon juice on the apple wedges so that they do not change color.
3. Unevenly chop walnuts. Combine the ingredients for the dressing in a bowl. Season with salt and pepper. Spread the lettuce on a plate and season with red pepper, red onions, apple wedges and walnuts.
4. Sprinkle bacon and cranberries over the salad. Drizzle the dressing over the salad and serve.

Nutrition: Calories: 70; Fat: 3 g; Carbohydrates: 6 g; Proteins: 7 g.

Sirt Fruit Salad

Preparation Time: 10 minutes
Cooking Time: 0 minutes
Servings: 1
Ingredients:
- 1/2 cup matcha green tea
- 1 teaspoon honey
- 1 orange, halved
- 1 apple, cored and roughly chopped
- 10 red seedless grapes
- 10 blueberries

Directions:
1. Stir the honey into half a cup of green tea and let it chill.
2. When chilled, add the juice of half an orange.
3. Slice the other half and put in a bowl with the chopped apple, blueberries and grapes.
4. Cover with tea and let rest in the fridge for 30 mins prior to serving.

Nutrition: Calories: 110; Fat: 0 g; Carbohydrates: 17 g; Proteins: 2 g.

Sprouts and Apples Snack Salad

Preparation Time: 10 minutes
Cooking Time: 0 minutes
Servings: 4
Ingredients:
- 1-pound Brussels sprouts, shredded
- 1 cup walnuts, chopped
- 1 apple, cored and cubed
- 1 red onion, chopped

- 3 tablespoons red vinegar
- 1 tablespoon mustard
- ½ cup olive oil
- 1 garlic clove, crushed
- Black pepper to taste

Directions:
1. In a salad container, combine sprouts with apple, onion as well as walnuts.
2. In another bowl, mix vinegar with mustard, oil, garlic and pepper; whisk well. Add this to your salad; toss well and serve as a snack.

Nutrition: Calories: 120; Fat: 2 g; Carbohydrates: 8 g; Proteins: 6 g.

Tomato and Avocado Salad

Preparation Time: 10 minutes
Cooking Time: 0 minutes
Servings: 1
Ingredients:
- 1 tomato
- 4 ounces cherry tomatoes
- 1/2 red onion
- 1 ripe avocado
- 1 teaspoon fresh oregano
- 1 tablespoon extra-virgin olive oil
- 1 teaspoon red wine vinegar
- 1 pinch Celtic Sea salt

Directions:
1. Cut the tomato into thick slices. Cut half of the cherry tomatoes into slices and the remaining in half. Cut the red onion into super-thin half rings (if you have it, use a mandolin slicer).
2. Cut the avocado into six parts. Spread the tomatoes on a plate; place the avocado on top.
3. Sprinkle red onion and oregano and drizzle olive oil, vinegar and a tweak of salt on the salad.

Nutrition: Calories: 165; Fat: 14 g; Carbohydrates: 7 g; Proteins: 5 g.

Avocado-Potato Salad

Preparation Time: 10 minutes
Cooking Time: 15 minutes
Servings: 2
Ingredients:
- 1 ripe avocado, mashed
- 6 Yukon gold or red potatoes
- 1/2 cup red onion, chopped
- 2 ribs of celery, chopped
- 1/2 cup sweet red bell pepper
- 1 handful parsley, chopped

Directions:
1. Steam as well as cook the potatoes until tender but not too soft. Stir thoroughly with all other ingredients.
2. Keep refrigerated until ready to serve.

Nutrition: Calories: 213; Fat: 9 g; Carbohydrates: 28 g; Proteins: 3 g.

Avocado with Raspberry Vinegar Salad

Preparation Time: 25 minutes
Cooking Time: 0 minutes
Servings: 2
Ingredients:

- 4 ounces raspberries
- 3 ounces red wine vinegar
- 1 teaspoon extra-virgin olive oil
- 2 firm-ripe avocados
- ¼ cup radicchio

Directions:

1. Put ½ the raspberries in a container. Heat the vinegar in a saucepan until it bubbles, pour it over the raspberries, and leave it too steep for 5 minutes.
2. After squeezing the fruit firmly with a spoon, sift the raspberry mixture to remove the pulp while keeping the juices.
3. After whisking the raspberry vinegar that has been filtered combined with the oils and toppings, put this aside.
4. To remove the stone from every avocado, first half it and then flip it.
5. Remove the skin, then slice the flesh in small pieces and add them directly to the topping.
6. To ensure that the avocados are completely coated within the seasoning, give the mixture a little toss.
7. Wrap it up airtight, and afterwards place it inside the refrigerator to cool for two hrs.
8. In the meantime, detach the petals of the radicchio. After being washed and drained, you should wipe these on some parchment paper. Place in a plastic cover and place in the refrigerator. When you're available to deliver, put a couple of radicchio leaf on each of the dishes.
9. Spread the avocado with the spatula. To finish, mix within the leftover raspberries then garnish using them.

Nutrition: Calories: 163; Fat: 4 g; Carbohydrates: 15 g; Proteins: 14 g.

Bitter Greens, Sprouts, Avocado and Orange Salad

Preparation Time: 5 minutes
Cooking Time: 0 minutes
Servings: 4
Ingredients:

- 1 cup baby spinach leaves
- 1 stir bitter greens (arugula, dandelion, watercress, etc.)
- 1 cup sprouts
- 1 orange, into wedges
- 1/2 cup diced avocado
- 1/4 cup walnuts, soaked
- 2 tablespoons extra-virgin olive oil
- 1 tablespoon lemon juice
- 1 teaspoon lemon zest
- Fresh split black pepper and salt to taste
- 1 tablespoon tahini
- 1/2 teaspoons diced fresh ginger

Directions:

1. Mix spinach leaves, bitter greens and sprouts within a container. Add the orange and avocado. In another bowl, whisk the lemon juice, olive oil, lemon zest, salt, pepper, ginger and tahini.
2. After pouring the dressings across the salads, swirl it to evenly cover the ingredients. Finish the dish off with the chopped walnuts, and serve right away.

Nutrition: Calories: 173; Fat: 4 g; Carbohydrates: 15 g; Proteins: 9 g.

Cannellini Bean Soup with Kale

Preparation Time: 15 minutes
Cooking Time: 25 minutes
Servings: 5
Ingredients:

- 1 tablespoon olive oil
- 1/2 teaspoons ginger, minced
- 1/2 teaspoons cumin seeds
- 1 red onion, chopped
- 1 carrot, trimmed and chopped
- 1 parsnip, trimmed and chopped
- 2 garlic cloves, minced
- 5 cups vegetable broth
- 12 ounces Cannellini beans, drained
- 2 cups kale, torn into pieces
- Sea salt and ground black pepper to taste

Directions:

1. Olive oil should be heated in a pan with a hefty lower part over moderate-high flame.
2. Then, heat some oil inside a skillet and fry the ginger with cumin for about a min.
3. After adding the onion, carrot, and parsnip, keep frying the veggies for a further three mins, or till they reach the desired degree of tenderness.
4. After adding the garlic, keep cooking the mixture for another min, or till the fragrance is released.
5. Next, add the vegetable stock, and carry the mixture back up to simmer.
6. As soon as it begins to boil, instantly turn the flame down to a boil and then let it stew for ten mins.
7. Fold the Cannellini beans and kale; continue simmering until the kale wilts and everything is thoroughly heated. Season with salt and pepper to taste.
8. Serve the soup in separate containers while it is still heated. "Bon appétit!"

Nutrition: Calories: 188; Fat: 4.1 g; Proteins: 11.1 g; Carbohydrates: 24.5 g.

Coconut Watercress Soup

Preparation Time: 10 minutes
Cooking Time: 20 minutes
Servings: 4
Ingredients:

- 1 teaspoon coconut oil
- 1 onion, diced
- 2 cups fresh or frozen peas
- 6 cups water, or vegetable stock
- 1 cup fresh watercress, chopped
- 1 tablespoon fresh mint, chopped
- Pinch sea salt
- Pinch freshly ground black pepper
- ¾ cup coconut milk

Directions:

1. Melt the coconut oil in a large pot over medium-high heat. Add the onion and cook until soft for about 5 minutes. Then add the peas and water. Bring to a boil; lower the heat. Then add the watercress, mint, salt and pepper. Cover and simmer for 5 minutes. Stir in the coconut milk.
2. Use a mixer or perhaps an electric processor to liquify the broth till it is completely homogeneous.

Try this soup with any other fresh, leafy green, anything from spinach to collard greens to arugula to Swiss chard.
Nutrition: Calories: 178; Fat: 10 g; Proteins: 6 g; Carbohydrates: 18 g.

Easy Borscht

Preparation Time: 30 minutes
Cooking Time: 45 minutes
Servings: 8
Ingredients:

- 6 cups shredded red cabbage
- 2 large potatoes, peeled and chopped
- 1 cup peeled julienned beets
- ¼ cup chopped fresh parsley
- 2 cloves garlic, crushed
- ¼ cup red-wine vinegar
- 1 onion, chopped
- 5 teaspoons chopped fresh dill
- 2 tablespoons maple syrup (optional)
- 1 teaspoon paprika
- Freshly ground pepper to taste
- 2 cups water
- Fresh dill for garnish

Directions:

1. In a big saucepan, add the entire components with the exception of the dill.
2. Raise the liquid to a boil. Coat, then bring the flame down to moderate & continue cooking for another forty-five mins.
3. Garnish with fresh dill and serve!

Nutrition: Calories: 127; Fat: 0.3 g; Proteins: 3.1 g; Carbohydrates: 29.5 g.

Potato and Corn Chowder

Preparation Time: 20 minutes
Cooking Time: 30 minutes
Servings: 4
Ingredients:

- 2 tbsps. low-sodium vegetables broth
- 1 medium yellow onion, diced
- 1 stalk celery, diced
- 1 small red bell pepper, diced
- two teaspoons minced fresh thyme leaves (about 4 sprigs) ½ teaspoon smoked paprika
- ½ teaspoon no-salt-added Old Bay seasoning
- 1 jalapeno pepper, seeded and minced
- 1 clove garlic, minced
- 1 pound (454 grams) new potatoes, diced
- 3 cups fresh corn kernels (about 4 fresh cobs) Salt (optional)
- Ground black or white pepper to taste
- 4 cups low-sodium vegetable broth
- 2 teaspoons white wine vinegar
- Chopped chives for garnish

Directions:

1. In a big saucepan set at moderate flame, bring the vegetable stew to a simmer. After adding the onions, continue to fry them for another four mins, or till they become transparent.
2. Include the red bell pepper, celery, paprika, thyme, jalapeno and Old Bay seasoning. Sauté for 1 minute or until the vegetables are tender.
3. After adding the garlic and continuing to fry for a further min, the garlic should become aromatic.
4. Put in the corn, potatoes, and vegetable stock. Season with salt and pepper, if preferred. Mix in order to get an even mixture. Raise to a boil, then immediately drop the flame to low and continue to cook for twenty-five more mins, or till the potatoes have reached the desired consistency.
5. Put one-half of the stew inside a mixer and run it through the machine till it is completely smooth and creamy. After the soup has enhance transparency, return it to the saucepan and stir in the white wine vinegar. Stir in order to get an even mixture.
6. Spread the cut chives on top and serve.

Nutrition: Calories: 733; Fat: 8.5 g; Carbohydrates: 148.5 g; Proteins: 20.4 g.

Pumpkin Soup

Preparation Time: 20 minutes
Cooking Time: 1 hour and 10 minutes
Servings: 8
Ingredients:

- 3 lbs of quartered, seeded sugar pumpkin
- 3 cups of vegetable broth
- 2 chopped large shallots

- 3 chopped fresh sage leaves
- 1/4 cup of Greek yogurt
- 6 springs of thyme
- 1 tablespoon of grated ginger
- 1/8 teaspoon of nutmeg
- 1 teaspoon of sea salt
- A pinch of ground pepper
- 1 (1/2) tablespoons of olive oil

Directions:
1. Heat your microwave to 450º Fahrenheit and spread some oil on a baking sheet.
2. Place pieces of pumpkin on the baking sheet. Drizzle them with olive oil and season with ground pepper and 1/4 teaspoon of sea salt. Put thyme sprigs on top.
3. Roast for about 1 hour, stirring halfway, and then let it cool and remove the skin.
4. Place a big saucepan on the stove over moderate flame, then add olive oil and allow it to heat up.
5. After adding the sliced shallots, continue to simmer the mixture for another five mins, mixing it regularly, till the shallots are cooked.
6. Mix in vegetable broth, pumpkin, ginger and sage. Season with the remaining salt and ground pepper to taste.
7. Raise the combination to a boil, and once it has reached a rolling boil, take it off the fire.
8. Puree with a blender until smooth consistency, and then pour in Greek yogurt and blend repeatedly.
9. Serve with some Greek yogurt and enjoy!

Nutrition: Calories: 145; Fat: 8 g; Carbohydrates: 16 g; Proteins: 3.5 g.

Cannellini Pesto Spaghetti

Preparation Time: 5 minutes
Cooking Time: 10 minutes
Servings: 4
Ingredients:
- 12 ounces whole-grain spaghetti, cooked, wearied as well as maintained its heat, half cup cooking liquid kept back
- 1 cup pesto
- Two cups prepared cannellini beans, drained and rinsed

Directions:
1. After the pasta has been boiled, transfer it to a big container and stir inside the pesto.
2. To finish, include the beans as well as the boiling fluid that you set aside earlier, then give everything a good shake.

Nutrition: Calories: 549; Proteins: 18.3 g; Carbohydrates: 45 g; Fat: 35 g.

Classic Tomato Soup

Preparation Time: 10 minutes
Cooking Time: 60 minutes
Servings: 6
Ingredients:

- 3 pounds of halved tomatoes
- 1 cup of canned crushed tomatoes
- 2-3 chopped carrots
- 2 chopped yellow onions
- 5 minced garlic cloves
- 2 ounces of basil leaves
- 2 teaspoons of thyme leaves
- 1 teaspoon of dry oregano
- ½ teaspoon of ground cumin
- ½ teaspoon of paprika
- 2 (½) cups of water
- Fresh lime juice to taste
- 2 tablespoons Extra virgin olive oil
- Salt to taste
- Black pepper to taste

Directions:
1. Prepare the microwave to 450 degrees Fahrenheit. In the bottom of a parchment paper spread oil.
2. Combine the carrots and tomatoes in a big basin and mix well. Include oil, salt, black pepper and stir.
3. The vegetable combination should be spread out within a thin sheet on the parchment paper.
4. Cook for a total of 40 mins, followed by an additional ten mins of resting time.
5. Place the baked veggies in a mixing bowl or a processor after they have been removed from the oven. Mix after adding a very small amount of water.
6. Put a big stockpot on a burner that is set to moderate-high flame. Put in two teaspoons of olive oil and bring it up to temperature. After the onions have been sliced and simmered for three mins, include the garlic that has been chopped, and continue to cook till it becomes golden.
7. After it has been combined, the mix should be poured into the stockpot. Include in the two and a half glasses of water, the tinned tomatoes, the thyme, the basil, and any more toppings. Raise it over to a boil, then immediately turn down the flame to low and cap it. Maintain a low boil for around twenty mins.
8. Serve with a splash of lime juice. Enjoy!

Nutrition: Calories: 104; Fat: 0.8 g; Carbohydrates: 23.4 g; Proteins: 4.3 g.

Minestrone Soup

Preparation Time: 10 minutes
Cooking Time: 1 hour and 5 minutes
Servings: 6
Ingredients:
- 2 chopped carrots
- 2 chopped celeries (ribs)
- 1 chopped yellow onion
- 2 cups of chopped seasonal vegetables
- 2 cups of greens (chopped kale, spinach, collard greens)
- 4 cups of vegetable broth
- 1 can (28 ounces) of diced tomatoes with liquid
- 1 can (15 ounces) of canned beans

- 1 cup of the whole-grain small shell, elbow or orecchiette pasta
- ¼ cup of tomato paste
- 2 teaspoons of lemon juice
- 2 minced garlic cloves
- ½ teaspoon of thyme
- ½ teaspoon of oregano
- 2 bay leaves
- 1 teaspoon of sea salt
- 4 tablespoons of Extra virgin olive oil
- 2 cups of water
- A pinch of red pepper
- Black pepper to taste

Directions:

1. Place a big saucepan or Dutch microwave on moderate flame. Pour 3 tablespoons of olive oil and warm. Add the chopped carrot, celery, onion, tomato paste and salt. Cook, stirring rapidly, for about 7-10 minutes until the vegetables are tender and onions become translucent.
2. Put in seasonal vegetables, thyme, oregano and garlic. Stir it and cook for 2 minutes until it smells fragrant.
3. Put vegetable broth, water as well as canned tomatoes with their liquid. Add red pepper, bay leaves, black pepper with salt and stir.
4. Increase to medium-high flame and raise it to a simmer. Then cover the pot with a lid, leaving a small 1-inch gap for steam escaping and reduce to low heat for simmering. Cook for 15 minutes.
5. Eradicate the lid and add beans, pasta and greens. Simmer for 20 minutes more until pasta is done.
6. Eliminate and take away bay leaves. Pour in 1 tablespoon of olive oil and lemon juice. Taste; add more seasonings if needed.
7. Serve and enjoy your Minestrone Soup.

Nutrition: Calories: 298; Fat: 10.5 g; Carbohydrates: 45.6 g; Proteins: 9.8 g.

CHAPTER 13:

VEGETABLES AND SIDE DISHES

Scallion and Mint Soup

Preparation Time: 5 minutes
Cooking Time: 15 minutes
Servings: 4
Ingredients:
- 6 cups vegetable broth
- ¼ cup fresh mint leaves, roughly chopped
- ¼ cup chopped scallions, white and green parts
- 3 garlic cloves, minced
- 3 tablespoons freshly squeezed lime juice

Directions:
1. In a large stockpot, combine the broth, mint, scallions, garlic and lime juice. Bring to a boil over medium-high heat.
2. Cover and reduce the heat to low. Simmer for 15 minutes and serve.

Nutrition: Calories: 55; Proteins: 5 g; Carbohydrates: 5 g; Fat: 2 g.

Green Pea Soup

Preparation Time: 5 minutes.
Cooking Time: 50 minutes.
Servings: 6
Ingredients:
- 1 (16 ounces) package dried green split peas, soaked overnight
- 5 cups vegetable broth or water
- 2 teaspoons garlic powder
- 2 teaspoons onion powder

- 1 teaspoon dried oregano
- 1 teaspoon dried thyme
- ¼ teaspoon freshly ground black pepper

Directions:
1. In a large stockpot, combine the split peas, broth, garlic powder, onion powder, oregano, thyme and pepper. Bring to a boil over medium-high heat.
2. Cover and reduce the heat to medium-low and simmer for 45 minutes, stirring every 5 to 10 minutes. Serve warm.

Nutrition: Calories: 297; Fat: 2 g; Carbohydrates: 48 g; Proteins: 23 g.

Avocado Chaat

Preparation Time: 15 minutes
Cooking Time: 5 minutes
Servings: 4
Ingredients:
- 4 avocados, peeled and diced into bite-sized chunks
- 2 teaspoons Chaat masala
- 1 lime, juiced
- ½ tsp sea salt
- Coconut yogurt to serve

Directions:
1. Place all together with the ingredients in a large bowl and shake them well.
2. Now serve it with some coconut yogurt if you desire.

Nutrition: Calories: 234; Fat: 21 g; Proteins: 3 g; Carbohydrates: 12 g.

Crispy Brinjal "Bacon"

Preparation Time: 15 minutes
Cooking Time: 40 minutes
Servings: 14
Ingredients:
- 1 medium eggplant
- 1 ½ tablespoon tamari
- 1 tablespoon vegan Worcestershire
- 1 teaspoon. smoked paprika
- 1 pinch garlic powder
- 1 tablespoon maple syrup
- 2 tablespoons avocado oil
- 2 teaspoons liquid smoke
- 1 pinch sea salt
- ½ tsp. black pepper, freshly cracked

Directions:

1. Take an eggplant and sliced it in half.
2. Chop down the eggplant in small size.
3. Prepare the sauce by adding Worcestershire sauce, maple syrup, paprika, garlic powder, sea salt, and black pepper into a bowl.
4. Place the sauce onto the eggplant and sprinkle black pepper.
5. Cook till the eggplant looks crispy and red.
6. For more crisps, let it cool down after you put away heat.

Nutrition: Calories: 28; Fat: 2 g; Proteins: 0.3 g; Carbohydrates: 2 g.

Pomegranate Flower Sprouts

Preparation Time: 15 minutes
Cooking Time: 15 minutes
Servings: 2
Ingredients:

- 3 tablespoons pomegranate molasses
- 150 g flower sprouts
- Vegetable oil for deep-frying
- A pinch of sea salt flakes
- A pinch pul biber

Directions:

1. Warm the oil in the pan, and when enough heat, add flower sprouts.
2. Just fry them for 30 seconds.
3. Add them into the bowl with other ingredients and mix.
4. Serve right away.

Nutrition: Calories: 202; Fat: 11 g; Proteins: 3 g; Carbohydrates: 19 g.

Banana Curry

Preparation Time: 15 minutes
Cooking Time: 15 minutes **Servings:** 3
Ingredients:

- 2 tablespoons olive oil
- 2 yellow onions, chopped
- 8 garlic cloves, minced
- 2 tablespoons curry powder
- 1 tablespoon ground ginger
- 1 tablespoon ground cumin
- 1 teaspoon ground turmeric
- 1 teaspoon ground cinnamon
- 1 teaspoon red chili powder
- Salt and ground black pepper, to taste
- 2/3 cup soy yogurt
- 1 cup tomato puree
- 2 bananas, peeled and sliced
- 3 tomatoes, chopped finely
- ¼ cup unsweetened coconut flakes

Directions:

1. In a large pan, heat the oil over medium heat and sauté onion for about 4–5 minutes.
2. Add the garlic, curry powder, and spices, and sauté for about 1 minute.

3. Add the soy yogurt and tomato sauce and bring to a gentle boil.
4. Stir in the bananas and simmer for about 3 minutes.
5. Stir in the tomatoes and simmer for about 1–2 minutes.
6. Stir in the coconut flakes and immediately remove them from the heat.
7. Serve hot.

Nutrition: Calories: 382; Fat: 18 g; Carbohydrates: 53 g; Proteins: 9 g.

Mushroom Curry

Preparation Time: 15 minutes
Cooking Time: 20 minutes
Servings: 3
Ingredients:

- 2 cups tomatoes, chopped
- 1 green chili, chopped
- 1 teaspoon fresh ginger, chopped
- ¼ cup cashews
- 2 tablespoons canola oil
- ½ teaspoon cumin seeds
- ¼ teaspoon ground coriander
- ¼ teaspoon ground turmeric
- ¼ teaspoon red chili powder
- 1½ cups fresh shiitake mushrooms, sliced
- 1½ cups fresh button mushrooms, sliced
- 1 cup frozen corn kernels
- 1¼ cups water
- ¼ cup unsweetened coconut milk
- Salt and ground black pepper, to taste

Directions:

1. In a food processor, add the tomatoes, green chili, ginger, and cashews. Pulse until smooth paste forms.
2. In a pan, heat the oil over medium heat and sauté the cumin seeds for about 1 minute.
3. Add the spices and sauté for about 1 minute.
4. Add the tomato paste and cook for about 5 minutes.
5. Stir in the mushrooms, corn, water, and coconut milk, and bring to a boil.
6. Cook for about 10–12 minutes, stirring occasionally.
7. Season with salt and black pepper and remove from the heat.
8. Serve hot.

Nutrition: Calories: 311; Fat: 20 g; Carbohydrates: 32 g; Proteins: 8 g.

Veggie Combo

Preparation Time: 15 minutes
Cooking Time: 25 minutes
Servings: 4
Ingredients:

- 1 tablespoon olive oil
- 1 small yellow onion, chopped
- 1 teaspoon fresh thyme, chopped
- 1 garlic clove, minced
- 8 ounces fresh button mushroom, sliced
- 1 pound Brussels sprouts
- 3 cups fresh spinach
- 4 tablespoons walnuts
- Salt and ground black pepper, to taste

Directions:

1. In a large skillet, heat the oil over medium heat and sauté the onion for about 3–4 minutes.
2. Add the thyme and garlic and sauté for about 1 minute.
3. Add the mushrooms and cook for about 15 minutes or until caramelized.
4. Add the Brussels sprouts and cook for about 2–3 minutes.
5. Stir in the spinach and cook for about 3–4 minutes.
6. Stir in the walnuts, salt, and black pepper, and remove from the heat.
7. Serve hot.

Nutrition: Calories: 153; Proteins: 8 g; Carbohydrates: 16 g; Fat: 9 g.

Squash Black Bean Bowl

Preparation Time: 5 minutes
Cooking Time: 30 minutes
Servings: 4
Ingredients:

- 1 large spaghetti squash, halved, seeded
- 1/3 cup water (or 2 tablespoons olive oil, rubbed on the inside of squash)
- Black bean filling
- 1 15-oz can of black beans, emptied and rinsed
- 1 cup fire-roasted corn (or frozen sweet corn)
- 1 cup thinly sliced red cabbage
- 3 tablespoons chopped green onion, green and white parts
- ¼ cup chopped fresh cilantro
- ½ lime, juiced or to taste
- Pepper and salt, to taste
- Avocado mash:
- 1 ripe avocado, mashed
- ½ lime, juiced or to taste
- ¼ tsp cumin
- Pepper and pinch of sea salt

Directions:

1. Preheat the oven to 400° F.
2. Chop the squash in part and scoop out the seeds with a spoon, like a pumpkin.
3. Fill the roasting pan with 1/3 cup of water. Lay the squash, cut side down, in the pan. Bake for 30 minutes until soft and tender.
4. While this is baking, mix all the ingredients for the black bean filling in a medium-sized bowl.

5. In a small dish, crush the avocado and blend in the ingredients for the avocado mash.
6. Eliminate the squash from the oven and let it cool for 5 minutes. Scrape the squash with a fork so that it looks like spaghetti noodles. Then, fill it with black bean filling and top with avocado mash.
7. Serve and enjoy.

Nutrition: Calories: 85; Fat: 0.5 g; Carbohydrates: 6 g; Proteins: 4 g.

Sherry Roasted King Trumpet

Preparation Time: 10 minutes
Cooking Time: 20 minutes
Servings: 4
Ingredients:

- 1 ½ pounds king trumpet mushrooms, cleaned and sliced in half lengthwise.
- 2 tablespoons olive oil
- 4 cloves garlic, minced or chopped
- 1/2 teaspoons dried rosemary
- 1/2 teaspoons dried thyme
- 1/2 teaspoons dried parsley flakes
- 1 teaspoon Dijon mustard
- 1/4 cup dry sherry
- Sea salt and freshly ground black pepper, to taste

Directions:

1. Start by preheating your oven to 390° F. Line a large baking pan with parchment paper.
2. In a mixing bowl, toss the mushrooms with the remaining ingredients until well coated on all sides.
3. Place the mushrooms in a single layer on the prepared baking pan.
4. Roast the mushrooms for approximately 20 minutes, tossing them halfway through the cooking.
5. Bon appétit!

Nutrition: Calories: 138; Fat: 8 g; Carbohydrates: 12 g; Proteins: 6 g.

Tomato and Basil Bruschetta

Preparation Time: 10 minutes
Cooking Time: 6 minutes
Servings: 2
Ingredients:

- 3 tomatoes, chopped
- ¼ cup chopped fresh basil
- 1 tablespoon extra-virgin olive oil
- A pinch of sea salt
- 1 baguette, cut into 12 slices
- 1 garlic clove, sliced in half

Directions:

1. In a small bowl, combine the tomatoes, basil, olive oil, and salt and stir to mix. Set aside. Preheat the oven to 400° F.

2. Place the baguette slices in a single layer on a baking sheet and toast in the oven until brown for about 6 minutes.
3. Flip the bread slices over once during cooking. Remove from the oven and rub the bread on both sides with the sliced clove of garlic.
4. Top with the tomato-basil mixture and serve immediately.

Nutrition: Calories: 120; Proteins: 12 g; Carbohydrates: 35 g; Fat:2 g.

Rosemary and Garlic Roasted Carrots

Preparation Time: 15 minutes
Cooking Time: 25 minutes
Servings: 4
Ingredients:

- 2 pounds carrots, trimmed and halved lengthwise
- 4 tablespoons olive oil
- 2 tablespoons champagne vinegar
- 4 cloves garlic, minced
- 2 sprigs rosemary, chopped
- Sea salt and ground black pepper, to taste
- 4 tablespoons pine nuts, chopped

Directions:

1. Begin by preheating your oven to 400° F.
2. Toss the carrots with olive oil, vinegar, garlic, rosemary, salt and black pepper. Arrange them in a single layer on a parchment-lined roasting sheet.
3. Roast the carrots in the preheated oven for about 20 minutes, until fork-tender.
4. Garnish the carrots with pine nuts and serve immediately. Bon appétit!

Nutrition: Calories: 228; Fat: 14 g; Carbohydrates: 24 g; Proteins: 3 g.

Sauté Cremini Mushrooms

Preparation Time: 10 minutes
Cooking Time: 10 minutes
Servings: 4
Ingredients:

- 4 tablespoons olive oil
- 4 tablespoons shallots, chopped
- 2 cloves garlic, minced
- 1 ½ pound Cremini mushrooms, sliced
- 1/4 cup dry white wine
- Sea salt and ground black pepper, to taste

Directions:

1. In a sauté pan, heat the olive oil over moderately high heat.
2. Now, sauté the shallot for 3 to 4 minutes or until tender and translucent. Add in the garlic and continue to cook for 30 seconds more or until aromatic.
3. Stir in the Cremini mushrooms, wine, salt and black pepper; continue sautéing an additional 6 minutes until your mushrooms are lightly browned.
4. Bon appétit!

Nutrition: Calories: 197; Fat: 15 g; Carbohydrates: 8 g; Proteins: 7 g.

Garlic and Herbs Mushrooms Skillet

Preparation Time: 10 minutes
Cooking Time: 10 minutes
Servings: 4
Ingredients:

- 4 tablespoons vegan butter
- 1 ½ pounds oyster mushrooms halved
- 3 cloves garlic, minced
- 1 teaspoon dried oregano
- 1 teaspoon dried rosemary
- 1 teaspoon dried parsley flakes
- 1 teaspoon dried marjoram
- 1/2 cup dry white wine
- Kosher salt and ground black pepper, to taste

Directions:

1. In a sauté pan, heat the olive oil over moderately high heat.
2. Now, sauté the mushrooms for 3 minutes or until they release the liquid. Add in the garlic and continue to cook for 30 seconds more or until aromatic.
3. Stir in the spices and continue sautéing for 6 minutes until your mushrooms are lightly browned.
4. Bon appétit!

Nutrition: Calories: 207; Fat: 15 g; Carbohydrates: 12 g; Proteins: 9 g.

Minted Peas

Preparation Time: 5 minutes
Cooking Time: 5 minutes
Servings: 4
Ingredients:

- 1 tablespoon extra-virgin olive oil
- Cups peas, fresh or frozen (not canned)
- ½ teaspoon sea salt
- Freshly ground black pepper
- 3 tablespoons chopped fresh mint

Directions:

1. In a large sauté pan, heat the olive oil over medium-high heat until hot. Add the peas and cook for about 5 minutes.
2. Remove the pan from heat. Stir in the salt, season with pepper, and stir in the mint.
3. Serve hot.

Nutrition: Calories: 53; Fat: 0.2 g; Proteins: 12 g; Carbohydrates: 15 g.

Cajun Sweet Potatoes

Preparation Time: 5 minutes
Cooking Time: 30 minutes
Servings: 4
Ingredients:

- 2 pounds sweet potatoes

- 2 teaspoons extra-virgin olive oil
- ½ teaspoon ground cayenne pepper
- ½ teaspoon smoked paprika
- ½ teaspoon dried oregano
- ½ teaspoon dried thyme
- ½ teaspoon garlic powder
- ½ teaspoon salt (optional)

Directions:
1. Preheat the oven to 400° F. Line a baking sheet with parchment paper.
2. Wash the potatoes, pat dry, and cut into ¾-inch cubes. Transfer to a large bowl, and pour the olive oil over the potatoes.
3. In a small bowl, combine the cayenne, paprika, oregano, thyme, and garlic powder.
4. Sprinkle the spices over the potatoes and combine until the potatoes are well coated. Spread the potatoes on the prepared baking sheet in a single layer. Season with salt (if using).
5. Roast for 30 minutes while stirring the potatoes after 15 minutes.
6. Divide the potatoes evenly among four single-serving containers. Let it cool completely before sealing.

Nutrition: Calories: 219; Fat: 3 g; Carbohydrates: 46 g; Proteins: 4 g.

Baked Brussel Sprouts

Preparation Time: 10 minutes
Cooking Time: 40 minutes
Servings: 4
Ingredients:

- 1 pound Brussels sprouts
- 2 teaspoons extra-virgin olive or canola oil
- 4 teaspoons minced garlic (about 4 cloves)
- 1 teaspoon dried oregano
- ½ teaspoon dried rosemary
- ½ teaspoon salt
- ¼ teaspoon freshly ground black pepper
- 1 tablespoon balsamic vinegar

Directions:
1. Preheat the oven to 400° F.
2. Line a rimmed baking sheet with parchment paper. Trim and halve the brussels sprouts. Transfer to a large bowl. Toss with olive oil, garlic, oregano, rosemary, salt, and pepper to coat well.
3. Transfer to the prepared baking sheet.
4. Bake for 35-40 minutes, shaking the pan occasionally to help with even browning until crisp on the outside and tender on the inside.
5. Remove from the oven and transfer to a large bowl.
6. Stir in balsamic vinegar.
7. Divide the brussels sprouts evenly among four single-serving containers. Let it cool before sealing the lids.

Nutrition: Calories: 77; Total fat: 3 g; Carbohydrates: 12 g; Proteins: 4 g.

Cauliflower Latke

Preparation Time: 15 minutes
Cooking Time: 30 minutes
Servings: 4
Ingredients:

- 12 oz. cauliflower rice, cooked
- 1 egg, beaten
- 1/3 c. cornstarch
- Salt and pepper to taste
- ¼ cup vegetable oil, divided
- Chopped onion chives

Directions:
1. Squeeze excess water from the cauliflower rice using paper towels.
2. Place the cauliflower rice in a bowl.
3. Stir in the egg and cornstarch.
4. Season with salt and pepper.
5. Fill 2 tablespoons of oil into a pan over medium heat.
6. Add 2–3 tablespoons of the cauliflower mixture into the pan.
7. Cook for 3 minutes on each side.
8. Repeat until you've used up the rest of the batter.
9. Garnish with chopped chives.

Nutrition: Calories: 209; Fiber: 1.9 g; Proteins: 3.4 g.

Roasted Brussels Sprouts

Preparation Time: 30 minutes
Cooking Time: 20 minutes
Servings: 4
Ingredients:

- 1 lb. Brussels sprouts, sliced in half
- 1 tablespoon olive oil
- Salt and pepper to taste
- 2 teaspoons balsamic vinegar
- ¼ c. pomegranate seeds
- ¼ c. goat cheese, crumbled

Directions:
1. Preheat your oven to 400° F.
2. Coat the Brussels sprouts with oil.
3. Sprinkle with salt and pepper.
4. Transfer to a baking pan.
5. Roast in the oven for 20 minutes.
6. Drizzle with vinegar.
7. Sprinkle with the seeds and cheese before serving.

Nutrition: Calories: 117; Fiber: 4.8 g; Proteins: 5.8 g.

Brussels Sprouts and Cranberries

Preparation Time: 10 minutes
Cooking Time: 0 minute
Servings: 6
Ingredients:

- 3 tablespoons lemon juice
- ¼ c. olive oil
- Salt and pepper to taste

- 1 lb. Brussels sprouts, sliced thinly
- ¼ c. dried cranberries, chopped
- ½ c. pecans, toasted and chopped
- ½ c. Parmesan cheese, shaved

Directions:
1. Mix the lemon juice, olive oil, salt, and pepper in a bowl.
2. Toss the Brussels sprouts, cranberries, and pecans in this mixture.
3. Sprinkle the Parmesan cheese on top.

Nutrition: Calories: 245; Proteins: 6.4 g; Fiber: 5 g.

Potato Latke

Preparation Time: 15 minutes
Cooking Time: 10 minutes
Servings: 6
Ingredients:
- 3 eggs, beaten
- 1 onion, grated
- 1 ½ teaspoon baking powder
- Salt and pepper to taste
- 2 lbs. potatoes, peeled and grated
- ¼ c. all-purpose flour
- 4 tablespoons vegetable oil
- Chopped onion chives

Directions:
1. Prep your oven to 400° F.
2. Scourge eggs, onion, baking powder, salt, and pepper.
3. Squeeze moisture from the shredded potatoes using a paper towel.
4. Add potatoes to the egg mixture.
5. Stir in the flour.
6. Heat the oil into a pan over medium setting.
7. Cook a small amount of the batter for 3–4 minutes per side.
8. Repeat. Garnish with the chives.

Nutrition: Calories: 266; Carbohydrates: 34.6 g; Proteins: 7.6 g.

Broccoli Rabe

Preparation Time: 15 minutes
Cooking Time: 15 minutes
Servings: 8
Ingredients:
- 2 oranges, sliced in half
- 1 lb. broccoli rabe
- 2 tablespoons sesame oil, toasted
- Salt and pepper to taste
- 1 tablespoon sesame seeds, toasted

Directions:
1. Heat the oil into a pan over medium setting.
2. Add the oranges and cook until caramelized.
3. Transfer to a plate.
4. Put the broccoli in the pan and cook for 8 minutes.
5. Squeeze the oranges to release juice in a bowl.
6. Stir in the oil, salt, and pepper.
7. Coat the broccoli rabe with the mixture.

8. Sprinkle seeds on top.
Nutrition: Calories: 59; Carbohydrates: 4.1 g; Proteins: 2.2 g.

Whipped Potatoes

Preparation Time: 20 minutes
Cooking Time: 35 minutes
Servings: 10
Ingredients:
- 4 cups water
- 3 lb. potatoes, sliced into cubes
- 3 garlic cloves, crushed
- 6 tablespoons butter
- 10 sage leaves
- ½ cup Greek yogurt
- ¼ cup low-fat milk
- Bay leaves

Directions:
1. Cook potatoes in water for 30 minutes.
2. Drain.
3. Cook garlic in butter for 1 minute over medium heat.
4. Add the sage and bay leaves and cook for 5 more minutes.
5. Discard the garlic and bay leaves.
6. Use a fork to mash the potatoes.
7. Whip using an electric mixer while gradually adding the butter, yogurt, and milk.
8. Season with salt.

Nutrition: Calories: 169; Carbohydrates: 22 g; Proteins: 4.2 g.

Quinoa Avocado Salad

Preparation Time: 15 minutes
Cooking Time: 4 minutes
Servings: 4
Ingredients:
- 2 tablespoons balsamic vinegar
- ¼ cup cream
- ¼ cup buttermilk
- 5 tablespoons lemon juice
- 1 clove garlic, grated
- 2 tablespoons shallot, minced
- Salt and pepper to taste
- 2 tablespoons avocado oil, divided
- 1 ¼ cup quinoa, cooked
- 2 heads endive, sliced
- 2 firm pears, sliced thinly
- 2 avocados, sliced
- ¼ cup fresh dill, chopped

Directions:
1. Combine the vinegar, cream, milk, 1 tablespoon lemon juice, garlic, shallot, salt, and pepper in a bowl.
2. Pour 1 tablespoon oil into a pan over medium heat.
3. Heat the quinoa for 4 minutes.
4. Transfer quinoa to a plate.
5. Toss the endive and pears in a mixture of remaining oil, remaining lemon juice, salt, and pepper.
6. Transfer to a plate.
7. Toss the avocado in the reserved dressing.

8. Add to the plate.
9. Top with the dill and quinoa.

Nutrition: Calories: 431; Fiber: 6 g; Proteins: 6.6 g.

Roasted Sweet Potatoes

Preparation Time: 20 minutes
Cooking Time: 20 minutes
Servings: 4
Ingredients:

- 2 potatoes, sliced into wedges
- 2 tablespoons olive oil, divided
- Salt and pepper to taste
- 1 red bell pepper, chopped
- ¼ cup fresh cilantro, chopped
- 1 garlic, minced
- 2 tablespoons almonds, toasted and sliced
- 1 tablespoon lime juice

Directions:

1. Preheat your oven to 425° F.
2. Toss the sweet potatoes in oil and salt.
3. Transfer to a baking pan.
4. Roast for 20 minutes.
5. In a bowl, combine the red bell pepper, cilantro, garlic, and almonds.
6. In another bowl, mix the lime juice, remaining oil, salt, and pepper.
7. Drizzle this mixture over the red bell pepper mixture.
8. Serve sweet potatoes with the red bell pepper mixture.

Nutrition: Calories: 146; Fiber: 2.9 g; Proteins: 2.3 g.

Cauliflower Salad

Preparation Time: 20 minutes
Cooking Time: 15 minutes
Servings: 4
Ingredients:

- 8 cups cauliflower florets
- 5 tablespoons olive oil, divided
- Salt and pepper to taste
- 1 cup parsley
- 1 garlic clove, minced
- 2 tablespoons lemon juice
- ¼ cup almonds, toasted and sliced
- 3 cups arugula
- 2 tablespoons olives, sliced
- ¼ cup feta, crumbled

Directions:

1. Preheat your oven to 425° F.
2. Toss the cauliflower in a mixture of 1 tablespoon olive oil, salt, and pepper.
3. Place in a baking pan and roast for 15 minutes.
4. Put the parsley, remaining oil, garlic, lemon juice, salt, and pepper in a blender.
5. Pulse until smooth.
6. Place the roasted cauliflower in a salad bowl. Stir in the rest of the ingredients along with the parsley dressing.

Nutrition: Calories: 198; Fiber: 4.1 g; Proteins: 5.4 g.

Garlic Mashed Potatoes and Turnips

Preparation Time: 20 minutes
Cooking Time: 30 minutes
Servings: 8
Ingredients:

- 1 head garlic
- 1 teaspoon olive oil
- 1 lb. turnips, sliced into cubes
- 2 lbs. potatoes, sliced into cubes
- ½ cup almond milk
- ½ cup Parmesan cheese, grated
- 1 tablespoon fresh thyme, chopped
- 1 tablespoon fresh chives, chopped
- 2 tablespoons butter

Directions:

1. Preheat your oven to 375° F.
2. Slice the tip off the garlic head.
3. Dash little oil and roast in the oven for 45 minutes. Boil the turnips and potatoes in a pot with water for 30 minutes or until tender.
4. Add all the ingredients into a food processor along with the garlic.
5. Pulse until smooth.

Nutrition: Calories: 141; Fiber: 3.1 g; Proteins: 4.6 g.

Green Beans

Preparation Time: 15 minutes
Cooking Time: 20 minutes
Servings: 8
Ingredients:

- 1 shallot, chopped
- 24 oz. green beans
- Salt and pepper to taste
- ½ teaspoon smoked paprika
- 1 teaspoon lemon juice
- 2 teaspoons vinegar

Directions:

1. Preheat your oven to 450°F.
2. Stir in the shallot and beans.
3. Season with salt, pepper, and paprika.
4. Roast for 10 minutes.
5. Drizzle with lemon juice and vinegar.
6. Roast for another 2 minutes.

Nutrition: Calories: 49; Fiber: 3 g; Proteins: 2.9 g.

Coconut Brussels Sprouts

Preparation Time: 15 minutes
Cooking Time: 10 minutes
Servings: 4
Ingredients:

- 1 lb. Brussels sprouts, trimmed and sliced in half

- 2 tablespoons coconut oil
- ¼ cup coconut water
- 1 tablespoon soy sauce

Directions:
1. In a skillet over medium heat, stir the coconut oil and cook the Brussels sprouts for 4 minutes.
2. Pour in the coconut water.
3. Cook for 3 minutes.
4. Add the soy sauce and cook for another 1 minute.

Nutrition: Calories: 114; Fiber: 4.3 g; Proteins: 4 g.

Creamy Polenta

Preparation Time: 5 minutes
Cooking Time: 50 minutes **Servings:** 8

Ingredients:
- 1 1/3 cup cornmeal
- 6 cups water
- Salt to taste

Directions:
1. Add all the ingredients to a pan over medium-high heat.
2. Boil and then simmer for 5 minutes.
3. Reduce the heat to low.
4. Stir until creamy for 45 minutes.
5. Let it sit before serving.

Nutrition: Calories: 74; Fiber: 3 g; Proteins: 1.6 g.

CHAPTER 14:

RICE AND GRAINS

Skillet Quinoa

Preparation Time: 20 minutes
Cooking Time: 25 minutes
Servings: 4
Ingredients:

- 1 cup sweet potato, cubed
- ½ cup water
- 1 tablespoon olive oil
- 1 onion, chopped
- 3 cloves garlic, minced
- 1 teaspoon ground cumin
- 1 teaspoon ground coriander
- ½ teaspoon chili powder
- ½ teaspoon dried oregano
- 15 oz. black beans, rinsed and drained
- 15 oz. roasted tomatoes
- 1 ¼ cup vegetable broth
- 1 cup frozen corn
- 1 cup quinoa (uncooked)
- Salt to taste
- ½ cup light sour cream
- ½ cup fresh cilantro leaves

Directions:

1. Add the water and sweet potato to a pan over medium heat.
2. Bring to a boil.
3. Decrease heat and cook sweet potatoes.
4. Add the oil and onion.
5. Cook for 3 minutes.
6. Cook garlic and spices for 1 minute.
7. Add the rest of the ingredients, except the sour cream and cilantro.
8. Cook for 20 minutes.
9. Serve with sour cream and top with the cilantro before serving.

Nutrition: Calories: 421; Fiber: 11 g; Proteins: 16 g.

Green Beans with Balsamic Sauce

Preparation Time: 10 minutes
Cooking Time: 15 minutes
Servings: 6
Ingredients:

- 2 shallots, sliced
- 8 cups green beans, trimmed
- 2 tablespoons olive oil
- Salt and pepper to taste
- 2 tablespoons balsamic vinegar
- ¼ cup parmesan cheese, grated

Direction:

1. Preheat your oven to 425° F.
2. Line you're baking with foil.
3. In the pan, toss the shallots and beans in oil, salt, and pepper.
4. Roast in the oven for 15 minutes.
5. Drizzle with vinegar and top with cheese.

Nutrition: Calories: 78; Fiber: 0.6 g; Proteins: 1.9 g.

Grain Dishes Cranberry and Walnut Brown Rice

Preparation Time: 10 minutes
Cooking Time: 15 minutes
Servings: 5
Ingredients:

- 1/4 cup water
- 1/4 cup dried cranberries
- 14 oz. vegetable broth
- 3/4 cup brown rice
- 1/4 cup chopped walnuts
- 1/8 teaspoon ground cinnamon
- Salt to taste

Directions:

1. To begin this recipe, you should first cook your brown rice in the vegetable broth according to the directions on the package.
2. Once this is done, allow the rice to cool slightly before adding it to a mixing bowl.
3. With the rice in place, add the walnuts and cranberries. Begin to season with the salt and ground cinnamon.
4. Once everything is in place, toss the flavors together, and your dish is set.

Nutrition: Calories: 150; Carbs: 25 g; Fat: 5 g; Proteins: 5 g.

Curried Rice

Preparation Time: 5 minutes
Cooking Time: 25 minutes **Servings:** 4
Ingredients:

- 1 tablespoon olive oil
- 1 broccoli, chopped
- 2 teaspoons ginger
- 1 cup spinach, chopped
- 1 tablespoon water
- 1 teaspoon curry powder
- 1 cup brown rice
- 2 garlic cloves, minced
- Salt to taste
- 2 carrots, chopped
- Pepper to taste

Directions:

1. Whether you are using this recipe as a base or a side, it is sure to offer a kick to any dish it is served with! To save yourself some time, you should prepare all the vegetables ahead of time.
2. When you are set to cook the dish, bring a skillet above moderate temperature and toss the oil, ginger, and garlic together. Once you can smell these ingredients, you can add the broccoli and carrot pieces. At this point, you should stir the ingredients and season to your fancy.
3. Next, flash steam the vegetables.
4. You can complete this task by placing one tablespoon of water into the bottom of the skillet and place a lid over the top for one minute.
5. When that is set, add your cooked brown rice along with the curry powder. Be sure to toss everything and coat the ingredients well.
6. If the rice is seasoned to your fancy, allow to cool off slightly and then serve.

Nutrition: Calories: 250; Carbs: 45 g; Fat: 5 g; Proteins: 10 g.

Cilantro and Avocado Lime Rice

Preparation Time: 5 minutes
Cooking Time: 20 minutes
Servings: 4
Ingredients:

- 2 avocados, sliced
- 5 cups brown rice, cooked
- 1/2 teaspoon cumin
- 1/4 cup cilantro, chopped
- 2 tablespoon lime juice
- 1 garlic clove, minced
- Salt to taste

Directions:

1. For a rice recipe with a twist, you need to try this recipe! Begin by taking out a mixing bowl and mashing down the avocado pieces until they are perfectly smooth.
2. Once the avocado is set, add in your seasonings, cilantro, and squeeze in the lime juice.
3. Finally, stir in your brown rice that has already been cooked and blend together well before serving.

Nutrition: Calories: 450; Carbs: 60 g; Fat: 15 g; Proteins: 5 g.

Fried Veggie Brown Rice

Preparation Time: 10 minutes
Cooking Time: 35 minutes
Servings: 4
Ingredients:

- 4 garlic cloves, chopped
- 1/2 teaspoon sesame oil
- 3 1/2 cups water
- 2 cups brown rice
- 4 green onions
- 1 cup green peas
- 1 carrot, diced
- 1/2 red bell pepper, diced
- 1 tablespoon rice vinegar
- 1 1/2 tablespoon soy sauce

Directions:

1. Fried rice is a classic dish; now you can make the healthy version of it! You should start this recipe cooking your rice in some water according to the directions on the package.
2. As the rice cooks, take out a skillet and bring it over high heat.
3. Once warm, add in the olive oil, scallions, ginger, and chopped garlic. When everything is in place, cook the ingredients for two or three minutes.
4. Next, toss in the peas, carrots, and the diced peppers. You will only be cooking these for another three minutes. Be sure to stir everything consistently to help avoid anything burning to the bottom.
5. With the vegetables all cooked, it is time to add in the rice vinegar, soy sauce, and the rice you just cooked. At this point, feel free to season the dish however you desire.
6. Finally, portion out your meal, and enjoy your rice.

Nutrition: Calories: 410; Carbs: 80 g; Fat: 4 g; Proteins: 10 g.

Vegetable Stir-fry

Preparation Time: 10 minutes
Cooking Time: 40 minutes
Servings: 3
Ingredients:

- 2 tablespoon olive oil
- 1/2 zucchini
- 1/2 red bell pepper
- 4 garlic cloves
- 1/2 broccoli
- 1 cup cabbage
- 1/2 cup brown rice
- 2 tablespoons tamari sauce

- 1 red chili pepper
- 1 teaspoon cayenne powder
- 1 parsley
- Optional: sesame seeds

Directions:

1. First things first, go ahead and cook your brown rice according to the directions provided on the package.
2. As the rice cooks, get out your frying pan and place some water at the bottom. Once it is boiling, add in all of the diced vegetables from the list above. Once in place, be sure the ingredients are covered by the water, and then cook everything for two minutes under high heat. Once done, drain the vegetables and place them to the side.
3. Next, put some olive oil in the pan and add garlic, cayenne, and parsley. After this has cooked for a minute or so, add the vegetables back in along with the tamari sauce and your rice.
4. Cook everything here for an additional two minutes before removing it from heat.
5. When it is ready, add some sesame seeds as garnish.

Nutrition: Calories: 280; Carbs: 35 g; Fat: 10 g; Proteins: 10 g.

Sweet Coconut Pilaf

Preparation Time: 5 minutes
Cooking Time: 30 minutes
Servings: 4
Ingredients:

- 2 tablespoons coconut oil
- 1 cinnamon stick
- 1 teaspoon ground cumin
- 1 cauliflower
- 1 onion, diced
- 3 garlic cloves
- 2 bay leaves
- 1 teaspoon ground coriander
- 1 cup coconut milk
- 1 1/2 teaspoon ground ginger
- 1 teaspoon ground cardamom
- 1 1/2 teaspoon ground turmeric
- 1 tablespoon ginger, grated

Directions:

1. If you are looking to switch up your grains, this is the perfect dish for you. Begin by heating your oven to 400° F.
2. As the oven begins to warm up, it is now time to prepare the cauliflower. Start by cutting the cauliflower into bite-sized pieces and then carefully place them onto your baking pan. Once in place, drizzle some coconut oil over the cauliflower and dash with salt, coriander, and cumin. When the cauliflower is set, pop the dish into the oven for about twenty-five minutes.
3. As the cauliflower cooks, take out a saucepan and begin heating up another tablespoon of coconut oil over medium heat. Once warm, you can also add in the ginger, garlic, onion, coriander, and a bit of salt. Cook these ingredients together for about five minutes.
4. With the garlic and onion cooked, add the rest of the spices before also throwing in the quinoa, a half cup of water, cinnamon, coconut milk, and the bay leaves. Throw a lid on top and simmer the ingredients for fifteen minutes.
5. When the quinoa is done, mix together the cauliflower and quinoa together, and your meal is set!

Nutrition: Calories: 150; Carbs: 20 g; Fat: 7 g; Proteins: 5 g.

Vegetable Quinoa Tots

Preparation Time: 5 minutes
Cooking Time: 1hour **Servings:** 4
Ingredients:

- 1 broccoli, cut
- 1/2 cup peas
- 2 carrots, chopped
- 1 cup quinoa, cooked
- 1 garlic powder
- 1/4 cup nutritional yeast
- Salt to taste
- 1/2 cup water
- 3/4 cup garbanzo bean flour

Directions:

1. These tots are easy to make and even easier to enjoy! You should start this recipe by prepping the oven to 400°F and getting out your sheet pan.
2. Before you begin creating the tots, cook the quinoa according to the directions provided on the package. In the meantime, take a small bowl and mix the flour and water. Once complete, set the bowl to the side.
3. Now, it is time to get your food processor out. Once you have this set, place the peas, carrot, and broccoli in. Blend these ingredients until the vegetables are broken down into tiny bits. When this step is complete, add it into the flour mixture along with the quinoa, salt, garlic powder, and nutritional yeast. Be sure to mix everything as well as possible.
4. When you are set, use your hands to create tots from the mixture. Once created, place them onto your baking sheet and pop the dish into the oven for twenty minutes.
5. After twenty minutes, take away the dish from the cooker and flip the tots over. Once they are all flipped, place the dish back into the oven for another twenty minutes, and by the end, you will have crispy and healthy tots.

Nutrition: Calories: 260; Carbs: 50 g; Fat: 3 g; Proteins: 15 g.

Easy Millet Nuggets

Preparation Time: 5 minutes
Cooking Time: 10 minutes
Servings: 4
Ingredients:

- 1/2 cup millet

- 3 scallions, sliced
- 1 lemon zest
- 1/4 cup mint
- 1 can chickpeas
- 2 tablespoons olive oil
- Pepper to taste

Directions:

1. Begin this recipe by first cooking the millet. You can do this by following the instructions provided on the packet.
2. As the millet cooks, place your chickpeas into a mixing dish and smash them down using a fork. When this is done, incorporate the remainder of the ingredients along with the cooked millet.
3. Next, use your hands to create nugget shapes from the mixture.
4. With this set, heat a skillet over intermediate heat and bake the nuggets for about five minutes on every side.
5. Finally, remove from the pan and dip in your favorite plant-friendly dipping sauce!

Nutrition: Calories: 250; Carbs: 35 g; Fat: 10 g; Proteins: 5 g.

Millet Fritters

Preparation Time: 5 minutes
Cooking Time: 20 minutes
Servings: 4
Ingredients:

- 2 tablespoons coconut oil
- 1/3 cup psyllium husk
- 1/2 cup chickpea flour
- 1 cup millet
- 1/8 teaspoon mustard powder
- Pepper to taste
- 1/2 teaspoon onion powder
- 1/2 teaspoon paprika
- 1 teaspoon dried parsley
- 1/8 teaspoon coriander
- Salt to taste

Directions:

1. To start this recipe, first cook your millet according to the directions on the package. Once this is cooked through, place the millet into a mixing bowl.
2. Next, add the flour, psyllium husk, and all of the seasonings into your bowl and mix everything well.
3. Once you have a "dough" formed, use your hands to create patties from the ingredients and set on a plate to the side.
4. When you bake the fritters, take a medium skillet and put it over a medium heat. As it warms up, add some coconut oil and your first batch of fritters into the pan.
5. You should grill the fritters for nearly five minutes on either side or up until the fritter is a nice, golden color and crunchy on the outer surface.
6. Finally, remove the dish from the stove and enjoy your creation!

Nutrition: Calories: 410; Carbs: 50 g; Fat: 15 g; Proteins: 10 g.

Classic Garlicky Rice

Preparation Time: 4 minutes
Cooking Time: 16 minutes
Servings: 4
Ingredients:

- 4 tablespoons olive oil
- 4 cloves garlic, chopped
- 1 ½ cups white rice
- 2 ½ cups vegetable broth

Directions:

1. In a saucepan, heat the olive oil over a moderately high flame. Add in the garlic and sauté for about 1 minute or until aromatic.
2. Add in the rice and broth. Bring to a boil; immediately turn the heat to a medium flame.
3. Cook for about 15 minutes or until all the liquid has been absorbed. Fluff the rice with a fork; season with salt and pepper, and serve hot!

Nutrition: Calories: 422; Fat: 15.1 g; Carbs: 61.1 g; Proteins: 9.3 g.

Brown Rice with Vegetables and Tofu

Preparation Time: 12 minutes
Cooking Time: 33 minutes
Servings: 4
Ingredients:

- 4 teaspoons sesame seeds
- 2 spring garlic stalks, minced
- 1 cup spring onions, chopped
- 1 carrot, trimmed and sliced
- 1 celery rib, sliced
- 1/4 cup dry white wine
- 10 ounces tofu, cubed
- 1 ½ cups long-grain brown rice, rinsed thoroughly
- 2 tablespoons soy sauce
- 2 tablespoons tahini
- 1 tablespoon lemon juice

Directions:

1. In a wok or large saucepan, heat 2 teaspoons of the sesame oil over medium-high fire. Now, cook the garlic, onion, carrot, and celery for about 3 minutes, stirring periodically to ensure even cooking.
2. Add the wine to deglaze the pan and push the vegetables to one side of the wok. Add in the remaining sesame oil and fry the tofu for 8 minutes, stirring occasionally.
3. Bring 2 ½ cups of water to a boil over medium-high heat. Bring to a simmer and cook the rice for about 30 minutes or until it is tender; fluff the rice and stir it with the soy sauce and tahini.
4. Stir the vegetables and tofu into the hot rice; add a few drizzles of the fresh lemon juice and serve warm. Bon appétit!

Nutrition: Calories: 410; Fat: 13.2 g; Carbs: 60 g; Proteins: 14.3 g.

Basic Amaranth Porridge

Preparation Time: 30 minutes
Cooking Time: 5 minutes
Servings: 4
Ingredients:

- 3 cups water
- 1 cup amaranth
- 1/2 cup coconut milk
- 4 tablespoons agave syrup
- A pinch of kosher salt
- A pinch of grated nutmeg

Directions:

1. Bring the water to a boil over medium-high heat; add in the amaranth and turn the heat to a simmer.
2. Let it cook for about 30 minutes, stirring periodically to prevent the amaranth from sticking to the bottom of the pan.
3. Stir in the remaining ingredients and continue to cook for 1 to 2 minutes more until cooked through. Bon appétit!

Nutrition: Calories: 261; Fat: 4.4 g; Carbs: 49 g; Proteins: 7.3 g.

Country Cornbread with Spinach

Preparation Time: 25 minutes
Cooking Time: 25 minutes
Servings: 8
Ingredients:

- 1 tablespoon flaxseed meal
- 1 cup all-purpose flour
- 1 cup yellow cornmeal
- 1/2 teaspoons baking soda
- 1/2 teaspoons baking powder
- 1 teaspoon kosher salt
- 1 teaspoon brown sugar
- A pinch of grated nutmeg
- 1 ¼ cups oat milk, unsweetened
- 1 teaspoon white vinegar
- 1/2 cup olive oil
- 2 cups spinach, torn into pieces

Directions:

1. Start by preheating your oven to 420° F. Now, coat a baking pan with a nonstick cooking spray.
2. To make the flax eggs, mix the flaxseed meal with 3 tablespoons of water. Stir and let it sit for about 15 minutes.
3. In a mixing bowl, thoroughly combine the flour, cornmeal, baking soda, baking powder, salt, sugar, and grated nutmeg.
4. Gradually add in the flax egg, oat milk, vinegar, and olive oil, whisking constantly to avoid lumps. Afterward, fold in the spinach.
5. Scrape the batter into the prepared baking pan. Bake your cornbread for about 25 minutes or until a tester inserted in the middle comes out dry and clean.
6. Let it stand for about 10 minutes before slicing and serving. Bon appétit!

Per Servings: Calories: 282; Fat: 15.4 g; Carbs: 30 g; Proteins: 4.6 g.

Rice Pudding with Currants

Preparation Time: 5 minutes
Cooking Time: 40 minutes
Servings: 4
Ingredients:

- 1 ½ cups water
- 1 cup white rice
- 2 ½ cups oat milk, divided
- 1/2 cup white sugar
- A pinch of salt
- A pinch of grated nutmeg
- 1 teaspoon ground cinnamon
- 1/2 teaspoons vanilla extract
- 1/2 cup dried currants

Directions:

1. In a saucepan, bring the water to a boil over medium-high heat. Immediately turn the heat to a simmer; add in the rice and let it cook for about 20 minutes.
2. Add the milk, sugar, and spices and continue to cook for 20 minutes more, stirring constantly to prevent the rice from sticking to the pan.
3. Top with dried currants and serve at room temperature. Bon appétit!

Nutrition: Calories: 423; Fat: 5.3 g; Carbs: 85 g; Proteins: 8.8 g.

Millet Porridge with Sultanas

Preparation Time: 5 minutes
Cooking Time: 20 minutes
Servings: 3
Ingredients:

- 1 cup water
- 1 cup coconut milk
- 1 cup millet, rinsed
- 1/4 teaspoon grated nutmeg
- 1/4 teaspoon ground cinnamon
- 1 teaspoon vanilla paste
- 1/4 teaspoon kosher salt
- 2 tablespoons agave syrup
- 4 tablespoons sultana raisins

Directions:

1. Place the water, milk, millet, nutmeg, cinnamon, vanilla, and salt in a saucepan; bring to a boil.
2. Turn the heat to a simmer and let it cook for about 20 minutes; fluff the millet with a fork and spoon into individual bowls.
3. Serve with agave syrup and sultanas. Bon appétit!

Nutrition: Calories: 353; Fat: 5.5 g; Carbs: 65.2 g; Proteins: 9.8 g

Quinoa Porridge with Dried Figs

Preparation Time: 5 minutes

Cooking Time: 20 minutes
Servings: 3
Ingredients:
- 1 cup white quinoa, rinsed
- 2 cups almond milk
- 4 tablespoons brown sugar
- A pinch of salt
- 1/4 teaspoon grated nutmeg
- 1/2 teaspoons ground cinnamon
- 1/2 teaspoons vanilla extract
- 1/2 cup dried figs, chopped

Directions:
1. Place the quinoa, almond milk, sugar, salt, nutmeg, cinnamon, and vanilla extract in a saucepan.
2. Bring it to a boil over medium-high heat. Turn the heat to a simmer and let it cook for about 20 minutes; fluff with a fork.
3. Divide between three serving bowls and garnish with dried figs. Bon appétit!

Nutrition: Calories: 414; Fat: 9 g; Carbs: 71.2 g; Proteins: 13.8 g.

Bread Pudding with Raisins

Preparation Time: 15 minutes
Cooking Time: 45 minutes
Servings: 4
Ingredients:
- 4 cups day-old bread, cubed
- 1 cup brown sugar
- 4 cups coconut milk
- 1/2 teaspoons vanilla extract
- 1 teaspoon ground cinnamon
- 2 tablespoons rum
- 1/2 cup raisins

Directions:
1. Start by preheating your oven to 360° F. Lightly oil a casserole dish with a nonstick cooking spray.
2. Place the cubed bread in the prepared casserole dish.
3. In a mixing bowl, thoroughly combine the sugar, milk, vanilla, cinnamon, rum, and raisins. Pour the custard evenly over the bread cubes.
4. Let it soak for about 15 minutes.
5. Bake in the preheated oven for about 45 minutes or until the top is golden and set. Bon appétit!

Nutrition: Calories: 474; Fat: 12.2 g; Carbs: 72 g; Proteins: 14.4 g.

Bulgur Wheat Salad

Preparation Time: 12 minutes
Cooking Time: 13 minutes **Servings:** 4
Ingredients:
- 1 cup bulgur wheat
- 1 ½ cups vegetable broth
- 1 teaspoon sea salt
- 1 teaspoon fresh ginger, minced
- 4 tablespoons olive oil

- 1 onion, chopped
- 8 ounces canned garbanzo beans, drained
- 2 large roasted peppers, sliced
- 2 tablespoons fresh parsley, roughly chopped

Directions:
1. In a deep saucepan, bring the bulgur wheat and vegetable broth to a simmer; let it cook, covered, for 12 to 13 minutes.
2. Let it stand for about 10 minutes and fluff with a fork.
3. Add the remaining ingredients to the cooked bulgur wheat; serve at room temperature or well-chilled. Bon appétit!

Nutrition: Calories: 359; Fat: 15.5 g; Carbs: 48.1 g; Proteins: 10.1 g.

Rye Porridge with Blueberry Topping

Preparation Time: 9 minutes
Cooking Time: 6 minutes
Servings: 3
Ingredients:
- 1 cup rye flakes
- 1 cup water
- 1 cup coconut milk
- 1 cup fresh blueberries
- 1 tablespoon coconut oil
- 6 dates, pitted

Directions:
1. Add the rye flakes, water, and coconut milk to a deep saucepan; bring to a boil over medium-high. Turn the heat to a simmer and let it cook for 5 to 6 minutes.
2. In a blender or food processor, puree the blueberries with coconut oil and dates.
3. Ladle into three bowls and garnish with the blueberry topping. Bon appétit!

Nutrition: Calories: 359; Fat: 11 g; Carbs: 56.1 g; Proteins: 12.1 g.

Coconut Sorghum Porridge

Preparation Time: 10 minutes
Cooking Time: 15 minutes **Servings:** 2
Ingredients:
- 1/2 cup sorghum
- 1 cup water
- 1/2 cup coconut milk
- 1/4 teaspoon grated nutmeg
- 1/4 teaspoon ground cloves
- 1/2 teaspoons ground cinnamon
- Kosher salt, to taste
- 2 tablespoons agave syrup
- 2 tablespoons coconut flakes

Directions:
1. Place the sorghum, water, milk, nutmeg, cloves, cinnamon, and kosher salt in a saucepan; simmer gently for about 15 minutes.

2. Spoon the porridge into serving bowls. Top with agave syrup and coconut flakes. Bon appétit!

Nutrition: Calories: 289; Fat: 5.1 g; Carbs: 57.8 g; Proteins: 7.3 g.

Dad's Aromatic Rice

Preparation Time: 5 minutes
Cooking Time: 15 minutes
Servings: 4
Ingredients:

- 3 tablespoons olive oil
- 1 teaspoon garlic, minced
- 1 teaspoon dried oregano
- 1 teaspoon dried rosemary
- 1 bay leaf
- 1 ½ cups white rice
- 2 ½ cups vegetable broth
- Sea salt and cayenne pepper, to taste

Directions:

1. In a saucepan, heat the olive oil over a moderately high flame. Add garlic, oregano, rosemary, and bay leaf; sauté for about 1 minute or until aromatic.
2. Add in the rice and broth. Bring to a boil; immediately turn the heat to a gentle simmer.
3. Cook for about 15 minutes or until all the liquid has been absorbed. Fluff the rice with a fork; season with salt and pepper, and serve immediately. Bon appétit!

Nutrition: Calories: 384; Fat: 11.4 g; Carbs: 60.4 g; Proteins: 8.3 g.

Every Day Savory Grits

Preparation Time: 5 minutes
Cooking Time: 30 minutes
Servings: 4
Ingredients:

- 2 tablespoons vegan butter
- 1 sweet onion, chopped
- 1 teaspoon garlic, minced
- 4 cups water
- 1 cup stone-ground grits
- Sea salt and cayenne pepper, to taste

Directions:

1. In a saucepan, melt the vegan butter over medium-high heat. Once hot, cook the onion for about 3 minutes or until tender.
2. Add in the garlic and continue to sauté for 30 seconds more or until aromatic; reserve.
3. Bring the water to a boil over moderately high heat. Stir in the grits, salt, and pepper.
4. Turn the heat to a simmer; cover, and cook for about 30 minutes or until cooked through.
5. Stir in the sautéed mixture and serve warm. Bon appétit!

Nutrition: Calories: 238; Fat: 6.5 g; Carbs: 38.7 g; Proteins: 3.7 g.

Greek-Style Barley Salad

Preparation Time: 5 minutes
Cooking Time: 30 minutes
Servings: 4
Ingredients:

- 1 cup pearl barley
- 2 ¾ cups vegetable broth
- 2 tablespoons apple cider vinegar
- 4 tablespoons extra-virgin olive oil
- 2 bell peppers, seeded and diced
- 1 shallot, chopped
- 2 ounces sun-dried tomatoes in oil, chopped
- 1/2 green olives, pitted and sliced
- 2 tablespoons fresh cilantro, roughly chopped

Directions:

1. Bring the barley and broth to a boil over medium-high heat; now, turn the heat to a simmer. Continue to simmer for about 30 minutes until all the liquid has absorbed; fluff with a fork.
2. Toss the barley with vinegar, olive oil, peppers, shallots, sun-dried tomatoes, and olives; toss to combine well.
3. Garnish with fresh cilantro and serve at room temperature or well-chilled. Enjoy!

Nutrition: Calories: 378; Fat: 15.6 g; Carbs: 50 g; Proteins: 10.7 g.

Easy Sweet Maize Meal Porridge

Preparation Time: 5 minutes
Cooking Time: 10 minutes **Servings:** 2
Ingredients:

- 2 cups water
- 1/2 cup maize meal
- 1/4 teaspoon ground allspice
- 1/4 teaspoon salt
- 2 tablespoons brown sugar
- 2 tablespoons almond butter

Directions:

1. In a saucepan, bring the water to a boil; then gradually add in the maize meal and turn the heat to a simmer.
2. Add in the ground allspice and salt. Let it cook for 10 minutes.
3. Add in the brown sugar and almond butter and gently stir to combine. Bon appétit!

Nutrition: Calories: 278; Fat: 12.7 g; Carbs: 37.2 g; Proteins: 3 g.

Mom's Millet Muffins

Preparation Time: 10 minutes
Cooking Time: 25 minutes **Servings:** 8
Ingredients:

- 2 cup whole-wheat flour
- 1/2 cup millet
- 2 teaspoons baking powder
- 1/2 teaspoons salt
- 1 cup coconut milk

- 1/2 cup coconut oil, melted
- 1/2 cup agave nectar
- 1/2 teaspoons ground cinnamon
- 1/4 teaspoon ground cloves
- A pinch of grated nutmeg
- 1/2 cup dried apricots, chopped

Directions:
1. Begin by preheating your oven to 400° F. Lightly oil a muffin tin with nonstick oil.
2. In a mixing bowl, mix all dry ingredients. In a separate bowl, mix the wet ingredients. Stir the milk mixture into the flour mixture; combine just until evenly moist and do not overmix your batter. Fold in the apricots and scrape the batter into the prepared muffin cups.
3. Bake the muffins in the preheated oven for about 15 minutes or until a tester inserted in the center of your muffin comes out dry and clean. Let it stand for 10 minutes on a wire rack before unmolding and serving. Enjoy!

Nutrition: Calories: 367; Fat: 15.9 g; Carbs: 53.7 g; Proteins: 6.5 g.

Ginger Brown Rice

Preparation Time: 15 minutes
Cooking Time: 30 minutes **Servings:** 4
Ingredients:

- 1 ½ cups brown rice, rinsed
- 2 tablespoons olive oil
- 1 teaspoon garlic, minced
- 1 (1-inch) piece ginger, peeled and minced
- 1/2 teaspoons cumin seeds
- Sea salt and ground black pepper, to taste

Directions:
1. Place the brown rice in a saucepan and cover it with cold water by 2 inches.
2. Bring to a boil.
3. Turn the heat to a simmer and continue to cook for about 30 minutes or until tender.
4. In a sauté pan, heat the olive oil over medium-high heat. Once hot, cook the garlic, ginger, and cumin seeds until aromatic. Stir the garlic/ginger mixture into the hot rice; season with salt and pepper and serve immediately. Bon appétit!

Nutrition: Calories: 318; Fat: 8.8 g; Carbs: 53.4 g; Proteins: 5.6 g.

Sweet Oatmeal "Grits"

Preparation Time: 5 minutes
Cooking Time: 15 minutes **Servings:** 4

Ingredients:

- 1 ½ cups steel-cut oats, soaked overnight
- 1 cup almond milk
- 2 cups water
- A pinch of grated nutmeg
- A pinch of ground cloves
- A pinch of sea salt
- 4 tablespoons almonds, slivered
- 6 dates, pitted and chopped
- 6 prunes, chopped

Directions:
1. In a deep saucepan, bring the steel-cut oats, almond milk, and water to a boil.
2. Add in the nutmeg, cloves, and salt. Immediately turn the heat to a simmer, cover, and continue cooking for about 15 minutes or until they've softened.
3. Then, spoon the grits into four serving bowls; top them with the almonds, dates, and prunes. Bon appétit!

Nutrition: Calories: 380; Fat: 11.1 g; Carbs: 59 g; Proteins: 14.4 g.

Freekeh Bowl with Dried Figs

Preparation Time: 15 minutes
Cooking Time: 35 minutes
Servings: 2
Ingredients:

- 1/2 cup freekeh, soaked for 30 minutes, drained
- 1 1/3 cups almond milk
- 1/4 teaspoon sea salt
- 1/4 teaspoon ground cloves
- 1/4 teaspoon ground cinnamon
- 4 tablespoons agave syrup
- 2 ounces dried figs, chopped

Directions:
1. Place the freekeh, milk, sea salt, ground cloves, and cinnamon in a saucepan.
2. Bring to a boil over medium-high heat.
3. Immediately turn the heat to a simmer for 30 to 35 minutes, stirring occasionally to promote even cooking.
4. Stir in the agave syrup and figs. Ladle the porridge into individual bowls and serve. Bon appétit!

Nutrition: Calories: 458; Fat: 6.8 g; Carbs: 90 g; Proteins: 12.4 g.

CHAPTER 15:

LEGUMES

Cornmeal Porridge with Maple Syrup

Preparation Time: 5 minutes
Cooking Time: 15 minutes
Servings: 4
Ingredients:

- 2 cups water
- 2 cups almond milk
- 1 cinnamon stick
- 1 vanilla bean
- 1 cup yellow cornmeal
- 1/2 cup maple syrup

Directions:

1. In a saucepan, bring the water and almond milk to a boil. Add in the cinnamon stick and vanilla bean.
2. Gradually add in the cornmeal, stirring continuously; turn the heat to a simmer. Let it simmer for about 15 minutes.
3. Drizzle the maple syrup over the porridge and serve warm. Enjoy!

Nutrition: Calories: 328; Fat: 4.8 g; Carbs: 63.4 g; Proteins: 6.6 g.

Garlic and White Bean Soup

Preparation Time: 1 hour
Cooking Time: 10 minutes
Servings: 4
Ingredients:

- 45 ounces cooked cannellini beans
- 1/4 teaspoon dried thyme
- 2 teaspoons minced garlic
- 1/8 teaspoon crushed red pepper
- 1/2 teaspoons dried rosemary
- 1/8 teaspoon ground black pepper
- 2 tablespoons olive oil
- 4 cups vegetable broth

Directions:

1. Place one-third of white beans in a food processor, then pour in 2 cups broth and pulse for 2 minutes until smooth.
2. Place a pot over medium heat, add oil and when hot, add garlic and cook for 1 minute until fragrant. Add pureed beans into the pan along with remaining beans, sprinkle with spices and herbs, pour in the broth, stir until combined, and bring the mixture to boil over medium-high heat. Switch heat to medium-low level. Simmer the beans for 15 minutes, and then mash them with a fork.
3. Taste the soup to adjust seasoning and then serve.

Nutrition: Calories: 222; Fat: 7 g; Carbs: 13 g; Fiber: 9.1 g; Proteins: 11.2 g.

Black Bean and Corn Salad with Cilantro Dressing

Preparation Time: 5 minutes
Cooking Time: 0 minutes
Servings: 4
Ingredients:

- 2 cups frozen corn, thawed
- 3 cups cooked or 2 (15.5-ounce) cans black beans, rinsed and drained
- ½ cup chopped red bell pepper
- ¼ cup minced red onion
- 1 (4-ounce) can chopped mild green chiles, drained
- 2 garlic cloves, crushed
- ¼ cup chopped fresh cilantro
- 1 teaspoon ground cumin
- ½ teaspoon salt (optional)
- ¼ teaspoon freshly ground black pepper
- 2 tablespoons fresh lime juice
- 2 tablespoons water
- ¼ cup extra-virgin olive oil

Directions:

1. In a large bowl, combine the corn, beans, bell pepper, onion, and chiles. Set aside.
2. In a blender or food processor, mince the garlic. Add the cilantro, cumin, salt, and black pepper, then pulse to blend. Add the lime juice, water, and oil and process until well blended.
3. Pour the dressing over the salad and toss to combine. Taste and adjust the seasonings, if necessary.
4. Finish and serve.

Nutrition: Proteins: 243g; Fat: 293g; Carbohydrates: 941 g.

Coconut Curry Lentils

Preparation Time: 15 minutes
Cooking Time: 40 minutes
Servings: 4
Ingredients:

- 1 cup brown lentils
- 1 small white onion, peeled, chopped
- 1 teaspoon minced garlic
- 1 teaspoon grated ginger
- 3 cups baby spinach
- 1 tablespoon curry powder
- 2 tablespoons olive oil
- 13 ounces coconut milk, unsweetened
- 2 cups vegetable broth

For Servings:

- 4 cups cooked rice
- 1/4 cup chopped cilantro

Directions:

1. Place a large pot over medium heat. Add oil and when hot, add ginger and garlic and cook for 1 minute until fragrant.
2. Add onion, cook for 5 minutes and stir in curry powder. Cook for 1 minute until toasted, add lentils and pour in broth.
3. Switch heat to medium-high level, bring the mixture to a boil. Then switch heat to the low level and simmer for 20 minutes until tender and all the liquid is absorbed.
4. Pour in milk and stir until combined. Turn heat to medium level, and simmer for 10 minutes until thickened.
5. Then remove the pot from heat and stir in spinach. Let it stand for 5 minutes until its leaves wilts and then top with cilantro.
6. Serve lentils with rice.

Nutrition: Calories: 184; Fat: 3.7 g: Carbs: 30 g; Proteins: 11.3 g; Fiber: 10.7 g.

Black Beans and Rice

Preparation Time: 10 minutes
Cooking Time: 30 minutes
Servings: 4
Ingredients:

- 3/4 cup white rice
- 1 medium white onion, peeled, chopped
- 3 1/2 cups cooked black beans
- 1 teaspoon minced garlic
- 1/4 teaspoon cayenne pepper
- 1 teaspoon ground cumin

- 1 teaspoon olive oil
- 1 1/2 cups vegetable broth

Directions:

1. Take a large pot over medium-high heat, add oil and when hot, add onion and garlic and cook for 4 minutes until sauté.
2. Then stir in rice, cook for 2 minutes, pour in the broth, bring it to a boil, switch heat to the low level and cook for 20 minutes until tender.
3. Stir in remaining ingredients. Cook for 2 minutes, and then serve straight away.

Nutrition: Calories: 140; Fat: 0.9 g: Carbs: 27.1 g; Proteins: 6.3 g; Fiber: 6.2 g.

Three-bean Cassoulet

Preparation Time: 10 minutes
Cooking Time: 60 minutes **Servings:** 4 to 6
Ingredients:

- 1 tablespoon extra-virgin olive oil
- 1 medium onion chopped
- 2 medium carrots chopped
- 1 celery rib chopped
- 3 garlic cloves minced
- 1½ cups cooked or 1 (15.5-ounce) cans Navy beans, drained and rinsed
- 1½ cups cooked or 1 (15.5-ounce) cans Great Northern beans, drained and rinsed
- 1½ cups cooked or 1 (15.5-ounce) cans cannellini beans drained and rinsed
- 1 (14.5-ounce) can crushed tomatoes
- 1 cup vegetable broth
- 1 tablespoon minced fresh parsley
- 1 teaspoon dried savory
- 1 teaspoon dried thyme
- 1 teaspoon salt
- ¼ teaspoon freshly ground black pepper
- ½ cup dry unseasoned bread crumbs

Directions:

1. Preparing the ingredients:
2. Preheat the oven to 375°F. Lightly oil a 3-quart casserole and set it aside.
3. In a large skillet, heat the oil over medium heat. Add the onion, carrots, celery, and garlic. Cover and cook until softened.
4. Transfer the vegetable mixture to the prepared casserole. Stir in the beans, tomatoes, broth, parsley, savory, thyme, salt, and pepper.
5. Cover tightly and bake until the vegetables are tender and the flavors are blended for about 45 minutes.
6. Finish and Serve
7. Remove the cassoulet from the oven, uncover, and top with the bread crumbs. Return to the oven and bake, uncovered, for 10 minutes longer to lightly brown the crumbs. Serve immediately.

Nutrition: Calories: 140; Fat: 0.9 g: Carbs: 27.1 g; Proteins: 6.3 g; Fiber: 6.2 g.

Pecan Rice

Preparation Time: 10 minutes
Cooking Time: 10 minutes
Servings: 4
Ingredients:

- 1/4 cup chopped white onion
- 1/4 teaspoon ground ginger
- 1/2 cup chopped pecans
- 1/4 teaspoon salt
- 2 tablespoons minced parsley
- 1/4 teaspoon ground black pepper
- 1/4 teaspoon dried basil
- 2 tablespoons vegan margarine
- 1 cup brown rice, cooked

Directions:

1. Take a skillet pan, place it over medium heat, add margarine and when it melts, add all the ingredients, except for rice, and stir until mixed.
2. Cook for 5 minutes, then stir in rice until combined and continue cooking for 2 minutes.
3. Serve straight away.

Nutrition: Calories: 280; Fat: 16.1 g; Carbs: 31 g; Proteins: 4.3 g; Fiber: 3.8 g.

Mediterranean Chickpea Casserole

Preparation Time: 15 minutes
Cooking Time: 60 minutes
Servings: 4
Ingredients:

- 3 cups baby spinach
- 2 medium red onions, peeled, diced
- 2 1/2 cups tomatoes
- 3 cups cooked chickpeas
- 1 ½ teaspoon minced garlic
- 1/3 teaspoon ground black pepper
- 1 ¼ teaspoon salt
- 1/4 teaspoon allspice
- 1 tablespoon coconut sugar
- 1 teaspoon dried oregano
- 1/4 teaspoon cayenne
- 1/4 teaspoon cloves
- 2 bay leaves
- 1 tablespoon coconut oil
- 2 tablespoons olive oil
- 1 cup vegetable stock
- 1 lemon, juiced
- 2 ounces vegan feta cheese

Directions:

1. Take a large skillet pan, place it over medium-high heat, add coconut oil and when it melts, add onion and cook for 5 minutes until softened.
2. Switch heat to medium-low level. Stir in garlic, cook for 2 minutes, then stir in tomatoes. Add all the spices and bay leaves. Pour in the stock, stir until mixed and cook for 20 minutes.

3. Then stir in chickpeas, simmer cooking for 15 minutes until the cooking liquid has reduced by one-third. Stir in spinach and cook for 3 minutes until it begins to wilt.
4. Then stir in olive oil, sugar and lemon juice. Taste to adjust seasoning, and remove and discard bay leaves.
5. When done, top chickpeas with cheese, broil for 5 minutes until cheese has melted and golden brown, then garnish with parsley and serve.

Nutrition: Calories: 257.8; Fat: 3.8 g; Carbs: 47.1 g; Proteins: 10.3 g; Fiber: 9.4 g.

Coconut-Peanut Chickpeas and Vegetables

Preparation Time: 10 minutes
Cooking Time: 13 minutes
Servings: 4
Ingredients:

- 1 tablespoon extra-virgin olive oil
- 1 medium onion chopped
- 1 medium red bell pepper chopped
- 3 garlic cloves minced
- 1 tablespoon hot or mild curry powder
- 2 tablespoons creamy peanut butter
- 1 (13.5-ounce) can unsweetened coconut milk
- 3 cups cooked or 2 (15.5-ounce) cans chickpeas drained and rinsed
- 1 (14.5-ounce) can diced tomatoes drained
- 3 cups fresh baby spinach
- Salt and freshly ground black pepper
- Crushed unsalted roasted peanuts, for garnish

Directions:

1. In a large saucepan, heat the oil over medium heat. Add the onion and bell pepper, cover, then cook until soft for about 10 minutes.
2. Add the garlic and curry powder, stirring until fragrant for about 30 seconds.
3. Add the peanut butter and gradually stir in the coconut milk until well blended. Add the chickpeas, tomatoes, and spinach, stirring to wilt the spinach for about 5 minutes. Season with salt and pepper.
4. Simmer until hot and the flavors are well blended for about 7 minutes.
5. Serve immediately and sprinkle with peanuts.

Nutrition: Calories: 140; Fat: 0.9 g; Carbs: 27.1 g; Proteins: 6.3 g; Fiber: 6.2 g.

Lentil and Wild Rice Soup

Preparation Time: 15 minutes
Cooking Time: 40 minutes
Servings: 4
Ingredients:

- 1/2 cup cooked mixed beans
- 12 ounces cooked lentils
- 2 stalks of celery, sliced
- 1 1/2 cup mixed wild rice, cooked

- 1 large sweet potato, peeled, chopped
- 1/2 medium butternut, peeled, chopped
- 4 medium carrots, peeled, sliced
- 1 medium onion, peeled, diced
- 10 cherry tomatoes
- 1/2 red chili, deseeded, diced
- 1 ½ teaspoon minced garlic
- 1/2 teaspoons salt
- 2 teaspoons mixed dried herbs
- 1 teaspoon coconut oil
- 2 cups vegetable broth

Directions:
1. Take a large pot, place it over medium-high heat, add oil and when it melts, add onion and cook for 5 minutes.
2. Stir in garlic and chili, cook for 3 minutes, then add remaining vegetables, pour in the broth, stir and bring the mixture to a boil.
3. Switch heat to medium-low heat, cook the soup for 20 minutes, then stir in remaining ingredients and continue cooking for 10 minutes until soup has reached to desired thickness.
4. Serve straight away.

Nutrition: Calories: 331; Fat: 2 g: Carbs: 54 g; Proteins: 13 g; Fiber: 12 g.

Five-spice Farro

Preparation Time: 20 minutes
Cooking Time: 35 minutes
Servings: 4
Ingredients:
- 1 cup dried farro, rinsed and drained
- 1 teaspoon five-spice powder

Directions:
Preparing the ingredients:
1. In a medium pot, combine the farro, five-spice powder, and enough water to cover.
2. Bring to a boil; reduce the heat to medium-low, and simmer for 30minutes. Drain off any excess water.
3. Finish and Serve
4. Transfer to a large storage container, or scoop 1 cup farro into each of 4 storage containers. Let cool before sealing the lids.
5. Place the airtight containers in the refrigerator for one week or freeze for up to 3 months. To thaw, refrigerate overnight. Reheat in the microwave for 1½ to 3 minutes.

Nutrition: Calories: 73; Fat: 0 g; Proteins: 3 g; Carbohydrates: 15 g; Fiber: 1 g; Sugar: 0 g; Sodium: 0 mg.

Quinoa and Chickpeas Salad

Preparation Time: 5 minutes
Cooking Time: 0 minutes
Servings: 4
Ingredients:
- 3/4 cup chopped broccoli
- 1/2 cup quinoa, cooked

- 15 ounces cooked chickpeas
- ½ teaspoon minced garlic
- 1/3 teaspoon ground black pepper
- 2/3 teaspoon salt
- 1 teaspoon dried tarragon
- 2 teaspoons mustard
- 1 tablespoon lemon juice
- 3 tablespoons olive oil

Directions:
1. Take a large bowl, place all the ingredients in it, and stir until well combined.
2. Serve straight away.

Nutrition: Calories: 264; Fat: 12.3 g: Carbs: 32 g; Proteins: 7.1 g; Fiber: 5.1 g.

Chickpeas with Lemon and Spinach

Preparation Time: 10 minutes
Cooking Time: 10 minutes **Servings:** 4
Ingredients:
- 3 tablespoons extra-virgin olive oil
- 1 15-ounce can chickpeas, drained and rinsed
- 10 ounces baby spinach
- ½ teaspoon sea salt
- Juice and zest of 1 lemon
- Freshly ground black pepper

Directions:
Preparing the ingredients:
1. In a large sauté pan, heat the olive oil over medium-high heat until it shimmers. Add the chickpeas and cook until they are heated for about 5 minutes.
2. Add the spinach and stir just until it wilts about 5 minutes.

Finish and Serve
3. Add the salt, lemon juice, lemon zest, and pepper and stir to combine.
4. Serve immediately.

Nutrition: Calories: 264; Fat: 12.3 g: Carbs: 32 g; Proteins: 7.1 g; Fiber: 5.1 g.

Broccoli and Rice Stir Fry

Preparation Time: 5 minutes
Cooking Time: 10 minutes **Servings:** 8
Ingredients:
- 16 ounces frozen broccoli florets, thawed
- 3 green onions, diced
- ½ teaspoon salt
- ¼ teaspoon ground black pepper
- 2 tablespoons soy sauce
- 1 tablespoon olive oil
- 1 ½ cups white rice, cooked

Directions:
1. Take a skillet pan, place it over medium heat, add broccoli, and cook for 5 minutes until tender-crisp.

2. Then add scallion and other ingredients. Toss until well mixed and cook for 2 minutes until hot. Serve straight away.

Nutrition: Calories: 187; Fat: 3.4 g: Carbs: 33 g; Proteins: 6.3 g; Fiber: 2.3 g.

Adzuki Beans and Vegetable Bowl

Preparation Time: 5 minutes
Cooking Time: 25 minutes
Servings: 4
Ingredients:

- 1 teaspoon sesame oil
- 2 cloves garlic, minced
- 1 teaspoon grated ginger
- 1 cup dried adzuki beans
- ½ cup brown rice
- ½ cup sliced shiitake mushrooms
- 2 cups shredded collard greens
- 1-inch strip kombu
- 3 cups water
- 3 umeboshi plums, mashed
- 1 tablespoon lemon juice
- 1 tablespoon tamari

Directions:

1. In the Instant Pot, heat the oil on Sauté mode.
2. Add the garlic and ginger and sauté for 2 minutes until the garlic is softened.
3. Stir in the adzuki beans, brown rice, mushrooms, greens, kombu, and water.
4. Secure the lid. Select Manual mode and set the cooking time for 22 minutes on High Pressure.
5. When the timer beeps, use a natural pressure release for 15 minutes, then release any remaining pressure.
6. Remove the cover and stir. Return to the pot, and simmer while stirring in the mashed umeboshi plums, lemon juice, and tamari on Sauté mode for 3 minutes.
7. Serve immediately.

Nutrition: Proteins: 151g; Fat: 54g; Carbohydrates: 659 g.

Almond Green Beans

Preparation Time: 5 minutes
Cooking Time: 5 minutes
Servings: 4
Ingredients:

- 1 teaspoon sesame oil
- 4 cloves garlic, thinly sliced
- 1 pound (454 g) green beans, cut into ½-inch pieces ¼ cup water
- ¼ teaspoon sea salt
- ¼ cup almond slivers

Directions:

1. In the Instant Pot, heat the oil on Sauté mode.
2. Add the garlic and sauté until soft, about 2 minutes.
3. Add the green beans and water.
4. Secure the lid. Select Manual mode and set the cooking time for 1minute on High Pressure.
5. When the timer beeps, use a quick pressure release.

6. Remove the lid, stir in the salt. Add the almond slivers, toss, and serve.

Nutrition: Proteins: 15g; Fat: 59g; Carbohydrates: 85 g.

Balsamic Black Beans with Parsnip

Preparation Time: 5 minutes
Cooking Time: 11 minutes **Servings:** 6
Ingredients:

- 1 cup dried black beans, soaked in water overnight, rinsed and drained
- 1 teaspoon olive oil
- 2 cloves garlic, minced
- 1 cup diced parsnip
- ½ teaspoon ground coriander
- ½ teaspoon ground cardamom
- 2 cups water
- 2 tablespoons balsamic vinegar

Directions:

1. In the Instant Pot, heat the oil on Sauté mode.
2. Add the garlic and sauté for a minute or until soft but not brown.
3. Add the parsnip, coriander, and cardamom and sauté for 5 minutes.
4. Add the black beans and water. Stir to combine.
5. Secure the lid. Select Manual mode and set the cooking time for 5 minutes on High Pressure.
6. When the timer beeps, use a natural pressure release for 5 minutes, then release any remaining pressure.
7. Remove the lid and stir in 2 tablespoons of balsamic vinegar.
8. Serve immediately.

Nutrition: Proteins: 59g; Fat: 12 g; Carbohydrates: 289 g.

Barbecue Northern Bean Bake

Preparation Time: 20 minutes
Cooking Time: 54 minutes **Servings:** 8
Ingredients:

- 1 cup barbecue sauce
- ¼ cup yellow mustard
- 2 tablespoons maple syrup
- 1¾ cups water
- 1½ teaspoons freshly ground black pepper
- 1½ teaspoons smoked paprika
- 3 tablespoons avocado oil
- 1 large yellow onion, diced
- 2 cloves garlic, minced
- 1 bay leaf

Directions:

1. In a small bowl, stir together the barbecue sauce, mustard, maple syrup, water, pepper, and smoked paprika.
2. Select the Sauté setting on the Instant Pot, add the oil, and heat for 2 minutes.
3. Add the onion and sauté for about 10 minutes, stirring often, until it begins to caramelize.
4. Add the garlic and sauté for about 2 minutes more until the garlic is no longer raw.

5. Add the barbecue sauce mixture, beans, and bay leaf. Stir to combine, using a wooden spoon to nudge lose any browned bits from the bottom of the pot.
6. Secure the lid. Select Bean/Chili setting and set the cooking time for 40 minutes at High Pressure.
7. When the timer beeps, let the pressure release naturally for 20 minutes, then release any remaining pressure. Open the pot, stir the beans, and discard the bay leaf.
8. Ladle the beans into bowls and serve hot.

Nutrition: Proteins: 25g; Fat: 410 g; Carbohydrates: 648 g.

Bean Tagine with Ras el Hanout

Preparation Time: 20 minutes
Cooking Time: 37 minutes
Servings: 8
Ingredients:

- 2½ cups (about 1 pound / 454 g) dried Northern beans, soaked in salted water overnight, rinsed and drained
- ¼ cup olive oil, plus more for serving
- 4 cloves garlic, minced
- 1 yellow onion, sliced
- 3 cups vegetable broth
- 8 medium carrots (about 1 pound / 454 g in total), peeled and cut into ½-inch rounds
- 1 tablespoon tomato paste
- 1 tablespoon fresh lemon juice
- Salt, to taste
- 2 tablespoons chopped fresh mint

Ras el Hanout:

- 2 teaspoons paprika
- ½ teaspoon ground cinnamon
- ½ teaspoon ground coriander
- ½ teaspoon ground cumin
- ¼ teaspoon cayenne pepper.

Ingredients:

1. Select the Sauté setting on the Instant Pot, add the oil and garlic, and heat for 2 minutes until the garlic is bubbling but not browned.
2. Add the onion and sauté for 5 minutes until the onion is softened and the garlic is toasty and brown.
3. Stir in the broth and use a wooden spoon to nudge lose any browned bits from the bottom of the pot.
4. Stir in the carrots, ingredients for the ras el hanout, and salt. Stir in the beans, making sure all of the beans are submerged in the cooking liquid.
5. Secure the lid. Select Bean/Chili setting and set the cooking time for 30 minutes at High Pressure.
6. When the timer beeps, let the pressure release naturally for 20 minutes, then release any remaining pressure.
7. Open the pot and stir in the tomato paste and lemon juice.
8. Ladle the tagine into bowls. Drizzle with oil and sprinkle with mint.
9. Serve hot.

Nutrition: Proteins: 710g; Fat: 853 g; Carbohydrates: 1417 g.

Beluga Lentils with Lacinato Kale

Preparation Time: 15 minutes
Cooking time: 40 minutes
Servings: 6
Ingredients:

- ¼ cup olive oil, plus more for serving
- 2 shallots, diced
- 5 cloves garlic, minced
- ½ teaspoon red pepper flakes
- ½ teaspoon ground nutmeg
- 1 teaspoon fine sea salt
- 2 bunches (about 1 pound / 454 g) lacinato kale, stems discarded and leaves chopped into 1-inch pieces
- 2 large carrots, peeled and diced
- 2½ cups water
- 1 cup beluga lentils, rinsed

Directions:

1. Select the Sauté setting on the Instant Pot, add the oil, and heat for 1 minute.
2. Add the shallots and garlic and sauté for about 4 minutes until the shallots soften.
3. Add the red pepper flakes, nutmeg, and salt and sauté for 1 minute more.
4. Stir in the kale and carrots and sauté for about 3 minutes until the kale fully wilts.
5. Stir in the water and lentils, scraping down the sides of the pot to make sure the lentils are submerged.
6. Secure the lid. Select Bean/Chili setting and set the cooking time for 30 minutes at High Pressure.
7. When the timer beeps, let the pressure release naturally for 10 minutes, then release any remaining pressure.
8. Open the pot and give the mixture a stir.
9. Ladle the lentils into serving dishes and drizzle with oil. Serve warm.

Nutrition: Proteins: 55g; Fat: 545 g; Carbohydrates: 153 g.

Black Bean and Pepper Tacos

Preparation Time: 10 minutes
Cooking Time: 23 minutes
Servings: 2
Ingredients:

- 1 tablespoon sesame oil
- ½ onion, chopped
- 1 teaspoon garlic, minced
- 1 sweet pepper, deseeded and sliced
- 1 jalapeño pepper, deseeded and minced
- 1 teaspoon ground cumin
- ½ teaspoon ground coriander
- 8 ounces (227 g) black beans, rinsed
- 2 (8-inch) whole wheat tortillas, warmed
- ½ cup cherry tomatoes, halved
- 1/3 cup coconut cream

Directions:

1. Press the Sauté button and heat the oil. Cook the onion, garlic, and peppers for 3 minutes or until tender and fragrant.
2. Add the ground cumin, coriander, and beans to the Instant Pot.
3. Secure the lid. Choose the Manual mode and cook for 20 minutes at High Pressure.
4. Once cooking is complete, use a natural pressure release for 10 minutes; then release any remaining pressure. Carefully remove the lid.
5. Serve the bean mixture in the tortillas, then garnish with cherry tomatoes and coconut cream.

Nutrition: Proteins: 243g; Fat: 924 g; Carbohydrates: 877 g.

Black Beans with Crumbled Tofu

Preparation Time: 15 minutes
Cooking Time: 23 minutes
Servings: 2
Ingredients:

- 1 cup canned black beans
- 2 cups vegetable broth
- 1 tablespoon avocado oil
- 1 small red onion, finely chopped
- 3 garlic cloves, minced
- 3 tomatoes, chopped
- 1 (14-ounce / 397-g) extra-firm tofu, crumbled
- 1 teaspoon turmeric powder
- 1 teaspoon cumin powder
- 1 teaspoon smoked paprika
- Salt and ground black pepper, to taste

Directions:
1. Pour the beans and broth into Instant Pot. Seal the lid, select Manual mode, and set the cooking time for 10 minutes on High Pressure.
2. When the timer beeps, do a quick pressure release. Transfer the beans to a medium bowl. Drain excess liquid and wipe Instant Pot clean.
3. Select Sauté mode. Heat the avocado oil and sauté onion, garlic, and tomatoes until softened, 4 minutes.
4. Crumble the tofu into the pan and cook for 5 minutes.
5. Season with turmeric, cumin, paprika, salt, and black pepper. Cook for 1 minute. Add black beans, stir, and allow heating for 3 minutes.
6. Serve immediately.

Nutrition: Proteins: 160g; Fat: 161 g; Carbohydrates: 608 g.

Black Beans with Lime

Preparation Time: 10 minutes
Cooking Time: 25 minutes
Servings: 4
Ingredients:

- 2½ cups black beans, uncooked
- 1 medium white onion, peeled and chopped
- 2 teaspoons minced garlic
- 1 teaspoon chili flakes
- 1 teaspoon ground cumin
- 1 teaspoon dried mint

- 1 teaspoon ground coriander
- 3 cups vegetable broth
- 1 teaspoon salt
- 1 lime, juiced

Directions:
1. Add all the ingredients, except for the lime juice, in the Instant Pot, stirring until mixed.
2. Secure Instant Pot, then press the Manual button, set the cooking time for 25 minutes on High Pressure.
3. When the timer beeps, do a natural pressure release for 10 minutes, then release any remaining pressure.
4. Carefully open the Instant Pot, stir the beans, drizzle with lime juice, and serve.

Nutrition: Proteins: 368g; Fat: 66 g; Carbohydrates: 1291 g.

Black-Eyed Peas with Spinach

Preparation Time: 10 minutes
Cooking Time: 13 minutes **Servings:** 6
Ingredients:

- 1 tablespoon peanut oil
- 1/8 teaspoon cumin seeds
- 1/8 teaspoon black mustard seeds
- 1 tablespoon minced garlic
- 1 tablespoon minced ginger
- 1 cup diced tomato
- ½ teaspoon ground turmeric
- ½ teaspoon ground cumin
- ½ teaspoon ground coriander
- ¼ teaspoon ground cayenne pepper
- 1 teaspoon salt
- 1 cup dried black-eyed peas
- 2 cups water - 4 cups raw spinach

Directions:
1. Set the Instant Pot to Sauté mode. When the Instant Pot is hot, add the oil and heat until shimmering.
2. Add the cumin seeds and mustard seeds and cook for 1 minute or until they sputter like popcorn popping. Add the garlic and ginger and sauté for 30 seconds.
3. Add the tomato and cook for 1 to 2 minutes until the tomato has softened.
4. Add the turmeric, cumin, coriander, cayenne, and salt, and mix well.
5. Add the black-eyed peas and water, and mix. Place the spinach on top.
6. Lock the lid. Select Manual mode. Set cooking time for 10 minutes on High Pressure.
7. When the timer beeps, allow 10 minutes of natural pressure release, then release any remaining pressure. Unlock the lid.
8. Serve immediately.

Nutrition: Proteins: 16g; Fat: 131 g; Carbohydrates: 62 g.

Braised Soybeans

Preparation Time: 15 minutes
Cooking Time: 35 minutes **Servings:** 4
Ingredients:

- 1 cup dried soybeans, soaked

- 4 cups water
- ½ cup soy sauce
- 1 tablespoon rice vinegar
- ¼ cup brown sugar
- 1 teaspoon sesame oil
- 2 garlic cloves, minced
- 2 teaspoons sesame seeds, for garnishing

Directions:

1. Pour soybeans and water in Instant Pot.
2. Seal the lid, select Manual and set the cooking time for 20 minutes on High Pressure.
3. When the timer beeps, do a natural pressure release for 10 minutes, then use a quick pressure release. Unlock the lid.
4. Meanwhile, in a bowl, combine soy sauce, rice vinegar, sugar, sesame oil, and garlic.
5. Press the Sauté button on the Instant Pot, add soy sauce mixture, stir and cook for 15 minutes.
6. Spoon beans onto a platter and garnish with sesame seeds. Serve immediately.

Nutrition: Proteins: 16g; Fat: 131 g; Carbohydrates: 62 g.

Chickpea Tagine with Pickled Raisins

Preparation Time: 30 minutes **Cooking Time:** 25 minutes
Servings: 4
Ingredients:
Spicy Pickled Raisins:

- 1/3 cup golden raisins
- 1/3 cup apple cider vinegar
- 2½ tablespoons organic cane sugar
- ¼ teaspoon crushed red pepper flakes, to taste

Tagine:

- 2 tablespoons olive oil
- 1 large yellow onion, diced
- 2 medium carrots, diced
- 5 garlic cloves, minced
- 2 teaspoons ground cinnamon
- 2 teaspoons ground coriander
- 1 teaspoon cumin seeds or ground cumin
- 1 teaspoon sweet paprika
- 2 bay leaves
- 1½ teaspoons kosher salt, plus more to taste
- 1¼ cups vegetable broth or water
- 3 cups peeled and finely diced peeled butternut squash (from one 1½ pound / 680 g butternut squash)
- ¼ cup finely diced dried apricots (about 8 apricots)
- 1 (14.5-ounce / 411 g) can crushed tomatoes
- 4 ounces (113 g) Tuscan kale, stems and midribs removed, roughly chopped
- ¼ cup roughly chopped fresh cilantro
- Zest and juice of 1 small lemon

Directions:

1. Place the raisins in a bowl. In a small saucepan, combine the vinegar, sugar, and pepper flakes and bring to a boil over medium-high heat, whisking until the sugar is dissolved.
2. Remove the vinegar mixture from the heat and carefully pour the hot vinegar mixture over the raisins. Leave the bowl uncovered and allow the mixture to come to room temperature. Set aside.
3. Select the Sauté setting on the Instant Pot and let the pot heat for a few minutes before adding the olive oil.
4. Once the oil is hot, add the onion and carrots. Cook until the vegetables have softened, 4 to 5 minutes.
5. Add the garlic and cook for 1 minute, stirring frequently.
6. Add the cinnamon, coriander, cumin seeds, paprika, bay leaves, and salt. Stir the spices into the vegetables for 30 seconds until the mixture is fragrant.
7. Pour in the broth, drained chickpeas, butternut squash, and dried apricots. Stir to combine all the ingredients. Pour the crushed tomatoes on top, but do not stir, allowing the tomatoes to sit on top.
8. Secure the lid. Select the Manual mode and set the cooking time for 12 minutes on High Pressure.
9. When the timer beeps, use a natural pressure release for 5 minutes, then release any remaining pressure.
10. Open the pot, discard the bay leaves, and stir in the kale. Select the Sauté setting and cook for 2 to 3 minutes to wilt the kale.
11. Add the cilantro and lemon zest and half of the lemon juice.
12. Transfer the tagine to bowls and add a few spoons of the spicy pickled raisins to each bowl. Serve immediately.

Nutrition: Proteins: 121g; Fat: 320 g; Carbohydrates: 1429 g.

Cinnamon Chickpeas Curry

Preparation Time: 15 minutes
Cooking Time: 35 minutes
Servings: 4
Ingredients:

- 1 cup dried chickpeas
- 1 tablespoon baking soda
- 4 cups water, divided
- 1 teaspoon olive oil
- 1 clove garlic, minced
- ¼ cup diced onion
- ½ teaspoon hot curry powder
- ¼ teaspoon ground cinnamon
- 1 bay leaf
- ½ teaspoon sea salt

Directions:

1. Add the chickpeas, baking soda, and 2 cups of water to a large bowl and soak for 1 hour. Rinse the chickpeas and drain.
2. In the Instant Pot, heat the oil on Sauté mode. Add the garlic and onion and sauté for 3 minutes.
3. Add the curry, cinnamon, and bay leaf and stir well. Stir in the chickpeas and 2 cups of water.
4. Cover the lid. Select Manual mode and set the cooking time for 32 minutes on High Pressure.

5. When the timer beeps, use a natural pressure release for 15 minutes, then release any remaining pressure.
6. Remove the lid and stir in the sea salt. Remove the bay leaf before serving.

Nutrition: Proteins: 144g; Fat: 143 g; Carbohydrates: 530 g.

Classic Langar Ki Dal

Preparation Time: 10 minutes
Cooking Time: 38 minutes
Servings: 8
Ingredients:

- 1 cup whole black urad dal
- ½ cup chana dal
- 5 cups water
- 1 teaspoon salt
- 1 teaspoon ground turmeric
- 1 tablespoon coconut oil
- 1 onion, chopped
- 1 tablespoon minced ginger
- 1 tablespoon minced garlic
- 2 tomatoes, chopped
- ½ teaspoon ground turmeric
- ½ teaspoon cumin seeds
- ½ teaspoon ground cayenne pepper, or more to taste
- 1 teaspoon salt
- ¼ cup water

Directions:

1. In the Instant Pot, combine the urad and chana dals. Add the water, salt, and turmeric, and stir to combine.
2. Lock the lid. Select the Bean/Chili setting and set the time for 30 minutes on High Pressure.
3. When the timer beeps, allow the pressure to release naturally for 10 minutes, then release any remaining pressure. Unlock the lid.
4. Use a spoon to crush the dals to get a creamy texture, leaving some whole deal in the mixture.
5. Meanwhile, heat a skillet over medium-high heat. When the pan is hot, add the oil.
6. When the oil is shimmering, add the onion and sauté for 30 seconds.
7. Add the ginger and garlic and cook for 5 minutes until the edges of the onion brown slightly.
8. Add the tomatoes, turmeric, cumin seeds, cayenne, and salt. Mix well. Add the water and mix again.
9. Cook, crushing the tomatoes with the back of a spoon, for 1 to 2 minutes. Set aside until the dals are cooked.
10. When cooking is complete, pour in the tomato-and-onion mixture and mix well before serving.

Nutrition: Proteins: 88g; Fat: 294 g; Carbohydrates: 202 g.

Coconut Tofu Curry

Preparation Time: 5 minutes

Cooking Time: 3 minutes
Servings: 4
Ingredients:

- 1 (13.5-ounce / 383-g) can coconut milk
- ¼ cup red or green curry paste
- ¼ teaspoon salt
- ¼ cup water
- 1 (14-ounce / 397-g) package extra-firm tofu, pressed and cubed
- 2 teaspoons unrefined sugar
- 2 cups chopped fresh spinach

Directions:

1. In the Instant Pot, combine the coconut milk, curry paste, salt, and water, stirring to mix well. Add the tofu.
2. Close the lid, then select Manual mode and set the cooking time for 3 minutes on High Pressure.
3. Once cooking is complete, quick release the pressure. Open the lid.
4. Stir in the sugar and spinach. Serve immediately.

Nutrition: Proteins: 43g; Fat: 86 g; Carbohydrates: 49 g.

Fast Navy Beans and Rice Bowls

Preparation Time: 10 minutes
Cooking Time: 15 minutes
Servings: 4
Ingredients:

- 1 cup dried navy beans, soaked in water overnight, rinsed and drained
- 1 teaspoon vegetable oil
- ½ cup diced red onion
- 3 cloves garlic, minced
- ½ cup short-grain white rice
- 4 cups loosely packed bite-size pieces kale
- 1 bay leaf
- 1 teaspoon dried thyme
- 2½ cups water
- 1 tablespoon lemon juice
- ½ teaspoon sea salt

Directions:

1. In the Instant Pot, heat the oil on Sauté mode.
2. Add the onion and garlic and sauté for 3 minutes, or until the onion is soft. Add the beans, rice, kale, bay leaf, thyme, and water to cover.
3. Secure the lid. Select Manual mode and set the cooking time for 7 minutes on High Pressure.
4. When the timer beeps, use a natural pressure release for 5 minutes, then release any remaining pressure.
5. Remove the lid and discard the bay leaf. Stir in the lemon juice and salt. Serve immediately.

Nutrition: Proteins: 87g; Fat: 20 g; Carbohydrates: 578 g.

CHAPTER 16:

UNIQUE DISHES

Green Bean and Arborio Risotto

Preparation Time: 5 minutes
Cooking Time: 10 minutes
Servings: 4
Ingredients:

- 1 teaspoon vegan butter
- 4 cloves of garlic, minced
- 1 cup chopped mushrooms
- 1 cup chopped fresh green beans
- 1 cup Arborio rice
- 2 cups vegetable broth
- ¼ teaspoon sea salt
- 2 tablespoons nutritional yeast
- 3 tablespoons lemon juice
- Fresh ground pepper, to taste

Directions:

1. Heat the vegan butter in the Instant Pot on Sauté function.
2. Add the garlic, mushrooms, and green beans. Sauté for about 3 minutes.
3. Add the rice, broth, and salt, and stir to combine well. Cover the pot.
4. Select the Manual function and set the timer for 7 minutes on High Pressure.
5. When the timer beeps, use a natural pressure release for 5 minutes, then release any remaining pressure.
6. Open the lid and stir in the nutritional yeast and lemon juice.
7. Serve with fresh ground black pepper.

Nutrition: Proteins: 107g; Fat: 308 g; Carbohydrates: 265 g.

Green Lentil Salad with Vinaigrette

Preparation Time: 15 minutes
Cooking Time: 20 minutes
Servings: 4 to 6
Ingredients:
Lentils:

- 1 cup green lentils, rinsed
- 3½ cups water, divided
- ½ teaspoon fine sea salt
- 1 large carrot, diced
- 1 red bell pepper, diced
- 2 ribs celery, diced
- ½ small red onion, diced
- ¼ cup chopped fresh flat-leaf parsley

Vinaigrette:

- 1 small shallot, minced

- 2 teaspoons Dijon mustard
- 1 teaspoon dried herbes de Provence
- ¼ cup fresh lemon juice
- 1½ teaspoons sugar
- ½ teaspoon fine sea salt
- ½ teaspoon freshly ground black pepper
- ½ cup olive oil

Directions:

1. In a heatproof bowl, stir together the lentils, 1½ cups of water, and salt.
2. Pour the remaining 2 cups of water into the Instant Pot and place a trivet in the pot. Put the bowl on the trivet.
3. Select Manual mode and set the cooking time for 20 minutes at High Pressure.
4. Meanwhile, in a bowl, combine the ingredients for the vinaigrette.
5. Stir to mix well. Set aside.
6. When the timer beeps, perform a quick pressure release. Open the pot and remove the bowl of lentils.
7. Drain the lentils in a colander, then return them to the bowl. While they are still warm, pour half of the vinaigrette over the lentils and stir gently. Let cool for 20 minutes.
8. In a serving bowl, toss the lentils, carrot, bell pepper, celery, onion, and parsley. Taste and add more vinaigrette as needed.
9. Serve immediately.

Nutrition: Proteins: 27g; Fat: 967 g; Carbohydrates: 153 g.

Hot Wings with Ranch

Preparation Time: 20 minutes
Cooking Time: 2 hours 45 minutes
Servings: 4
Ingredients:

- ½ cup chickpea flour
- ½ cup water
- 1 teaspoon garlic powder
- ½ teaspoon salt
- 1 head cauliflower, chopped
- 1 teaspoon avocado oil
- 2/3 cup hot sauce
- ½ cup roasted cashews
- 4 teaspoons lime juice
- ½ teaspoon dill
- ¼ teaspoon garlic powder
- ¼ teaspoon paprika

- Salt - Pepper

Directions:
1. Place the cashews in a bowl and add 2 teaspoons of lime juice. Add enough water to cover cashews and a little more. Let soak for 2 hours, then drain and rinse well.
2. In a strong blender, add cashews, ¼ cup of water, dill, garlic powder, paprika, 2 teaspoons lime juice, a pinch of salt, and a pinch of pepper to taste. Blend until smooth. Set aside in the fridge until ready to use.
3. Preheat the oven to 450° F. Grease a large baking tray.
4. Chop the cauliflower into bite-sized florets.
5. Whisk together the flour, water, garlic powder, and salt.
6. Dip the florets in the batter, coating each piece thoroughly. Place carefully on the baking tray and cook for 8 minutes. Flip florets over and cook another 8 minutes.
7. While the cauliflower is cooking, whisk together the oil and hot sauce.
8. When the cauliflower is done, move the florets to the bowl with the sauce and coat thoroughly. Place the sauce-covered cauliflower back on the baking sheet and cook for 25 minutes or until crispy.
9. Serve the cauliflower with cold sauce.

Nutrition: Proteins: 117g; Fat: 648 g; Carbohydrates: 356 g.

Breaded Tempeh Bites

Preparation Time: 15 minutes
Cooking Time: 35 minutes
Servings: 4
Ingredients:

- 8 oz package tempeh
- ¼ cup oat milk
- ¼ cup nutritional yeast
- 1 tablespoon pre-blended spice mix
- 1 teaspoon arrowroot powder
- 1 teaspoon fresh lime juice
- ¼ tsp. pepper
- ¼ tsp. hot sauce
- ¼ tsp. salt
- 1 cup panko

Directions:
1. Preheat the oven to 400° F. Grease a large baking pan.
2. Cut the tempeh in half and cut into eight pieces. Squish each piece lightly to flatten slightly.
3. In a bowl, combine the milk, nutritional yeast, seasoning blend, arrowroot powder, lime juice, pepper, hot sauce, and salt. Add the tempeh bits and let soak for 5 minutes. Make sure each piece is evenly coated.
4. Pour the panko on a plate. Dip each piece of tempeh from the batter to roll in the panko. Place on the prepared baking pan.
5. Cook for 15 minutes. Flip all pieces, then cook for another 15 minutes or until golden brown.

Nutrition: Proteins: 227g; Fat: 226 g; Carbohydrates: 189 g.

Cumin Chili Chickpeas

Preparation Time: 20 minutes
Cooking Time: 45 minutes
Servings: 6
Ingredients:

- 1 can chickpeas
- 1 tablespoon paprika powder
- 1 tablespoon cumin powder
- 2 teaspoons red chili flakes
- 2 tablespoons honey
- 3 tablespoons lemon juice
- 1 tablespoon avocado oil
- Sea salt - Black pepper

Directions:
1. Preheat oven to 395° F.
2. Drain and rinse the chickpeas, then spread them on a large oven pan.
3. Mix the paprika, cumin, chili flakes, and a pinch of salt and pepper. Evenly powder over the chickpeas.
4. Mix the honey, lemon juice, and oil, then pour over the chickpeas. Stir the mixture to make sure the chickpeas are fully coated.
5. Cook for 45 minutes, or until browned and crisp.

Quick tip: Use these delicious chickpeas on your salads!
Nutrition: Proteins: 99g; Fat: 263 g; Carbohydrates: 391 g.

Summer Sushi

Preparation Time: 10 minutes
Cooking Time: 10 minutes
Servings: 6
Ingredients:

- 2 cucumbers
- 2 avocados
- 4 tablespoons lime juice
- 2 tablespoons extra-virgin olive oil
- Sea salt
- Black pepper

Directions:
1. Peel the cucumber skin off and throw it away.
2. Peel or slice each cucumber length-wise, going from the bottom to the top. Discard the very middle of the cucumber, as it is not strong enough to shape.
3. After the cucumbers are sliced, take each slice and tightly roll it from the bottom up.
4. Cut open the avocado and discard the pit. Cut the avocado flesh into tiny squares and put it inside the cucumber circles. Cram as much in as possible for a more stable roll.
5. After you've completed your rolls, lightly cover with lime juice and olive oil. Sprinkle a pinch of salt and pepper on top and serve!

Nutrition: Proteins: 65g; Fat: 662 g; Carbohydrates: 172 g.

Almond Milk Ricotta

Preparation Time: 10 minutes
Cooking Time: 30 minutes
Servings: 8
Ingredients:

- 2 cups almond flour
- 4 tablespoons onion powder
- Water
- 1 teaspoon light soy sauce
- 1 tablespoon poppy seeds
- 5 teaspoons agar powder
- ½ cup bell pepper
- ½ cup raw cashews
- 1 1/3 cup nutritional yeast
- 4 tablespoons lemon juice
- ½ tsp. mustard

Directions:

1. Preheat the oven to 350° F.
2. To make the crackers, mix together the flour, 3 tablespoons onion powder, 3 tablespoons water, soy sauce, and poppy seeds. Form into a ball.
3. Cover a baking tray with parchment paper and place the ball on top.
4. Press it down as flat as possible, then place another piece of parchment sheet on top.
5. On top of the second sheet of parchment, use a rolling pin to roll the cracker mix to about 1/4th inch thick.
6. Remove the second sheet of parchment and cook in the oven for about 15 minutes.
7. When the crackers are done baking, let cool and cut into cracker-sized pieces. Store in an airtight container.
8. Put the agar and 1 ½ cups of water into a small pot over high heat. Wait for it to boil and whisk continuously until the mixture becomes thick like custard.
9. Remove from heat and scoop into a blender.
10. Roughly chop pepper and add to the blender along with the cashews, nutritional yeast, lemon juice, 2 teaspoons onion powder, and mustard.
11. Pulse until smooth.
12. Pour the blended mix into a bread pan lined with parchment paper and refrigerate for at least 30 minutes before serving.

Nutrition: Proteins: 466g; Fat: 699 g; Carbohydrates: 589 g.

3-Ingredient Flatbread

Preparation Time: 10 minutes
Cooking Time: 25 minutes
Servings: 5

Ingredients:

- 1 cup tri-color quinoa
- 1½ cups water
- 1 teaspoon onion powder

Directions:

1. Before starting, preheat the oven to 400° F.
2. In a blender, put all ingredients. Blend until smooth with no lumps.
3. Line a baking pan with parchment paper (make sure the pan has a small lip).
4. Evenly spread the quinoa blend on the baking sheet and put it in the oven for 20-25 minutes.
5. Remove from oven and allow to cool.
6. Lift the bread out of the pan using the parchment paper and carefully peel bread from the paper.

Quick tip: This is delicious as a sandwich or with a curry!
Nutrition: Proteins: 124g; Fat: 148 g; Carbohydrates: 444 g.

Spicy Homemade Tortilla Chips

Preparation Time: 13 minutes
Cooking Time: 16 minutes
Servings: 6
Ingredients:

- 12 corn tortillas
- 1 teaspoon olive oil
- ¼ teaspoon chili powder
- ¼ teaspoon cumin powder
- ¼ teaspoon garlic powder
- ¼ teaspoon paprika powder
- Himalayan sea salt

Directions:

1. Before starting, preheat the oven to 425° F.
2. Line 2 large baking pans with parchment paper.
3. Slice each tortilla into six triangles, then place them on the baking pans, trying not to overlap. Place in oven and cook for 10 minutes.
4. Take the baking pans out of the oven and delicately brush oil over the surface side of the chips (use only a little, otherwise, the chips won't be crispy).
5. Mix the spices and salt together and sprinkle over the chips.
6. Put the chips back in the oven for another 6 minutes, or until crispy and golden.

Nutrition: Proteins: 73g; Fat: 166 g; Carbohydrates: 519 g.

Healthy Cereal Bars

Preparation Time: 15 minutes
Cooking Time: 30 minutes
Servings: 9
Ingredients:

- ½ cup toasted almonds
- 1 ½ cup oats
- ½ cup almond flour
- ½ cup pure maple syrup
- ½ cup raisins
- ¼ cup almond butter
- 2 tablespoons chia seeds

- 1 tablespoon fractionated coconut oil
- 1 teaspoon vanilla extract
- ½ teaspoon cinnamon powder
- ¼ teaspoon Himalayan pink sea salt
- 1/ teaspoon nutmeg powder

Directions:
1. Go ahead and preheat the oven to 325° F.
2. Use an 8x8 inch baking tin and grease and line with non-stick parchment paper.
3. Slice the almonds and add to a large bowl alongside the oats, almond flour, syrup, raisins, almond butter, chia seeds, oil, vanilla, cinnamon, salt, and nutmeg. Mix until it all sticks together.
4. Pat the almond mix into the pan, making sure the top is even. Put in the oven for 25 to 30 minutes, or until the edges of the pan are golden.
5. Allow to cool completely before cutting into even squares. Store in an airtight container.

Nutrition: Proteins: 119g; Fat: 558 g; Carbohydrates: 687 g.

Black Bean Taquitos

Preparation Time: 10 minutes
Cooking Time: 20 minutes **Servings:** 12
Ingredients:

- Olive oil - 1 onion
- 1 poblano chili pepper
- 1 jalapeño chili pepper
- 4 garlic cloves - 1 can black beans
- ½ cup cilantro leaves
- 1 teaspoon chili powder
- 1 teaspoon cumin powder
- 1 teaspoon sea salt - 24 corn tortillas

Directions:
1. Preheat your oven to 400° F.
2. Use a large baking pan and line it with parchment paper, then grease with oil.
3. Chop your onion into quarters. Half both peppers and deseed them before chopping into quarters.
4. Using a food processor, add onion, poblano pepper, jalapeño pepper, and garlic. Use the chopping blade and pulse three times before adding the black beans, cilantro, chili powder, cumin, and salt.
5. Pulse another three times or until the mixture is finely chopped (you can pulse more if you want a smoother mix).
6. Put the tortillas on a pan and heat them in the oven for about a minute or until soft and pliable.
7. Smear a large tablespoon of bean mixes across each tortilla. Tightly roll like a burrito with open edges and put on a baking pan with the edge facing down. Leave a smidge of space between each tortilla and cook for 20 minutes or until golden.

Quick tip: These are great with dips like queso or salsa!
Nutrition: Proteins: 129g; Fat: 203 g; Carbohydrates: 1121 g.

Vegetable Tacos

Preparation Time: 20 minutes

Cooking Time: 35 minutes
Servings: 6
Ingredients:

- 1 head of cauliflower
- 1 sweet potato
- 1 onion
- 2 tablespoons olive oil
- 1/ tsp. Himalayan Sea salt
- 1/ tsp. black pepper
- 1 can chickpeas
- ½ cup BBQ

Directions:
1. Preheat your oven to 425° F and put a sheet of parchment paper on a large baking tray.
2. Chop the cauliflower into small florets, the sweet potato into inch-sized cubes, and dice the onion into small pieces.
3. Evenly place the cauliflower, sweet potato, and onion across the baking tray. Sprinkle oil, salt, and pepper across and mix to coat. Put in the oven for 10 to 15 minutes.
4. Take the tray out of the oven and dump the chickpeas on top. Pour ½ cup of BBQ sauce on top and stir to coat. Bake for another 8 minutes, or until the vegetable is soft.

Quick tip: This is great with any kind of taco, but especially on a corn tortilla with avocado, cilantro, coleslaw, and tomatoes!
Nutrition: Proteins: 106g; Fat: 360 g; Carbohydrates: 324 g.

Savory Sweet Potatoes

Preparation Time: 20 minutes
Cooking Time: 35 minutes
Servings: 2
Ingredients:

- 2 sweet potatoes
- 1 teaspoon garlic powder
- 1/2 teaspoons cumin powder
- 1/2 teaspoons chili powder
- 1/2 teaspoons Himalayan Sea salt
- 1/2 teaspoons black pepper

Directions:
1. Before starting, preheat your oven to 425° F.
2. Peel the sweet potatoes and quarter lengthwise.
3. In a pot, put a couple of inches of water and bring to a boil. Put a steamer tray on top of the pot (make sure it is above the water) and put the potato pieces in the steamer. Put a lid on and steam for 7 minutes or until the potatoes have just become soft.

4. Put a sheet of parchment paper on a large baking pan before moving the potatoes onto the pan. Make sure there is a bit of space between each piece.
5. Whisk together the garlic, cumin, chili, salt, and pepper. Evenly powder over the potato pieces.
6. Put the tray in the oven for 10 minutes, then turn all the pieces and cook for another 10 minutes.
7. Serve!

Nutrition: Proteins: 129g; Fat: 203 g; Carbohydrates: 1121 g.

Winter Greens

Preparation Time: 15 minutes
Cooking Time: 1 hour 20 minutes
Servings: 6
Ingredients:

- 1/2 can chickpeas
- 1 cup scallions
- 4 garlic cloves
- 1 cup kale
- 1 1/ cups dandelion leaves
- 3 cups spinach
- ¾ cup Swiss chard
- 1 teaspoon jalapeño
- 2/ cup bunch dill
- ¼ tsp. ground cloves
- ¼ tsp. cinnamon powder
- 1 teaspoon lemon juice
- Himalayan sea salt

Directions:

1. Finely chop the scallions, garlic, kale, dandelion, spinach, Swiss chard, and jalapeño. Destem the dill and chop finely.
2. Put the chickpeas in a pot with 1 cup of water and bring to a boil before reducing heat to a simmer. Leave with a lid halfway on for 30-45 minutes until tender. Drain the water and set the chickpeas aside.
3. In a large pot, add the scallions, garlic, and ½ cup of water. Cover and simmer over medium heat for 10 minutes.
4. In the pot with the scallions, add all the greens, jalapeño, cloves, cinnamon, lemon juice, a pinch of salt, and another cup of water. Keep at a simmer for another 10 minutes and stir every so often.
5. Transfer the greens to a blender and pulse until a chunky puree, but not so much it becomes a sauce.
6. Put the blended greens back into the pot and add the chickpeas. Stir over medium heat for another 5 minutes.
7. Serve hot!

Nutrition: Proteins: 106g; Fat: 360 g; Carbohydrates: 324 g.

Lettuce Bean Burritos

Preparation Time: 5 minutes
Cooking Time: 5 minutes
Servings: 4

Ingredients:

- 1 can white beans
- Head of romaine lettuce
- 1 red onion
- 1/2 cup basil
- 1 organic tomato
- 2 tablespoons lemon juice
- Himalayan pink salt
- Black pepper

Directions:

1. Rinse and drain the beans.
2. Pull off 8 of the largest lettuce leaves, chop the hard stem off the bottom, and set aside. Finely chop the onion and basil. Core and dice the tomato.
3. Mix together the beans, onion, tomato, basil, lemon juice, and a pinch of salt and pepper.
4. To shape the wraps, spread a spoonful of the white bean mixture down the middle of each lettuce leaf and roll the leaf like a burrito.
5. Place seam-side down on a platter and serve.

Nutrition: Proteins: 56g; Fat: 77 g; Carbohydrates: 142 g.

Mango Chutney Wraps

Preparation Time: 5 minutes
Cooking Time: 8 minutes
Servings: 8
Ingredients:

- 3 ripe mangoes
- 1 avocado
- 4 tablespoons lime juice
- 2 tablespoons coconut oil
- 2 tablespoons tahini
- 1 teaspoon chili flakes
- ½ cup coriander leaves
- Sea salt
- 1 tablespoon fresh ginger
- 16 sheets of rice paper
- 3 carrots
- 2 bell peppers
- 1 cucumber
- Black pepper

Directions:

1. Peel the skin off the mangos and cut the mango meat off the pit, keeping one mango flesh separate. Cut the avocado in half, remove the pit, and scoop out the flesh.
2. Add the mango flesh of 2 mangos to a blender along with the avocado, 2 tablespoons lime juice, oil, tahini, chili, coriander leaves, and a pinch of salt.
3. Peel the skin off the ginger and roughly chop it before adding to the blender. Pulse, then blend until smooth.
4. Pour the blended mango into a bowl and refrigerate until serving.
5. Chop the remaining mango flesh into slices.
6. To prepare the wraps, carefully dip the rice paper into hot water for no more than 10 seconds; then lay them flat and let them dry for 2 minutes.

7. While you wait, thinly slice your carrots, peppers, and cucumber.
8. After the wraps have dried, spread a tablespoon of mango dip down the middle of each sheet of rice paper. Put the dried mango slices and vegetable slices in the middle. Dribble some lime juice on top and a smidge of salt and pepper, then roll up like a burrito.
9. Serve with more mango dip on the side!

Quick Tip: If you don't have access to rice paper, try using sushi seaweed strips for a twist! Instead of dipping it in water, just lightly brush some across.

Nutrition: Proteins: 75g; Fat: 683 g; Carbohydrates: 225 g.

Thanksgiving Herb Gravy

Preparation Time: 15 minutes
Cooking Time: 20 minutes
Servings: 6
Ingredients:

- 3 cups vegetable broth
- 1 ½ cups brown rice, cooked
- 6 ounces Cremini mushrooms, chopped
- 1 teaspoon dried basil
- 1 teaspoon dried oregano
- 1/2 teaspoons dried rosemary
- 1/2 teaspoons dried thyme
- 1/2 teaspoons garlic, minced
- 1/4 cup unsweetened plain almond milk
- Sea salt and freshly ground black pepper

Directions:

1. Bring the vegetable broth to a boil over medium-high heat; add in the rice and mushrooms and reduce the heat to a simmer.
2. Let it simmer for about 12 minutes until the mushrooms have softened. Remove from the heat.
3. Then, blend the mixture until creamy and uniform.
4. Add the remaining ingredients and heat your gravy over medium heat until everything is cooked through.
5. Serve with mashed potatoes or vegetables of choice. Bon appétit!

Nutrition: Calories: 165; Fat: 1.6 g; Carbs: 33.8 g; Proteins: 6.8 g.

Grilled Tofu Mayo Sandwiches

Preparation Time: 10 minutes
Cooking Time: 15 minutes
Servings: 2
Ingredients:

- ¼ cup tofu mayonnaise
- 2 slices whole-grain bread
- ¼ cucumber, sliced
- ½ cup lettuce, chopped
- ½ tomato, sliced
- 1 teaspoon olive oil, divided

Directions:

1. Spread the vegan mayonnaise over a bread slice. Top with the cucumber, lettuce and tomato, and finish with the other slice. Heat the oil in a skillet over medium heat.
2. Place the sandwich and grill for 3 minutes; then flip over and cook for a further 3 minutes.
3. Cut the sandwich in half and serve.

Nutrition: Proteins: 75g; Fat: 683 g; Carbohydrates: 225 g.

Tamari Toasted Almonds

Preparation Time: 5 minutes
Cooking Time: 8 minutes
Servings: 1
Ingredients:

- ½ cup raw almonds, or sunflower seeds
- 2 tablespoons tamari, or soy sauce
- 1 teaspoon toasted sesame oil

Directions:

1. Heat a dry skillet to medium-high heat, then add the almonds, stirring very frequently to keep them from burning.
2. Once the almonds are toasted, 7 to 8 minutes for almonds, or 3 to 4 minutes for sunflower seeds, pour the tamari and sesame oil into the hot skillet and stir to coat.
3. You can turn off the heat, and as the almonds cool, the tamari mixture will stick to and dry on the nuts.

Nutrition: Calories: 89; Total Fat: 8 g; Carbs: 3 g; Fiber: 2 g; Proteins: 4 g.

Chocolate Mousse Cake

Preparation Time: 20 minutes
Cooking Time: 40 minutes
Servings: 4
Ingredients:

- 2/3 cup toasted almond flour
- ¼ cup unsalted plant butter, melted
- 2 cups unsweetened chocolate bars, broken into pieces 2 ½ cups coconut cream
- Fresh raspberries or strawberries for topping

Directions:

1. Lightly grease a 9-inch springform pan with some plant butter and set it aside.
2. Mix the almond flour and plant butter in a medium bowl and pour the mixture into the springform pan. Use the spoon to spread and press the mixture into the bottom of the pan. Place in the refrigerator to firm for 30 minutes.
3. Meanwhile, pour the chocolate in a safe microwave bowl and melt for 1 minute stirring every 30 seconds.
4. Remove from the microwave and mix in the coconut cream and maple syrup.
5. Remove the cake pan from the oven. Pour the chocolate mixture on top, and shake the pan and even the layer. Chill further for 4 to 6 hours.
6. Take out the pan from the fridge, release the cake and garnish with the raspberries or strawberries.
7. Slice and serve.

Nutrition: Calories 608; Fat: 60.5 g; Carbs: 19.8 g; Proteins: 6.3 g.

Mushroom Steaks

Preparation Time: 20 minutes
Cooking Time: 24 minutes
Servings: 4
Ingredients:

- 1 tablespoon vegan butter
- ½ cup vegetable broth
- ½ small yellow onion, diced
- 1 large garlic clove, minced
- 3 tablespoons balsamic vinegar
- 1 tablespoon mirin
- ½ tablespoon soy sauce
- ½ tablespoon tomato paste
- 1 teaspoon dried thyme
- ½ teaspoon dried basil
- A dash of ground black pepper
- 2 large, whole portobello mushrooms

Directions:

1. Melt butter in a saucepan over medium heat and stir in half of the broth.
2. Bring to a simmer, then add garlic and onion. Cook for 8 minutes.
3. Whisk the rest of the ingredients except the mushrooms in a bowl.
4. Add this mixture to the onion in the pan and mix well.
5. Bring this filling to a simmer, then remove from the heat.
6. Clean the mushroom caps inside and out and divide the filling between the mushrooms.
7. Place the mushrooms on a baking sheet and top them with the remaining sauce and broth.
8. Cover with foil, then place it on a grill to smoke.
9. Cover the grill and broil for 16 minutes over indirect heat.
10. Serve warm.

Nutrition: Proteins: 35 g; Fat: 170 g; Carbohydrates: 72 g.

Baked Potatoes & Asparagus & Pine Nuts

Preparation Time: 20 minutes
Cooking Time: 50 minutes
Servings: 4
Ingredients:

- 1 bunch of asparagus, sliced
- 2 tablespoons olive oil
- 2 garlic cloves, minced
- 5 cups fresh baby spinach
- Salt and black pepper to taste
- 1 teaspoon dried basil
- ½ tsp dried thyme
- 2 potatoes, sliced
- ½ cup vegetable broth
- 2 tablespoons nutritional yeast

- ½ cup ground pine nuts

Directions:

1. Preheat oven to 370° F.
2. Heat half of the oil in a skillet over medium heat. Place in garlic, spinach, salt, and pepper and cook for 4 minutes until the spinach wilts. Add in basil and thyme. Set aside.
3. Arrange half of the potato slices on a greased casserole and season with salt and pepper. Top with the asparagus slices and finish with the spinach mixture. Cover with the remaining potato slices.
4. Whisk the broth with nutritional yeast in a bowl. Pour over the vegetables. Sprinkle with remaining oil and pine nuts. Cover with foil and bake for 40 minutes. Uncover and bake for another 10 minutes until golden brown. Serve warm.

Nutrition: Calories: 326; Fat: 2.3 g; Carbs: 57.4 g; Proteins: 6.5 g Fiber: 20 g

Sweet Tang' And Chia Smoothie

Preparation Time: 15 minutes
Cooking Time: 0 minutes
Servings: 2
Ingredients:

- 4 large plums
- 2 tablespoon chia seeds
- 1/2 cup pineapple chunks
- 1/2 cup ice cubes
- 3/4 cup coconut water

Directions:

1. Place all the ingredients in the order in a food processor or blender and then pulse for 2 to 3 minutes at high speed until smooth.
2. Pour the smoothie into two glasses and then serve.

Nutrition: Calories: 406; Fat: 9.3 g; Carbs: 77.4 g; Proteins: 6.3 g Fiber: 13 g.

Kale and Lemon Salad

Preparation Time: 15 minutes
Cooking Time: 10 minutes
Servings: 4
Ingredients:

- 5 cups of chopped kale
- 1 teaspoon of minced garlic
- ½ a tablespoon of maple syrup
- 2 tablespoons of lemon juice, freshly squeezed

Directions:

1. Combine the garlic, maple syrup and lemon juice in a large bowl and whisk to combine.
2. Add the kale and massage the dressing into it for two minutes before serving.

Nutrition: Calories: 216; Fat: 12.1 g; Carbs: 66.5 g; Proteins: 7 g

Cuban-style Millet

Preparation Time: 20 minutes
Cooking Time: 40 minutes
Servings: 4
Ingredients:

- 2 tablespoons olive oil
- 1 onion, chopped
- 2 zucchinis, chopped
- 2 garlic cloves, minced
- 1 teaspoon dried thyme
- ½ tsp ground cumin
- 1 (15.5-oz) can black-eyed peas
- 1 cup millet
- 2 tablespoons chopped fresh cilantro

Directions:

1. Heat the oil in a pot over medium heat. Place in onion and sauté for 3 minutes until translucent. Add in zucchinis, garlic, thyme, and cumin and cook for 10 minutes. Put in peas, millet and 2 ½ cups hot water.
2. Bring to a boil, then lower the heat and simmer for 20 minutes. Fluff the millet using a fork. Serve garnished with cilantro.

Nutrition: Calories: 476; Fat: 50 g; Carbs: 65 g; Proteins: 4.8 g.

Mediterranean Chickpeas with Vegetables

Preparation Time: 20 minutes
Cooking Time: 40 minutes
Servings: 6
Ingredients:

- 3 tablespoons olive oil
- 1 red onion, chopped
- 2 carrots, chopped
- 1 celery stalk, chopped
- 2 garlic cloves, minced
- 1 teaspoon grated fresh ginger
- 1 teaspoon ground cumin
- ½ tsp turmeric
- 2 parsnips, peeled and chopped
- 8 oz green beans, chopped
- 1 (15.5-oz) can chickpeas, drained
- 1 (14.5-oz) can diced tomatoes
- 1 ½ cups vegetable broth
- 2 tablespoons minced cilantro
- 1 teaspoon fresh lemon juice

Directions:

1. Heat the oil in a pot over medium heat. Place in onion, carrots, celery, garlic, and ginger. Sauté for 5 minutes. Add in cumin, turmeric, parsnips, green beans, chickpeas, tomatoes and juices, and broth.
2. Bring to a boil, then lower the heat and sprinkle with salt and pepper. Simmer for 30 minutes.
3. Sprinkle with lemon juice and cilantro and serve.

Nutrition: Calories: 426; Fat: 15.1 g; Carbs: 56 g; Proteins: 6 g.

Teff Porridge with Dried Figs

Preparation Time: 20 minutes
Cooking Time: 25 minutes **Servings:** 4
Ingredients:

- 1 cup whole-grain teff
- 1 cup water
- 2 cups coconut milk
- 2 tablespoons coconut oil
- 1/2 teaspoons ground cardamom
- 1/4 teaspoon ground cinnamon
- 4 tablespoons agave syrup
- 7-8 dried figs, chopped

Directions:

1. Bring the whole-grain teff, water and coconut milk to a boil.
2. Turn the heat to a simmer and add in the coconut oil, cardamom and cinnamon.
3. Let it cook for 20 minutes or until the grain has softened and the porridge has thickened. Stir in the agave syrup and stir to combine well. Top each serving bowl with chopped figs and serve warm. Bon appétit!

Nutrition: Calories: 356; Fat: 12.1 g; Carbs: 56.5 g; Proteins: 6.8 g.

Coconut Pumpkin Soup

Preparation Time: 10 minutes
Cooking Time: 30 minutes
Servings: 6
Ingredients:

- 2 cups pumpkin puree
- 1 teaspoon curry powder
- 2 shallots, chopped
- ½ onion, chopped
- 1 cup coconut cream
- 4 cups vegetable broth
- ½ tsp ground ginger
- 4 tablespoons olive oil
- Pepper
- Salt

Directions:

1. Heat oil in a saucepan over medium heat.
2. Add onion and shallot and sauté until softened.
3. Add ginger and curry powder and stir well.
4. Add broth, pumpkin puree, and coconut cream and stir well. Simmer for 10 minutes.
5. Puree the soup using a blender until smooth. Season with pepper and salt.

Serving Suggestion: Sprinkle pumpkin seeds on top of the soup and serve.
Variation Tip: Add a teaspoon of maple syrup for a little sweetness.
Nutrition: Calories 231; Fat 20.1 g; Sodium: 547 mg; Carbs 10.6 g; Fiber 3.6 g; Sugar: 4.9 g; Protein 5.2 g.

Garlic Basil Tomato Soup

Preparation Time: 10 minutes
Cooking Time: 5 minutes
Servings: 4
Ingredients:

- 28 oz can tomato, diced
- 1 tablespoon dried oregano
- 1 teaspoon garlic, minced
- 2 tablespoons olive oil
- 1 tablespoon balsamic vinegar
- 1 tablespoon dried basil
- Pepper
- Salt

Preparation:

1. Heat oil in a saucepan over medium flame.
2. Add garlic, basil, and oregano and sauté for 30 seconds.
3. Add tomatoes, vinegar, pepper, and salt and simmer for 3-5 minutes.

Serving Suggestion: Serve hot with crusty bread.
Variation Tip: Add some chili flakes for more flavor.
Nutrition: Calories 108; Fat 7.1 g; Sodium: 462 mg; Carbs 11.2 g; Fiber 3.9 g; Sugar: 6.8 g; Protein 2 g.

Cauliflower Carrot Soup

Preparation Time: 10 minutes

Cooking Time: 25 minutes
Servings: 8
Ingredients:

- 1 cauliflower head, chopped
- 8 cups vegetable broth
- 1 onion, diced
- 4 carrots, shredded
- ½ tsp turmeric powder
- ½ tbsp ginger, grated
- 5 oz coconut milk
- 1 tablespoon olive oil
- 1 tablespoon curry powder
- Pepper
- Salt

Preparation:

1. Heat oil in a saucepan over medium heat.
2. Add onion and sauté for 5 minutes. Add cauliflower, carrots, and broth and bring to boil.
3. Turn heat to medium-low and simmer until vegetables are softened.
4. Add curry powder, turmeric, and ginger and stir well.
5. Puree the soup using a blender until smooth.
6. Add coconut milk and stir well. Season with pepper and salt.

Serving Suggestion: Sprinkle some paprika on top of the soup and serve.
Variation Tip: You can also add vegetable stock instead of broth.
Nutrition: Calories 125; Fat 7.5 g; Sodium: 817 mg; Carbs 8.7 g; Fiber 2.6 g; Sugar: 4.2 g; Protein 6.5 g.

CHAPTER 17:

SNACKS AND APPETIZERS

Cauliflower Spinach Rice

Preparation Time: 10 minutes
Cooking Time: 10 minutes
Servings: 4
Ingredients:
- 5 oz baby spinach
- 4 cups cauliflower rice
- ¼ tsp chili powder
- 1 teaspoon garlic, minced
- 3 tablespoons olive oil
- 1 fresh lime juice
- ¼ cup vegetable broth
- Pepper
- Salt

Preparation:
1. Heat oil in a pan over medium heat. Add garlic and sauté for 30seconds.
2. Add cauliflower rice, chili powder, pepper, and salt and cook for 2minutes.
3. Add broth and lime juice and stir well.
4. Add spinach and cook until spinach is wilted.

Serving Suggestion: Serve warm.
Variation Tip: You can also add some sautéed mushrooms.
Nutritional: Calories 127; Fat 10.9 g; Sodium: 146 mg; Carbs 7 g; Fiber 3.4 g; Sugar: 2.6 g; Protein 3.4 g.

Basil Zucchini Noodles

Preparation Time: 10 minutes
Cooking Time: 10 minutes
Servings: 2
Ingredients:
- 1 zucchini, spiralized
- ¼ cup pine nuts
- 1/3 cup water
- 1¼ cup fresh basil
- ¾ cup cherry tomatoes, halved
- 1 avocado, chopped
- 2 tablespoons fresh lemon juice
- Pepper
- Salt

Preparation:
1. Add zucchini noodles and tomatoes into the bowl. Add remaining ingredients into the blender and blend until smooth.
2. Pour blended mixture over zucchini noodles. Toss well.

Serving Suggestion: Serve immediately.
Variation Tip: You can also add grape tomatoes instead of cherry tomatoes.
Nutrition: Calories 355; Fat 31.8 g; Sodium: 102 mg; Carbs: 17.5 g; Fiber 9.6 g; Sugar: 5 g; Protein 6.6 g.

Hummus

Preparation Time: 10 minutes
Cooking Time: 40 minutes **Servings:** 2 cups
Ingredients:
- 1 can chickpeas
- ½ cup tahini
- ¼ cup lemon juice
- 1 chopped garlic clove
- ½ teaspoon ground cumin
- ½ teaspoon baking soda
- ½ teaspoon sea salt
- 1 tablespoon extra-virgin olive oil
- 2–4 tablespoons ice water

Directions:
1. Put chickpeas (with baking soda) in a medium saucepan on high heat. Pour water to cover chickpeas by several inches and bring it to a boil. Cook for 20 minutes until they look bloated.
2. Drain chickpeas using a fine-mesh strainer and cool with running cold water for 20–30 seconds.
3. Meanwhile, add garlic, lemon juice, and salt in a food processor or a blender. Blend until garlic clove is finely minced. Set aside. Let it rest for 10 minutes to enhance the flavor.
4. Put tahini into the empty machine and blend until you reach a thick, creamy consistency.

5. Pour 2 tablespoons of ice water into the machine and blend until it has ultra-smooth consistency. If it's too thick, add more water.
6. Add chickpeas with cumin into the processor, blend for 2 minutes until super smooth consistency. Drizzle the olive oil while processing.
7. Taste, add more salt or lemon juice if needed.
8. Serve and enjoy your Hummus!

Nutrition: Calories: 151; Fat: 11 g; Proteins: 5 g; Carbohydrates: 11 g.

Eggplant Sticks

Preparation Time: 10 minutes
Cooking Time: 15 minutes
Servings: 4
Ingredients:

- 10 ounces eggplants
- ½ cup breadcrumbs
- 2 tablespoons grated parmesan cheese
- 1 large egg white
- 1 teaspoon extra virgin olive oil
- ½ teaspoon salt and black pepper

Directions:

1. Preheat your oven to 450° F. Cover 2 baking sheets with a piece of parchment paper and lightly spread some oil.
2. Cut eggplants into large strips. Transfer them to a large mixing bowl. Add seasonings with olive oil, and toss. Set aside.
3. Mix parmesan cheese with breadcrumbs in a bowl. Put egg whites into another bowl.
4. Dip a couple of eggplants into the egg whites and transfer them into the breadcrumb's mixture. Then spread them on the baking sheet in one layer. Repeat the same with the remaining part. Spritz with olive oil.
5. Bake for 10 minutes. Turn it over and continue cooking for 5 minutes.
6. Serve warm and enjoy.

Nutrition: Calories: 87; Fat: 3 g; Proteins: 4 g; Carbohydrates: 12 g.

Cauliflower Popcorn

Preparation Time: 10 minutes
Cooking Time: 12 hours
Servings: 2
Ingredients:

- 2 heads of cauliflower
- Spicy Sauce
- ½ cup filtered water
- ½ teaspoon of turmeric
- 1 cup dates
- 2-3 tablespoons nutritional yeast
- ¼ cup sun-dried tomatoes
- 2 tablespoons raw tahini
- 1-2 teaspoons cayenne pepper
- 2 teaspoons onion powder
- 1 tablespoon apple cider vinegar

- 2 teaspoons garlic powder

Directions:

1. Chop the cauliflower into small pieces.
2. Put all the ingredients for the spicy sauce in a blender and create a mixture with a smooth consistency.
3. Coat the cauliflower florets in the sauce. See that each piece is properly covered.
4. Put the spicy florets in a dehydrator tray.
5. Add some salt and your favorite herb if you want.
6. Dehydrate the cauliflower for 12 hours at 115° F. Keep dehydrating until it is crunchy.
7. Enjoy cauliflower popcorn, which is a healthier alternative!

Nutrition: Calories: 491; Fat: 13 g; Carbohydrates: 86 g; Proteins: 20 g.

Sweet Potato Hummus

Preparation Time: 15 minutes
Cooking Time: 55 minutes **Servings:** 4
Ingredients:

- 2 cups cooked chickpeas
- 2 medium sweet potatoes
- 3 tablespoons tahini
- 3 tablespoons olive oil
- 3 freshly peeled garlic gloves
- Freshly squeezed lemon juice
- Ground sea salt
- ¼ teaspoon cumin
- Zest from half a lemon
- ½ teaspoon smoked paprika
- 1 ½ teaspoon cayenne pepper

Directions:

1. Set the oven to 400° F. Add the sweet potatoes to the middle rack of the oven and bake them for about 45 minutes. You may also bake the potatoes in a baking dish. You will know that they are ready when they become soft and squishy.
2. Allow the sweet potatoes to cool. Add all the other ingredients in a food processor, then blend.
3. After the sweet potatoes have sufficiently cooled down, use a knife to peel off the skin.
4. Add the sweet potatoes to a blender and blend well with the rest of the ingredients.
5. Once you have a potato mash, sprinkle some sesame seeds and cayenne pepper and serve it!

Nutrition: Calories: 376; Fat: 20 g; Carbohydrates: 40 g; Proteins: 12 g.

Roasted Chickpeas

Preparation Time: 10 minutes
Cooking Time: 25 minutes
Servings: 4
Ingredients:

- 1 can make chickpea, rinsed, and drained
- 2 teaspoons freshly squeezed lemon juice
- 2 teaspoons tamari
- ½ tsp fresh rosemary, chopped

- 1/8 teaspoons sea salt
- 1/8 teaspoons pure maple syrup or agave nectar

Directions:
1. Preheat the stove to 400° F. Line a baking sheet with parchment paper.
2. Toss all ingredients together and spread the chickpeas out on the baking sheet.
3. Roast for around 25 minutes, stirring the chickpeas every 5 minutes or so. Note, until the tamari and lemon juice dry up, the chickpeas will seem delicate, not crunchy.
4. Serve hot or at room warmth for a snack.

Nutrition: Calories: 290; Proteins: 11 g; Carbohydrates: 40 g; Fat: 10 g.

Tamari Almonds

Preparation Time: 5 minutes
Cooking Time: 25 minutes **Servings:** 8
Ingredients:
- 1-pound raw almonds
- 3 tablespoons tamari or soy sauce
- 2 tablespoons extra-virgin olive oil
- 1 tablespoon nutritional yeast
- 1 to 2 teaspoons chili residue, to taste

Directions:
1. Preheat the oven to 400° F. Line a baking sheet with parchment paper.
2. In a medium bowl, combine the almonds, tamari, and olive oil until well coated. Spread the almonds on the prepared baking sheet and roast for 10 to 15 minutes, until browned.
3. Cool for 10 minutes, then season with the nutritional yeast and chili powder.
4. Transfer to a glass jar and close tightly with a lid.

Nutrition: Calories: 364; Fat: 32 g; Carbohydrates: 13 g; Proteins: 13 g.

Spiced and Herbs Nuts

Preparation Time: 10 minutes
Cooking Time: 12 minutes
Servings: 12
Ingredients:
- 1½ cups whole almonds
- 1½ cups pistachios
- 1 cup pecan halves
- 1 cup walnut halves
- 1 cup cashews
- 1/3 cup extra-virgin olive oil
- 2 tablespoons fresh rosemary, chopped
- 2 tablespoons fresh thyme, chopped
- 2 tablespoons fresh oregano, chopped
- 1 tablespoon smoked paprika
- 1 teaspoon cayenne pepper
- 2 teaspoons garlic powder
- Salt, to taste

Directions:

1. Preheat your oven to 350° F and line a large baking sheet with parchment paper.
2. In a bowl, place all ingredients and toss to coat well.
3. Transfer the nut mixture onto the prepared baking sheet and spread in a single layer.
4. Roast for about 10–12 minutes, flipping after every 5 minutes.
5. Remove from the oven and set the baking sheet aside to cool completely before serving.

Nutrition: Calories: 369; Fat: 34 g; Carbohydrates: 12 g; Proteins: 10 g.

Nuts and Seeds Squares

Preparation Time: 20 minutes
Cooking Time: 5 minutes
Servings: 8
Ingredients:
- ½ cup hazelnuts, toasted
- ½ cup walnuts, toasted
- ½ cup almonds, toasted
- ½ cup white sesame seeds
- ½ cup pumpkin seeds, shelled
- 1 cup unsweetened dried cherries
- 2 cups unsweetened dried coconut flakes
- ¼ cup coconut oil
- 1/3 cup maple syrup
- ½ teaspoon ground cinnamon
- ½ teaspoon salt

Directions:
1. Line a 13x9-inch baking dish with parchment paper. Set aside.
2. In a large bowl, add the hazelnuts, walnuts, and almonds and mix well.
3. Transfer 1 cup of the nut mixture into another large bowl and chop them roughly.
4. In the food processor, add the remaining nut mixture and pulse until finely ground.
5. Now, transfer the ground nut mixture into the bowl of the chopped nuts.
6. Add the seeds and coconut flakes and mix well.
7. In a small pan, add the oil, maple syrup, and cinnamon over medium-low heat and cook for about 3–5 minutes or until it starts to boil, stirring continuously.
8. Remove from the heat and immediately pour over the nut mixture, stirring continuously until well combined.
9. Set aside to cool slightly.
10. Now, place the mixture into the prepared baking dish evenly, and with the back of a spoon, smooth the top surface by pressing slightly.
11. Refrigerate for about 1 hour or until set completely.
12. Remove from refrigerator and cut into equal-sized squares and serve.

Nutrition: Calories: 496; Proteins: 10 g; Carbohydrates: 24 g; Fat: 42 g.

Zucchini Chips

Preparation Time: 10 minutes

Cooking Time: 2 hours
Servings: 5
Ingredients:

- 1 large zucchini
- 2 tablespoons of olive oil
- Sea salt, to taste

Directions:

1. Preheat your oven to 225º F. Cover 2 baking sheets with a piece of parchment paper.
2. Slice zucchini on a mandolin (use medium thickness.
3. Place zucchini slices on a paper towel, cover them with another piece, and press. It will help you to squeeze in extra water.
4. Spread zucchini slices on the covered baking sheets in a single layer. Brush each piece with olive oil by using a baking brush.
5. Sprinkle salt on the top.
6. Bake for about 2 hours until brown and crisp.
7. Serve and enjoy!

Nutrition: Calories: 54; Fat: 5 g; Proteins: 0 g; Carbohydrates: 1 g.

Seed Bars

Preparation Time: 15 minutes
Cooking Time: 15 minutes
Servings: 10
Ingredients:

- 1¼ cups creamy salted peanut butter
- 5 Medjool dates, pitted
- ½ cup unsweetened vegan protein powder
- 2/3 cup hemp seeds
- 1/3 cup chia seeds

Directions:

1. Line a loaf pan with parchment paper. Set aside.
2. In a food processor, add the peanut butter and dates and pulse until well combined.
3. Add the protein powder, hemp seeds, and chia seeds and pulse until well combined.
4. Now, place the mixture into the prepared loaf pan and, with the back of a spoon, smooth the top surface.
5. Freeze for at least 10–15 minutes, or until set.
6. Cut into ten equal-sized bars and serve.

Nutrition: Calories: 308; Fat: 21 g; Carbohydrates: 17 g; Proteins: 16 g.

Chocolate Protein Bites

Preparation Time: 10 minutes
Cooking Time: 20 minutes
Servings: 12
Ingredients:

- ½ cup chocolate protein powder
- 1 avocado, medium
- 1 tablespoon chocolate chips
- 1 tablespoon almond butter
- 1 tablespoon cocoa powder
- 1 teaspoon vanilla extract
- Dash of salt

Directions:

1. Begin by blending avocado, almond butter, vanilla extract, and salt in a high-speed blender until you get a smooth mixture.
2. Next, spoon in the protein powder, cocoa powder, and chocolate chips to the blender.
3. Blend again until you get a smooth dough-like consistency mixture.
4. Now, check for seasoning and add more sweetness if needed.
5. Finally, with the help of a scooper, scoop out dough to make small balls.

Nutrition: Calories: 46; Fat: 2 g; Carbohydrates: 2 g; Proteins: 2 g.

Chocolate Almond Bars

Preparation Time: 10 minutes
Cooking Time: 20 minutes
Servings: 12
Ingredients:

- 1 cup almonds
- 1 ½ cup rolled oats
- 1/3 cup maple syrup
- ¼ tsp. sea salt
- 5 oz. protein powder
- 1 teaspoon cinnamon

Directions:

1. For making these delicious vegan bars, you first need to place ¾ cup of the almonds and salt in the food processor.
2. Process them for a minute or until you get them in the form of almond butter.
3. Now, stir in the rest of the ingredients to the processor and process them again until smooth.
4. Next, transfer the mixture to a greased parchment paper-lined baking sheet and spread it across evenly.
5. Press them slightly down with the back of the spoon.
6. Chop down the remaining ¼ cup of the almonds and top it across the mixture.
7. Finally, place them in the refrigerator for 20 minutes or until set.

Nutrition: Calories: 166; Fat: 6 g; Carbohydrates: 17 g; Proteins: 13 g.

Spicy Nuts and Seeds Snack Mix

Preparation Time: 5 minutes
Cooking Time: 10 minutes
Servings: 4
Ingredients:

- ¼ tsp garlic powder
- ¼ tsp nutritional yeast
- ½ tsp smoked paprika
- ¼ tsp sea salt
- ¼ tsp dried parsley
- ½ cup slivered almonds
- ½ cup cashew pieces
- ½ cup sunflower seeds

- ½ cup pepitas

Directions:
1. In a small bowl, mix the garlic powder, nutritional yeast, paprika, salt, and parsley. Set aside.
2. In a large skillet, add the almonds, cashews, sunflower seeds, pepitas and heat over low heat until warm and glistening, 3 minutes.
3. Turn the heat off and stir in the parsley mixture.
4. Allow complete cooling and enjoy!

Nutrition: Calories: 385; Fat: 33 g; Proteins: 12 g; Carbohydrates: 16 g.

Almond, Date Energy Bites

Preparation Time: 10 minutes
Cooking Time: 15 minutes
Servings: 24
Ingredients:

- 1 cup dates, pitted
- 1 cup unsweetened shredded coconut
- ¼ cup chia seeds
- ¾ cup ground almonds
- ¼ cup cocoa nibs, or non-dairy chocolate chips

Directions:
1. Purée everything in a food processor until crumbly and sticking together, pushing down the sides whenever necessary to keep it blending. If you don't have a food processor, you can mash soft Medjool dates. But if you're using harder baking dates, you'll have to soak them, then try to purée them in a blender.
2. Form the mix into 2 balls and place them on a baking sheet lined with parchment or waxed paper. Put in the fridge to set for about 15 minutes. Use the softest dates you can find. Medjool dates are the best for this purpose. The hard dates you see in the baking aisle of your supermarket will take a long time to blend up. If you use those, try soaking them in water for at least an hour before starting and then start draining.
3. Finish and serve.

Nutrition: Calories: 152; Fat: 11 g; Carbohydrates: 13 g; Proteins: 3 g.

Banana Nut Bread Bars

Preparation Time: 5 minutes
Cooking Time: 30 minutes **Servings:** 9
Ingredients:

- Nonstick cooking spray (optional)
- 2 large ripe bananas
- 2 tablespoon maple syrup
- ½ teaspoon vanilla extract
- 2 cups old-fashioned rolled oats
- ½ teaspoons salt
- ¼ cup chopped walnuts

Directions:
1. Preheat the oven to 350° F. Lightly coat a 9x9-inch baking pan with nonstick cooking spray (if using) or line with parchment paper for oil-free baking.

2. In a medium bowl, mash the bananas with a fork. Add the maple syrup and vanilla extract and mix well. Add the oats, salt, and walnuts, mixing well.
3. Transfer the batter to the baking pan and bake for 25 to 30 minutes, until the top is crispy. Cool completely before slicing into 9 bars. Transfer to an airtight storage container or a large plastic bag.

Nutrition: Calories: 73; Total fat: 1 g; Carbohydrates: 15 g; Proteins: 2 g.

Rosemary and Lemon Zest Popcorn

Preparation Time: 10 minutes
Cooking Time: 0 minutes **Servings:** 2
Ingredients:

- 1/3 cup popcorn kernels
- 2 tablespoon vegan butter, melted
- 1 tablespoon chopped rosemary
- 1 teaspoon lemon zest
- ¼ teaspoon salt

Directions:
1. Pop the kernels, and when done, transfer them into a large bowl.
2. Drizzle butter over the popcorns, sprinkle with salt, lemon zest, and rosemary, and then toss until combined.
3. Serve straight away.

Nutrition: Calories: 201; Proteins: 3 g; Carbohydrates: 25 g; Fat: 10 g.

Strawberry Avocado Toast

Preparation Time: 5 minutes
Cooking Time: 0 minutes
Servings: 4
Ingredients:

- 1 avocado, peeled, pitted, and quartered
- **4**whole-wheat bread slices, toasted
- 4 ripe strawberries, cut into ¼-inch slices
- 1 tablespoon balsamic glaze or reduction

Directions:
1. Mash one-quarter of the avocado on a slice of toast. Layer one-quarter of the strawberry slices over the avocado, and finish with a drizzle of balsamic glaze.
2. Repeat with the remaining ingredients, and serve.

Nutrition: Calories: 150; Fat: 8 g; Carbohydrates: 17 g; Proteins: 5 g.

Strawberry Watermelon Ice Pops

Preparation Time: 5 minutes + 6 hours to freeze
Cooking Time: 0 minutes
Servings: 6
Ingredients:

- 4 cups diced watermelon
- 4 strawberries, tops removed
- 2 tablespoons freshly squeezed lime juice

Directions:

1. In a blender, combine the watermelon, strawberries, and lime juice.
2. Blend for 1 to 2 minutes, or until well combined.
3. Pour evenly into six ice-pop molds, insert ice-pop sticks, and freeze for at least 6 hours before serving.

Nutrition: Calories: 61; Fat: 0 g; Carbohydrates: 15 g; Proteins: 1 g.

Carrot Energy Balls

Preparation Time: 10 minutes + chilling
Cooking Time: 0 minutes
Servings: 8
Ingredients:

- 1 large carrot, grated carrot
- 1 ½ cups old-fashioned oats
- 1 cup raisins
- 1 cup dates, pitied
- 1 cup coconut flakes
- 1/4 teaspoon ground cloves
- 1/2 teaspoons ground cinnamon

Directions:

1. In your food processor, pulse all ingredients until it forms a sticky and uniform mixture.
2. Shape the batter into equal balls.
3. Place in your refrigerator until ready to serve. Bon appétit!

Nutrition: Calories: 495; Proteins: 22 g; Carbohydrates: 58 g; Fat: 21 g.

Sweet Potato Bites

Preparation Time: 10 minutes + chilling
Cooking Time: 25 minutes
Servings: 4
Ingredients:

- 4 sweet potatoes, peeled and grated
- 2 chia eggs
- 1/4 cup nutritional yeast
- 2 tablespoons tahini
- 2 tablespoons chickpea flour
- 1 teaspoon shallot powder
- 1 teaspoon garlic powder
- 1 teaspoon paprika
- Sea salt and ground black pepper, to taste

Directions:

1. Start by preheating your oven to 395° F. Line a baking pan with parchment paper or a Silpat mat.
2. Thoroughly combine all the ingredients until everything is well incorporated.
3. Roll the batter into equal balls and place them in your refrigerator for about 1 hour.
4. Bake these balls for approximately 25 minutes, turning them over halfway through the cooking time. Bon appétit!

Nutrition: Calories: 215; Fat: 4.5 g; Carbohydrates: 35 g; Proteins: 9 g.

Banana Bulgur Bars

Preparation Time: 10 minutes
Cooking Time: 30 minutes
Servings: 9
Ingredients:

- 2 large ripe bananas
- 1 tablespoon pure maple syrup
- ½ teaspoon pure vanilla extract
- 1 cup rolled oats
- 1 cup medium-grind or coarse bulgur
- ¼ cup chopped walnuts

Directions:

1. Preheat the oven to 350° F. Line an 8-inch square baking pan with parchment paper.
2. In a medium bowl, mash the bananas with a fork. Add the maple syrup and vanilla and mix well. Add the oats, bulgur, and walnuts and mix until combined.
3. Transfer the mixture to the prepared baking pan and bake for 25 to 30 minutes until the top is crispy.
4. Let cool completely, then cut into 9 bars and transfer to an airtight container or a large zip-top plastic bag. Store at room temperature for up to 5 days.

Nutrition: Calories: 142; Fat: 3 g; Carbohydrates: 26 g; Proteins: 4 g.

Italian Tomato Snack

Preparation Time: 10 minutes
Cooking Time: 60 minutes
Servings: 6
Ingredients:

- 50 oz canned tomatoes, drained
- A pinch of salt and black pepper
- ¼ cup extra virgin olive oil
- 15 basil leaves, sliced
- 1 tablespoon burgundy or merlot wine vinegar
- A pinch of stevia
- 10 baguette pieces, toasted.

Directions:

1. Spread the tomatoes on the lined baking sheet, drizzle half of the oil, season with salt and pepper and bake them at 300° F for one hour. Slice the tomatoes into cubes, put them inside a bowl. Add the oil, basil, vinegar and stevia, and toss.
2. Split the tomatoes on each baguette slice and serve as a snack.

Nutrition: Calories: 191; Fat: 4 g; Carbohydrates: 9 g; Proteins: 7 g

Rosemary-Onion Jam

Preparation Time: 5 minutes
Cooking Time: 6 to 7 hours on High or 10 to 12 hours on Low
Servings: 3 to 4 cups
Ingredients:

- 4 to 6 large sweet onions (about 3 pounds), sliced into half-moons

- 2 garlic cloves, minced
- ½ cup maple syrup
- ¼ cup balsamic vinegar
- 1 teaspoon finely chopped fresh rosemary (about 2 sprigs), or dried

Directions:
1. Put the onions in the slow cooker. Add the garlic.
2. In a small bowl, stir together the maple syrup, vinegar, and rosemary. Pour the mixture into the slow cooker and toss gently to coat the onions. Cover and cook on High for 6 to 7 hours or on Low for 10 to 12 hours, until the onions are deep brown.
3. Transfer the mixture to a blender, or use an immersion blender, and blend into a chunky jam consistency. Store in glass jars or plastic containers in the refrigerator for up to 1 month.

Nutrition: Calories: 76; Fat: <1 g; Carbohydrates: 19 g; Proteins: 1 g; Fiber: 1 g; Sodium: 12 mg.

Pineapple, Peach, and Mango Salsa

Preparation Time: 15 minutes
Cooking Time: 2 to 3 hours on Low
Servings: about 6 cups
Ingredients:

- 1 medium onion, finely diced
- 2 garlic cloves, minced
- 1 medium orange, red, or yellow bell pepper, finely diced
- 1 (20-ounce) can crushed pineapple in juice
- 1 (15-ounce) can no-sugar-added mango in juice, drained and finely diced
- 1 (15-ounce) can no-sugar-added sliced peaches in juice, drained and finely diced
- ½ teaspoon ground cumin
- 1 teaspoon paprika
- Juice of 1 lime
- 3 to 4 tablespoons chopped fresh mint (about 10 to 15 leaves)

Directions:
1. Put the onion, garlic, and bell pepper in the slow cooker. Add the pineapple and its juices, the mango, and the peaches. Sprinkle the cumin and paprika into the slow cooker. Add the lime juice and stir well to combine.
2. Cover and cook on Low for 2 to 3 hours, or until the onion and peppers are ready and softened. Let the salsa cool slightly, then stir in the mint just before serving.

Variation Tip: For a spicy Southwestern flair, replace the mint with cilantro and incorporate one finely diced jalapeño pepper, ½teaspoon of chili powder, and an extra clove of minced garlic (optional) at the beginning of the cooking time. Stir in the cilantro after slightly cooling the finished dish.

Nutrition: Calories: 36; Fat: <1 g; Carbohydrates: 9 g; Proteins: 1 g; Fiber: 1 g; Sodium: 2 mg.

Spinach-Artichoke Dip

Preparation Time: 20 minutes
Cooking Time: 2 hours on Low
Servings: about 5 cups
Ingredients:

- 1 cup water
- ¾ cup raw cashews
- 1 (8-ounce) can water chestnuts, drained
- 1 (12-ounce) package frozen quartered or chopped artichoke hearts
- 1 (12-ounce) package frozen spinach
- ¼ cup finely chopped onion
- 2 garlic cloves, minced
- 11/2 cups unsweetened plant-based milk
- 3 tablespoons nutritional yeast
- 1 tablespoon Plant-Based Worcestershire Sauce or store-bought
- 1 tablespoon white miso paste
- 1 tablespoon lemon juice
- ½ teaspoon paprika

Directions:
1. Boil the water and put the cashews in a medium bowl. Pour the hot water over the cashews and let soak to soften while preparing the rest of the ingredients for at least 15 minutes.
2. Meanwhile, coarsely chop the water chestnuts and any artichoke hearts that are larger than bite-size. Add the water chestnuts, artichoke hearts, spinach, and onion to the slow cooker.
3. Drain the cashews. Put the cashews, garlic, milk, nutritional yeast, Worcestershire sauce, miso paste, lemon juice, and paprika in a blender. Blend on high until the sauce is very smooth and creamy.
4. Pour the sauce into the slow cooker and stir well to combine. The sauce will look a bit too thin at this stage, but it will thicken as the dip cooks. Cover and cook on Low for 2 hours, or until heated through.
5. Store leftovers in the refrigerator for up to 4 days and reheat in the microwave until warmed through.

Nutrition: Calories: 53; Fat: 3 g; Carbohydrates: 6 g; Proteins: 3 g; Fiber: 2 g; Sodium: 81 mg.

White Bean Tzatziki Dip

Preparation Time: 10 minutes
Cooking Time: 1 to 2 minutes
Servings: about 8 cups
Ingredients:

- 4 (14.5-ounce) cans white beans, drained and rinsed
- 8 garlic cloves, minced
- 1 medium onion, coarsely chopped
- ¼ cup Low-Sodium Vegetable Broth or store-bought, plus more as needed
- Juice from one lemon, divided
- 2 teaspoons dried dill, divided
- Salt (optional)
- 1 cucumber, peeled and finely diced

Directions:

1. Place the beans, garlic, onion, broth, and half the lemon juice in a blender. Blend until creamy, about 1 minute, adding up to ¼ cup of additional broth as needed to make the mixture creamy.
2. Transfer the mixture to the slow cooker, stir in 1 teaspoon of dill, and season with salt (if using). Cover and cook on Low for 1 to 2 hours until heated through.
3. Meanwhile, in a medium bowl, mix the cucumber with the remaining 1 teaspoon of dill and the remaining half of the lemon juice. Toss to coat. Season with salt (if using). Spoon the dip from the slow cooker into a serving bowl and top with the cucumber mixture before serving.

Nutrition: Calories: 59; Fat: <1 g; Carbohydrates: 11 g; Proteins: 3 g; Fiber: 4 g; Sodium: 1 mg.

Buffalo Cauliflower Dip

Preparation Time: 20 minutes
Cooking Time: 2 hours on Low
Servings: about 5 cups
Ingredients:

- 1 cup water
- 1 cup raw cashews
- 2 tablespoons white vinegar
- ¼ teaspoon cayenne powder
- ½ cup unsweetened plant-based milk
- ¼ cup Low-Sodium Vegetable Broth or store-bought
- 1 (14.5-ounce) can cannellini or Great Northern white beans, drained and rinsed
- 3 tablespoons nutritional yeast
- ¼ cup diced onion
- 3 garlic cloves, minced
- 1 (12-ounce) package frozen riced cauliflower
- 1 recipe Shredded Tofu Meaty Crumbles (optional) Salt (optional)
- 12 celery stalks, cut into 3-inch-long sticks, for serving

Directions:

1. Boil the water and put the cashews in a medium bowl. Pour the hot water over the cashews and let soak to soften for at least 15 minutes.
2. Meanwhile, in a small bowl, stir together the vinegar and cayenne.
3. Transfer the cayenne mixture to a blender or food processor, then add the milk, broth, beans, nutritional yeast, onion, and garlic. Drain the cashews and add them to the blender. Mix until creamy.
4. In the slow cooker, combine the cauliflower and tofu crumbles (if using). Season with salt (if using) and cover with the sauce. Mix well to combine. Cover and cook on Low for 2 hours, or until heated through.

5. Serve with the celery sticks for dipping.

Nutrition: Calories: 68; Fat: 3 g; Carbohydrates: 7 g; Proteins: 4 g; Fiber: 2 g; Sodium: 36 mg.

Creamy Southwestern Salsa Bean Dip

Preparation Time: 10 minutes
Cooking Time: 2 hours on High or 4 hours on Low
Servings: 12 cups
Ingredients:

- 1 medium onion, diced
- 1 medium green bell pepper, diced
- 3 garlic cloves, minced
- 1 (1-pound) bag frozen corn
- 2 (14.5-ounce) cans no-salt-added diced tomatoes
- 1 (14.5-ounce) can black beans, drained and rinsed
- 1 (14.5-ounce) can pinto beans, drained and rinsed
- 1 tablespoon chili powder
- 2 teaspoons ground cumin
- 1 cup Cheese Sauce or store-bought cheese sauce
- Juice of ½ lime
- Salt (optional)
- Ground black pepper
- 2 scallions, green and white parts, chopped
- ¼ cup fresh cilantro, chopped

Directions:

1. Place the onion, bell pepper, garlic, corn, tomatoes, black beans, pinto beans, chili powder, and cumin in the slow cooker. Cover and cook on High for 2 hours or on Low for 4 hours.
2. During the last 30 minutes of cooking, stir in the cheese sauce.
3. Before serving, stir in the lime juice and season with salt (if using) and black pepper. Transfer the dip to a bowl, top with the scallions and cilantro, and serve warm.

Nutrition: Calories: 72; Fat: 1 g; Carbohydrates: 14 g; Proteins: 4 g; Fiber: 4 g; Sodium: 45 mg.

Eggplant Caponata Bruschetta

Preparation Time: 20 minutes
Cooking Time: 2 to 3 hours on High or 5 to 6 hours on Low
Servings: 4 to 8
Directions:

- 1 medium eggplant, unpeeled and chopped
- 1 medium onion, diced
- 2 small zucchinis, diced
- 3 celery stalks, diced
- 4 garlic cloves, minced
- 1 cup sliced pitted green olives
- 2 (14.5-ounce) cans diced tomatoes
- 2 tablespoons capers, drained
- ¼ cup red wine vinegar
- 1 tablespoon maple syrup
- 1 teaspoon dried basil

- 1 teaspoon dried oregano
- Ground black pepper
- Salt (optional)
- 1 long thin loaf crusty whole-grain bread
- 3 tablespoons chopped fresh flat-leaf parsley

Directions:

1. Put the eggplant, onion, zucchini, celery, garlic, and olives in the slow cooker. Pour in the tomatoes. Add the capers, vinegar, maple syrup, basil, oregano, pepper, and salt (if using). Stir well to combine. Cover and cook on High for 2 to 3 hours or on Low for 5 to 6 hours.
2. Preheat the oven to 375° F. Slice the bread into ½-inch slices and place them on a baking sheet. Toast in the oven, keeping an eye on the bread, so it doesn't burn. Flip the bread and toast the other side to make it into crostini.
3. After the caponata finishes cooking, stir in the parsley. Spoon about 2 tablespoons of caponata onto each piece of crostini and serve immediately.

Nutrition: Calories: 405; Fat: 8 g; Carbohydrates: 72 g; Proteins: 14 g; Fiber: 11 g; Sodium: 1,493 mg.

Sweet 'n' Spicy Crunchy Snack Mix

Preparation Time: 5 minutes
Cooking Time: 1½ hours on Low
Servings: 5½ cups
Ingredients:

- 1 cup raw cashews
- 1 cup raw almonds
- 1 cup raw pecan halves
- 1 cup walnuts - ½ cup raw pepitas
- ½ cup raw sunflower seeds
- ¼ cup aquafaba
- ¼ cup maple syrup
- 1 teaspoon miso paste
- 1 teaspoon garlic powder
- 1 teaspoon paprika
- 2 teaspoons ground ginger

Directions:

1. Put the cashews, almonds, pecans, walnuts, pepitas, and sunflower seeds in the slow cooker.
2. In a deep bowl, whisk or use an immersion blender to beat the aquafaba until foamy, about 1 minute. Add the maple syrup, miso paste, garlic powder, paprika and ginger, and whisk or blend to combine. Pour over the nuts in the slow cooker and gently toss, making sure all the nuts and seeds are coated.
3. Stretch a clean dish towel or several layers of paper towels over the top of the slow cooker, but not touching the food, and place the lid on top. Cook on Low for 1½ hours, stirring every 20 to 30 minutes to keep the nuts from burning. After each stir, dry any condensation under the lid and replace the towels before re-covering.
4. Line a rimmed baking sheet with parchment paper. Transfer the snack mix to the baking sheet to cool. Store in an airtight container for up to 2 weeks.

Nutrition: Calories: 182; Fat: 16 g; Carbohydrates: 8 g; Proteins: 5 g; Fiber: 2 g; Sodium: 12 mg.

CHAPTER 18:

SMOOTHIE RECIPES

Max Power Smoothie

Preparation Time: 5 minutes
Cooking Time: 0 minutes **Servings:** 4
Ingredients:

- 1 banana
- ¼ cup rolled oats or 1 scoop plant protein powder
- 1 tablespoon flaxseed or chia seeds
- 1 cup raspberries or other berries
- 1 cup chopped mango (frozen or fresh)
- ½ cup non-dairy milk (optional)
- 1 cup water

Directions:

1. Purée everything in a blender until smooth, adding more water (or non-dairy milk) if needed.

Nutrition: Calories: 550; Fat: 9 g; Carbs: 116 g; Fiber: 29 g; Proteins: 13 g.

Chai Chia Smoothie

Preparation Time: 5 minutes
Cooking Time: 0 minutes **Servings:** 3
Ingredients:

- 1 banana
- ½ cup coconut milk
- 1 cup water
- 1 cup alfalfa sprouts (optional)
- 1 to 2 soft Medjool dates, pitted
- 1 tablespoon chia seeds, or ground flax or hemp hearts ¼ teaspoon ground cinnamon
- A pinch of ground cardamom
- 1 tablespoon grated fresh ginger or ¼ teaspoon ground ginger

Directions:

1. Purée everything in a blender until smooth, adding more water (or coconut milk) if needed.

Nutrition: Calories: 477; Fat: 29 g; Carbs: 57 g; Fiber: 14 g; Proteins: 8 g.

Trope-Kale Breeze

Preparation Time: 5 minutes
Cooking Time: 0 minutes
Servings: 4
Ingredients:

- 1 cup chopped pineapple (frozen or fresh)
- 1 cup chopped mango (frozen or fresh)
- ½ to 1 cup kale, chopped
- ½ avocado

- ½ cup coconut milk
- 1 cup water (or coconut water)
- 1 teaspoon matcha green tea powder (optional)

Directions:

1. Purée everything in a blender until smooth, add more water (or coconut milk) if needed.

Nutrition: Calories: 566; Fat: 36 g; Carbs: 66 g; Fiber: 12 g; Proteins: 8 g.

Hydration Station

Preparation Time: 5 minutes
Cooking Time: 0 minutes
Servings: 4
Ingredients:

- 1 banana
- 1 orange, peeled and divided, or 1 cup pure orange juice
- 1 cup strawberries (frozen or fresh)
- 1 cup chopped cucumber
- ½ cup coconut water
- 1 cup water
- ½ cup ice

Directions:

1. Purée everything in a blender until smooth, adding more water if needed.
2. Add bonus boosters, as desired, and purée until blended.

Nutrition: Calories: 320; Fat: 3 g; Carbs: 76 g; Fiber: 13 g; Proteins: 6 g.

Mango Madness

Preparation Time: 5 minutes
Cooking Time: 0 minutes
Servings: 4
Ingredients:

- 1 banana
- 1 cup chopped mango (frozen or fresh)
- 1 cup chopped peach (frozen or fresh)
- 1 cup strawberries
- 1 carrot, peeled and chopped (optional)
- 1 cup water

Directions:

1. Purée everything in a blender until smooth, adding more water if needed.

Nutrition: Calories: 376; Fat: 2 g; Carbs: 95 g; Fiber: 14 g; Proteins: 5 g.

Chocolate PB Smoothie

Preparation Time: 5 minutes
Cooking Time: 0 minutes
Servings: 4
Ingredients:

- 1 banana
- ¼ cup rolled oats, or 1 scoop plant protein powder
- 1 tablespoon flaxseed or chia seeds
- 1 tablespoon unsweetened cocoa powder
- 1 tablespoon peanut butter, or almond or sunflower seed butter
- 1 tablespoon maple syrup (optional)
- 1 cup alfalfa sprouts or spinach, chopped (optional) ½ cup non-dairy milk (optional)
- 1 cup water

Directions:

1. Purée everything in a blender until smooth, add more water (or non-dairy milk) if needed. Add bonus boosters, as desired, and purée until blended.

Nutrition: Calories: 474; Fat: 16 g; Carbs: 79 g; Fiber: 18 g; Proteins: 13 g.

Pink Panther Smoothie

Preparation Time: 5 minutes
Cooking Time: 0 minutes
Servings: 3
Ingredients:

- 1 cup strawberries
- 1 cup chopped melon (any kind)
- 1 cup cranberries or raspberries
- 1 tablespoon chia seeds
- ½ cup coconut milk or other non-dairy milk
- 1 cup water

Directions:

1. Purée everything in a blender until smooth, add more water (or coconut milk) if needed.

Nutrition: Calories: 459; Fat: 30 g; Carbs: 52 g; Fiber: 19 g; Proteins: 8 g.

Banana Nut Smoothie

Preparation Time: 5 minutes
Cooking Time: 0 minutes **Servings:** 3
Ingredients:

- 1 banana
- 1 tablespoon almond butter, or sunflower seed butter
- ¼ teaspoon ground cinnamon
- A pinch of ground nutmeg

- 1 to 2 tablespoons dates, or maple syrup
- 1 tablespoon ground flaxseed, or chia or hemp hearts
- ½ cup non-dairy milk (optional)
- 1 cup water

Directions:

1. Purée everything in a blender until smooth, add more water (or non-dairy milk) if needed.

Nutrition: Calories: 343; Fat: 14 g; Carbs: 55 g; Fiber: 8 g; Proteins: 6 g.

Light Ginger Tea

Preparation Time: 5 minutes
Cooking Time: 10 minutes **Servings:** 2
Ingredients:

- 1 small ginger knob, sliced into four 1-inch chunks
- 4 cups water
- Juice of 1 large lemon
- Maple syrup to taste

Directions:

1. Add the ginger knob and water in a saucepan, then simmer over medium heat for 10 to 15 minutes.
2. Turn off the heat, then mix in the lemon juice. Strain the liquid to remove the ginger, then fold in the maple syrup and serve.

Nutrition: Calories: 32; Fat: 0.1 g; Carbs: 8.6 g; Fiber: 0.1 g; Proteins: 0.1 g.

Kale Smoothie

Preparation Time: 5 minutes
Cooking Time: 0 minutes **Servings:** 2
Ingredients:

- 2 cups chopped kale leaves
- 1 banana, peeled
- 1 cup frozen strawberries
- 1 cup unsweetened almond milk
- 4 Medjool dates, pitted and chopped

Directions:

1. Put all the ingredients in a food processor, then blitz until glossy and smooth.
2. Serve immediately or chill in the refrigerator for 1 hour before serving.

Nutrition: Calories: 663; Fat: 10 g; Carbs: 142.5 g; Fiber: 19 g; Proteins: 17.4 g.

Hot Tropical Smoothie

Preparation Time: 5 minutes
Cooking Time: 0 minutes **Servings:** 4
Ingredients:

- 1 cup frozen mango chunks
- 1 cup frozen pineapple chunks
- 1 small tangerine, peeled and pitted
- 4 cups spinach leaves
- 1 cup coconut water
- ¼ teaspoon cayenne pepper, optional

Directions:

1. Add all the ingredients to a food processor, then blitz until the mixture is smooth and combined well.
2. Serve immediately or chill in the refrigerator for 1 hour before serving.

Nutrition: Calories: 283, Fat: 1.9 g; Carbs: 67.9 g; Fiber: 10.4 g; Proteins: 6.4 g.

Berry Smoothie

Preparation Time: 5 minutes
Cooking Time: 0 minutes
Servings: 4
Ingredients:

- 1 cup berry mix (strawberries, blueberries and cranberries)
- 4 Medjool dates, pitted and chopped
- 1 ½ cups unsweetened almond milk, plus more as needed

Directions:
1. Add all the ingredients to a blender, then process until the mixture is smooth and well mixed.
2. Serve immediately or chill in the refrigerator for 1 hour before serving.

Nutrition: Calories: 473; Fat: 4 g; Carbs: 103.7 g; Fiber: 9.7 g; Proteins: 14.8 g.

Cranberry and Banana Smoothie

Preparation Time: 5 minutes
Cooking Time: 0 minutes
Servings: 4
Ingredients:

- 1 cup frozen cranberries
- 1 large banana, peeled
- 4 Medjool dates, pitted and chopped
- 1 ½ cups unsweetened almond milk

Directions:
1. Add all the ingredients to a food processor, then process until the mixture is glossy and well mixed.
2. Serve immediately or chill in the refrigerator for 1 hour before serving.

Nutrition: Calories: 616; Fat: 8 g; Carbs: 132.8 g; Fiber: 14.6 g; Proteins: 15.7 g.

Pumpkin Smoothie

Preparation Time: 5 minutes
Cooking Time: 0 minutes
Servings: 2
Ingredients:

- ½ cup pumpkin purée
- 4 Medjool dates, pitted and chopped

- 1 cup unsweetened almond milk
- ¼ teaspoon vanilla extract
- ¼ teaspoon ground cinnamon
- ½ cup ice
- A pinch of ground nutmeg

Directions:
1. Add all the ingredients to a blender, then process until the mixture is glossy and well mixed.
2. Serve immediately.

Nutrition: Calories: 417; Fat: 3 g; Carbs: 94.9 g; Fiber: 10.4 g; Proteins: 11.4 g.

Super Smoothie

Preparation Time: 5 minutes
Cooking Time: 0 minutes **Servings:** 4
Ingredients:

- 1 banana, peeled
- 1 cup chopped mango
- 1 cup raspberries
- ¼ cup rolled oats
- 1 carrot, peeled
- 1 cup chopped fresh kale
- 2 tablespoons chopped fresh parsley
- 1 tablespoon flaxseeds
- 1 tablespoon grated fresh ginger
- ½ cup unsweetened soy milk
- 1 cup water

Directions:
1. Put all the ingredients in a food processor, then blitz until glossy and smooth.
2. Serve immediately or chill in the refrigerator for 1 hour before serving.

Nutrition: Calories: 550; Fat: 39 g; Carbs: 31 g; Fiber: 15 g; Proteins: 13 g.

Kiwi and Strawberry Smoothie

Preparation Time: 5 minutes
Cooking Time: 0 minutes **Servings:** 3
Ingredients:

- 1 kiwi, peeled
- 5 medium strawberries
- ½ frozen banana
- 1 cup unsweetened almond milk
- 2 tablespoons hemp seeds
- 2 tablespoons peanut butter
- 1 to 2 teaspoons maple syrup
- ½ cup spinach leaves
- Handful broccoli sprouts

Directions:
1. Put all the ingredients in a food processor, then blitz until creamy and smooth.
2. Serve immediately or chill in the refrigerator for 1 hour before serving.

Nutrition: Calories: 562; Fat: 28.6 g; Carbs: 63.6 g; Fiber: 15.1 g; Proteins: 23.3 g.

Banana and Chai Chia Smoothie

Preparation Time: 5 minutes
Cooking Time: 0 minutes
Servings: 3
Ingredients:
- 1 banana
- 1 cup alfalfa sprouts
- 1 tablespoon chia seeds
- ½ cup unsweetened coconut milk
- 1 to 2 soft Medjool dates, pitted
- ¼ teaspoon ground cinnamon
- 1 tablespoon grated fresh ginger
- 1 cup water
- A pinch of ground cardamom

Directions:
1. Add all the ingredients to a blender, then process until the mixture is smooth and creamy. Add water or coconut milk if necessary.
2. Serve immediately.

Nutrition: Calories: 477; Fat: 41 g; Carbs: 31 g; Fiber: 14 g; Proteins: 8 g.

Chocolate and Peanut Butter Smoothie

Preparation Time: 5 minutes
Cooking Time: 0 minutes
Servings: 4
Ingredients:
- 1 tablespoon unsweetened cocoa powder
- 1 tablespoon peanut butter
- 1 banana
- 1 teaspoon maca powder
- ½ cup unsweetened soy milk
- ¼ cup rolled oats
- 1 tablespoon flaxseeds
- 1 tablespoon maple syrup
- 1 cup water

Directions:
1. Add all the ingredients to a blender, then process until the mixture is smooth and creamy. Add water or soy milk if necessary.
2. Serve immediately.

Nutrition: Calories: 474; Fat: 16 g; Carbs: 27 g; Fiber: 18 g; Proteins: 13 g.

Golden Milk

Preparation Time: 5 minutes
Cooking Time: 0 minutes
Servings: 4
Ingredients:
- ¼ teaspoon ground cinnamon
- ½ teaspoon ground turmeric
- ½ teaspoon grated fresh ginger
- 1 teaspoon maple syrup

- 1 cup unsweetened coconut milk
- Ground black pepper to taste
- 2 tablespoons water

Directions:
1. Combine all the ingredients in a saucepan. Stir to mix well.
2. Heat over medium heat for 5 minutes. Keep stirring during the heating.
3. Allow to cool for 5 minutes, then pour the mixture into a blender.
4. Pulse until creamy and smooth. Serve immediately.

Nutrition: Calories: 577; Fat: 57.3 g; Carbs: 19.7 g; Fiber: 6.1 g; Proteins: 5.7 g.

Mango Agua Fresca

Preparation Time: 5 minutes
Cooking Time: 0 minutes
Servings: 2
Ingredients:
- 2 fresh mangoes, diced
- 1 ½ cups water
- 1 teaspoon fresh lime juice
- Maple syrup to taste
- 2 cups ice
- 2 slices fresh lime for garnish
- 2 fresh mint sprigs for garnish

Directions:
1. Put the mangoes, lime juice, maple syrup and water into a blender.
1. Process until creamy and smooth.
2. Divide the beverage into two glasses, then garnish each glass with ice, lime slice and mint sprig before serving.

Nutrition: Calories: 230; Fat: 1.3 g; Carbs: 57.7 g; Fiber: 5.4 g; Proteins: 2.8 g.

Fruity Smoothie

Preparation Time: 10 minutes
Cooking Time: 0 minute
Servings: 1
Ingredients:
- ¾ cup soy yogurt
- ½ cup pineapple juice
- 1 cup pineapple chunks
- 1 cup raspberries, sliced
- 1 cup blueberries, sliced

Directions:
1. Process the ingredients in a blender.
2. Chill before serving.

Nutrition: Calories: 279; Total Fat 2 g; Saturated Fat: 0 g; Cholesterol: 4 mg; Sodium: 149 mg; Total Carbohydrates: 56 g; Dietary Fibers: 7 g; Proteins: 12 g; Total Sugars: 46 g; Potassium: 719 mg.

Pineapple, Banana & Spinach Smoothie

Preparation Time: 10 minutes
Cooking Time: 0 minute
Servings: 1
Ingredients:

- ½ cup almond milk
- ¼ cup soy yogurt
- 1 cup spinach
- 1 cup banana
- 1 cup pineapple chunks
- 1 tablespoon chia seeds

Directions:

1. Add all the ingredients to a blender.
2. Blend until smooth.
3. Chill in the refrigerator before serving.

Nutrition: Calories: 297; Total Fat: 6 g; Saturated Fat: 1 g; Cholesterol: 4 mg; Sodium: 145 mg; Total Carbohydrates: 54 g; Dietary Fiber: 10 g; Proteins: 13 g; Total Sugars: 29 g; Potassium: 1038 mg.

Kale & Avocado Smoothie

Preparation Time: 10 minutes
Cooking Time: 0 minute
Servings: 1
Ingredients:

- 1 ripe banana
- 1 cup kale
- 1 cup almond milk
- ¼ avocado
- 1 tablespoon chia seeds
- 2 teaspoons honey
- 1 cup ice cubes

Directions:

1. Blend all the ingredients until smooth.

Cantaloupe Smoothie Bowl

Preparation Time: 5 minutes
Cooking Time: 0 minutes **Servings:** 2
Ingredients:

- ¾ cup carrot juice
- 4 cups cantaloupe, frozen & cubed
- Mellon balls or berries to serve
- Pinch sea salt

Directions:

1. Blend everything together until smooth.

Nutrition: Calories: 135; Proteins: 3 g; Fat: 1 g; Carbs: 32 g.

Berry & Cauliflower Smoothie

Preparation Time: 10 minutes
Cooking Time: 0 minutes **Servings:** 2
Ingredients:

- 1 cup rice cauliflower, frozen
- 1 cup banana, sliced & frozen
- ½ cup mixed berries, frozen

Nutrition: Calories: 343; Total Fat: 14 g; Saturated Fat: 2 g; Cholesterol: 0 mg; Sodium: 199 mg; Total Carbohydrates: 55 g; Dietary Fiber 12 g; Proteins: 6 g; Total Sugars: 29 g; Potassium: 1051 mg.

Coconut & Strawberry Smoothie

Preparation Time: 10 minutes
Cooking Time: 0 minutes **Servings:** 1
Ingredients:

- 1 cup strawberries, frozen & thawed slightly
- 1 ripe banana, sliced & frozen
- ½ cup coconut milk, light
- ½ cup vegan yogurt
- 1 tablespoon chia seeds
- 1 teaspoon lime juice, fresh
- 4 ice cubes

Directions:

1. Blend everything until smooth, and serve immediately.

Nutrition: Calories: 278; Proteins: 14 g; Fat: 2 g; Carbs: 57 g.

Pumpkin Chia Smoothie

Preparation Time: 5 minutes
Cooking Time: 0 minutes **Servings:** 1
Ingredients:

- 3 tablespoons pumpkin puree
- 1 tablespoon MCT oil
- ¾ cup coconut milk, full fat
- ½ avocado, fresh
- 1 teaspoon vanilla, pure
- ½ teaspoon pumpkin pie spice

Directions:

1. Combine all ingredients together until blended.

Nutrition: Calories: 726; Proteins: 5.5 g; Fat: 69.8 g; Carbs: 15 g.

- 2 cups almond milk, unsweetened
- 2 teaspoons maple syrup, pure & optional

Directions:

1. Blend until mixed well.

Nutrition: Calories: 149; Proteins: 3 g; Fat: 3 g; Carbs: 29 g.

Green Mango Smoothie

Preparation Time: 5 minutes
Cooking Time: 0 minutes **Servings:** 1
Ingredients:

- 2 cups spinach
- 1-2 cups coconut water
- 2 mangos, ripe, peeled and diced

Directions:

1. Blend everything together until smooth.

Nutrition: Calories: 417; Proteins: 7.2 g; Fat: 2.8 g; Carbs: 102.8 g.

Chia Seed Smoothie

Preparation Time: 5 minutes
Cooking Time: 0 minutes
Servings: 3
Ingredients:

- ¼ teaspoon cinnamon
- 1 tablespoon ginger, fresh & grated
- Pinch cardamom
- 1 tablespoon chia seeds
- 2 Medjool dates, pitted
- 1 cup alfalfa sprouts
- 1 cup water
- 1 banana
- ½ cup coconut milk, unsweetened

Directions:

1. Blend everything together until smooth.

Nutrition: Calories: 477; Proteins: 8 g; Fat: 29 g; Carbs: 57 g.

Mango Smoothie

Preparation Time: 5 minutes
Cooking Time: 0 minutes
Servings: 3
Ingredients:

- 1 carrot, peeled and chopped
- 1 cup strawberries
- 1 cup water
- 1 cup peaches, chopped
- 1 banana, frozen and sliced
- 1 cup mango, chopped

Directions:

1. Blend everything together until smooth.

Nutrition: Calories: 376; Proteins: 5 g; Fat: 2 g; Carbs: 95 g.

CHAPTER 19:

SAUCES AND CONDIMENTS

Thai Peanut Sauce

Preparation Time: 5 minutes
Cooking Time: 0 minutes
Servings: 3
Ingredients:
- 2 tablespoons apple cider vinegar
- 1/4 cup Thai Red curry paste
- 1 cup peanut butter
- 1 ½ cup coconut milk
- 1 tablespoon lime juice
- 1/4 cup brown sugar
- 2 tablespoons soy sauce

Directions:
1. For a quick and easy sauce, simply place everything into a food processor and meld until soft.
2. Be sure you keep any sauce and dressing in the fridge to keep fresh!

Nutrition: Calories: 250; Carbs: 10 g; Fat: 13 g; Proteins: 5 g.

Simple Marinara Sauce

Preparation Time: 10 minutes
Cooking Time: 1 hour
Servings: 6
Ingredients:
- 1 can 56 oz crushed tomatoes
- 8 garlic cloves, sliced
- 1 tablespoon olive oil
- 2 teaspoons salt
- 4 basil leaves, torn
- 2 teaspoons balsamic vinegar

Directions:
1. While you could just buy some marinara sauce from the store, the packaged stuff is typically filled with sugar! Now, with some basic ingredients, you will be able to make your own from scratch!
2. You should begin by heating a large saucepan over low heat.
3. As it warms up, you can throw in the olive oil, garlic, and the basil. Go ahead and sauté until the garlic begins to turn a nice golden color.
4. Next, add in the tomatoes and gently bring everything to a stew before you add in the salt and reduce the heat.

5. For the next fifty minutes, let the sauce simmer and condense. At the end of this time, stir in your vinegar, and then your sauce will be set for serving.
Nutrition: Calories: 110; Carbs: 20 g; Fat: 4 g; Proteins: 5 g.

Green Cilantro Sauce

Preparation Time: 5 minutes
Cooking Time: 20 minutes
Servings: 10
Ingredients:
- 1 cup olive oil
- 1 cup cilantro
- 5 tablespoons water
- 4 garlic cloves
- 1/4 teaspoon ground cumin
- Sherry vinegar to taste

Directions:
1. To begin this sauce, you should crush your garlic cloves and place them into a food processor, along with the cilantro.
2. After you have processed these two ingredients together, slowly begin adding in your olive oil and blend everything smoothly.
3. If you would like, feel welcome to combine as much or as little water as you would like, along with the sherry vinegar for some extra flavor.
4. Finally, add in your ground cumin, stir, and the sauce will be prepared.

Nutrition: Calories: 200; Carbs: 4 g; Fat: 20 g; Proteins: 2 g.

General Tso Sauce

Preparation Time: 5 minutes
Cooking Time: 10 minutes
Servings: 4
Ingredients:
- 1/4 cup rice vinegar
- 1/2 cup water
- 1 ½ tablespoon sriracha sauce
- 1/4 cup soy sauce
- 1 ½ tablespoon corn starch
- 1/2 cup sugar

Directions:
1. General Tso Sauce is a classic, and you can now make a healthier version of it! All you have to do is take out your saucepan and place all of the ingredients in.

2. Once in place, bring everything over medium heat and whisk together for ten minutes or until the sauce begins to get thick.
3. Finally, remove from heat and enjoy!

Nutrition: Calories: 150; Carbs: 30 g; Fat: 0 g; Proteins: 2 g.

Cashew Cheese Sauce

Preparation Time: 5 minutes
Cooking Time: 0 minutes
Servings: 8
Ingredients:
- 1 tablespoon olive oil
- 1/2 cup water
- 3/4 cup raw cashews
- 1 tablespoon lemon juice
- 1/2 teaspoon tamari sauce
- Salt to taste

Directions:
1. As you begin a plant-based diet, you may be thinking you will miss your cheese. Luckily, this cashew cheese is an excellent replacement!
2. All you will have to do is take the rest of the components, place them into a blender, and combine until completely smoothed out.
3. Once you are done, place it in the fridge and enjoy!

Nutrition: Calories: 90; Carbs: 5 g; Fat: 10 g; Proteins: 5 g.

Tartar Sauce

Preparation Time: 3 minutes
Cooking Time: 3 minutes
Servings: 4
Ingredients:
- 2 egg yolks
- 250 ml groundnut oil
- 250 ml olive oil
- 1 teaspoon Dijon mustard
- Juice of ½ a lemon
- 1 tablespoon chopped tarragon
- 1 tablespoon chopped gherkins
- 2 tablespoons chopped parsley
- 1 tablespoon rinsed capers

Directions:
1. Start by preparing a mayonnaise of the two egg yolks, Dijon mustard, salt, and pepper. Slowly pour in the groundnut oil and olive oil in a steady stream and whisk.
2. Pour in the lemon juice followed by tarragon, gherkins, capers, and parsley. Check for adequate seasoning at this point. Chill and serve.

Nutrition: Calories: 114; Fat: 6.72 g; Carbs: 1.24 g; Fiber: 0.2 g; Proteins: 11.68 g.

Grilled Seitan with Creole Sauce

Preparation Time: 10 minutes.
Cooking Time: 14 minutes.
Servings: 4

Ingredients:
Grilled seitan kebabs:
- 4 cups seitan, diced
- 2 medium onions, diced into squares
- 8 bamboo skewers
- 1 can coconut milk
- 2 (½) tablespoons creole spice
- 2 tablespoons tomato paste
- 2 cloves of garlic

Creole spice mix:
- 2 tablespoons paprika
- 12 dried Peri chili peppers
- 1 tablespoon salt
- 1 tablespoon freshly ground pepper
- 2 teaspoons dried thyme
- 2 teaspoons dried oregano

Directions:
1. Prepare the creole seasoning by blending all the ingredients and preserve them in a sealable jar.
2. Thread seitan and onion on the bamboo skewers in an alternating pattern.
3. On a baking sheet, mix coconut milk with creole seasoning, tomato paste, and garlic.
4. Soak the skewers in the milk marinade for 2 hours. Prepare and set up a grill over medium heat. Grill the skewers for 7 minutes per side. Serve.

Nutrition: Calories: 407; Total fat: 42 g; Carbs: 13 g Net carbs: 6 g; Fiber: 1 g; Proteins: 4 g.

Scotch Bonnet Pepper Sauce

Preparation Time: 6 minutes
Cooking Time: 6 minutes **Servings:** 4
Ingredients:
- Scotch Bonnet Hot Peppers (about 4-6 cups chopped)
- 6 cloves garlic
- 1/2 cup chopped cilantro
- 1 teaspoon sea salt
- 1 cup white vinegar

Directions:
1. Wash and trim the peppers and roughly chop them up. If you wish for the sauce to be fiery, leave the seeds in, otherwise, de-seed the peppers before using.
2. Roughly chop up the garlic and cilantro as well. If using a mill to make the sauce, then adjust the settings accordingly. This is a traditional method to make the sauce.
3. Add the garlic and cilantro slowly as you run the mill. If not, put all the ingredients in a food processor and pulse it roughly.

Nutrition: Calories: 24; Fat: 0.06 g; Carbs: 3.18 g; Fiber: 0.3 g; Proteins: 0.55 g.

Sambal Sauce

Preparation Time: 10 minutes
Cooking Time: 10 minutes
Servings: 8
Ingredients:

- 2 pounds dried red or fresh jalapeños, stemmed and chopped very roughly
- 10 fresh Thai chilies, or 1 tablespoon red pepper flakes
- 1 cup minced garlic
- 1/4 cup canola oil
- 2 cups rice wine vinegar
- 1 teaspoon sugar
- 2 teaspoons salt

Directions:
1. Take a medium pan, mix in the jalapenos, garlic, oil, and Thai chilies, and cook on low heat until the ingredients are mixed in thoroughly. Once the mixture is reduced in half, slowly add the vinegar and cook it again on a slow flame.
2. Now take it off the heat and add the salt and sugar, then cool to room temperature. Move this mixture to a food processor, and pulse to an accepted texture. Store in the fridge in a jar till further use.

Nutrition: Calories: 578; Fat: 27.95 g; Carbs: 86.16 g; Fiber: 11.1 g; Proteins: 3.19 g.

Louisiana Hot Sauce

Preparation Time: 8 minutes
Cooking Time: 5 minutes
Servings: 8
Ingredients:
- 1-1/4 lb. fresh red chilies, such as cayenne, Tabasco, or Serrano
- 1 teaspoon finely chopped fresh basil
- 4 medium garlic cloves, halved and peeled
- Kosher salt and freshly ground black pepper
- 1/4 teaspoons ground celery seeds
- 1 cup white vinegar
- 1 teaspoon finely chopped fresh oregano

Directions:
1. Place the chilies on a pan in an oven and broil for about five minutes on each side before flipping them over. Bring them out and let them cool down to room temperature.
2. Now skin the chilies and place them along with the seeds in a food processor. Add to this the oregano, basil, garlic, celery seeds, salt, and pepper and run the food processor.
3. Pour the vinegar in a steady stream through the tube and process until the consistency is a smooth mixture.
4. Your sauce is ready to be served and stored in bottles.

Nutrition: Calories: 93; Fat: 5.23 g; Carbs: 10.01 g; Fiber: 2 g; Proteins: 1.98 g.

Harissa Sauce

Preparation Time: 9 minutes
Cooking Time: 7 minutes
Servings: 7
Ingredients:
- 4 ounces dried chilies of your choice (cayenne, ancho, chili de arbor or guajillo)

- 3 to 4 garlic cloves, peeled
- 1 teaspoon cumin seeds
- 1 teaspoon coriander seeds
- 1 teaspoon caraway seeds
- 2 tablespoons extra virgin olive oil, plus more for storing
- 1 teaspoon kosher salt, or to taste

Directions:
1. To start with, you need to soften the chilies by immersing them in hot water for about 30 minutes. Meanwhile, roast the caraway, cumin, and coriander seeds in a dry pan on low heat until they let out an aromatic fragrance.
2. Then grind them into a dry powder. Drain the soaked chilies, de-seed and de-stem them and make a paste of it along with garlic, salt and the roasted spices in a food processor, allowing a steady drizzle of olive oil into the jar.
3. Once you achieve your desired texture, turn off the processor and adjust the seasoning accordingly
4. Serve immediately or store in a jar with additional olive oil.

Nutrition: Calories: 93; Fat: 5.23 g; Carbs: 10.01 g; Fiber: 2 g; Proteins: 1.98 g.

Piri Sauce

Preparation Time: 6 minutes
Cooking Time: 4 minutes
Servings: 4
Ingredients:
- 4 to 8 fresh hot chilies, depending on the heat
- Juice of 1 lemon
- 2 garlic cloves, minced
- 1/2 to 1 cup extra-virgin olive oil, depending on how thin you want it
- Pinch of salt

Directions:
1. Roughly chop up the peppers by discarding the stems, and place them in the food processor along with garlic, salt, lemon juice, oil, and puree until your desired consistency.
2. Your sauce is now ready to be served and also stored in an air-tight jar for at least a week in the fridge.

Nutrition: Calories: 110; Fat: 11.64 g; Carbs: 1.32 g; Fiber: 0.1 g; Proteins: 0.24 g.

Barbeque Sauce

Preparation Time: 5 minutes
Cooking Time: 5 minutes
Servings: 8
Ingredients:
- 2 cups chopped onions
- 1 cup ketchup
- 1 cup Worcestershire sauce
- 1 cup strong black coffee

- 1/2 cup cider vinegar
- 1/2 cup brown sugar
- 1/4 cup hot chili peppers, minced
- 6 cloves garlic, minced
- 3 tablespoons chili powder
- 2 teaspoons salt

Directions:
1. Place all of the above ingredients in a blender simmer for about half an hour.
2. After a while, it will release a great flavor. Turn off the heat and let it cool down, after which you can puree it with the mixer.

Nutrition: Calories: 138; Fat: 0.55 g; Carbs: 33.75 g; Fiber: 1.7 g; Proteins: 1.3 g

.

Roasted Veggies in Lemon Sauce

Preparation Time: 15 minutes
Cooking Time: 20 minutes
Servings: 5
Ingredients:

- 2 cloves garlic, sliced
- 1 ½ cups broccoli florets
- 1 ½ cups cauliflower florets
- 1 tablespoon olive oil
- Salt to taste
- 1 teaspoon dried oregano, crushed
- ¾ cup zucchini, diced
- ¾ cup red bell pepper, diced
- 2 teaspoons lemon zest

Directions:
1. Preheat your oven to 425° F.
2. In a baking pan, add garlic, broccoli, and cauliflower.
3. Toss in oil and season with salt and oregano.
4. Roast in the oven for 10 minutes.
5. Add the zucchini and bell pepper to the pan.
6. Stir well.
7. Roast for another 10 minutes.
8. Sprinkle lemon zest on top before serving.
9. Transfer to a food container and reheat before serving.

Nutrition: Calories: 52; Fat: 3 g; Carbs: 5 g; Fiber: 2 g; Proteins: 2 g.

Hemp Falafel with Tahini Sauce

Preparation Time: 10 minutes
Cooking Time: 10 minutes
Servings: 6
Ingredients:

- 80 g raw hemp hearts
- 4 g chopped cilantro
- 4 g chopped basil
- 2 cloves garlic, minced
- 2 g ground cumin seeds
- 3 g chili powder
- 14 g flax meal + 30 ml filtered water
- Sea salt and pepper, to taste

- Avocado or coconut oil, to fry

Sauce:
- 115 g tahini
- 60 ml fresh lime juice
- 115 ml filtered water
- 30 ml extra-virgin olive oil
- Sea salt, to taste
- A good pinch ground cumin seed

Directions:
1. Mix flax with filtered water in a small bowl.
2. Place aside for 10 minutes.
3. In the meantime, combine raw hemp hearts, cilantro, basil, garlic, cumin, chili, and seasonings in a food processor.
4. Process until it just comes together. Add the flax seeds mixture and process until finely blended and uniform.
5. Heat approximately 2 tablespoons of avocado oil in a skillet. Shape 1 tablespoon mixture into balls and fry for 3-4 minutes or until deep golden brown.
6. Remove from the skillet and place on a plate lined with paper towels.
7. Make the sauce; combine all ingredients in a food blender. Blend until smooth and creamy.
8. Serve falafel with fresh lettuce salad and tahini sauce.

Nutrition: Calories: 347; Fat: 29.9 g; Carbs: 7.2 g; Fiber: 4.3 g; Proteins: 13.8 g.

Red Applesauce and Beet

Preparation Time: 5 minutes
Cooking Time: 10 minutes
Servings: 6
Ingredient

- 2 cups unpeeled apple, diced or grated
- 1 cup boneless cherries or mixed berries
- 1 cup unpeeled grated beets
- 1 tablespoon date paste
- ½ teaspoon cinnamon
- 2 tablespoons of water

Directions:
1. Place all the ingredients in a saucepan.
2. Take to a boil and cook until apples and beets have softened for 10-15 minutes.
3. Crush with a potato masher or process in a food processor for a smoother consistency.
4. Serve alone or use it to decorate Halloween treats.

Nutrition: Calories: 247; Fat: 26.3 g; Carbs: 7 g; Fiber: 3 g; Proteins: 13.8 g.

Tomatillo Green Sauce

Preparation Time: 5 minutes
Cooking Time: 10 minutes **Servings:** 6
Ingredients:

- 8 small tomatillos (approximately 1 pound or 453 grams)
- ½ white onion, cut in half
- 1½ teaspoon ground garlic (approximately 3 small teeth)

- 1 jalapeño, cut in half, and seeded
- 1/3 cup full of chopped cilantro
- 1 can (4 ounces or 113 grams) of chopped soft green chiles

Optional Additions:

- ½ tablespoon ground cumin
- Salt and pepper to taste
- Jalapeño Seeds (to add spicily)

Directions:

1. Preheat the grill. Cover a large baking sheet with foil.
2. Prepare the tomatillos: remove their lanterns, wash them, and cut them in half.
3. Place the tomatillos and onion upside down on the prepared baking sheet.
4. Add the garlic and jalapeño to the tray.
5. Roast for five to seven minutes or until everything is uniformly charred.
6. In a blender or food processor, mix the charred ingredients, cilantro, and chills until the sauce is smooth.

Nutrition: Calories: 223; Fat: 25 g; Carbs: 8 g; Fiber: 6 g; Proteins: 14 g.

Cranberry and Orange Sauce

Preparation Time: 15 minutes
Cooking Time: 5 minutes **Servings:** 4
Ingredients:

- Zest and juice of an orange
- ½ cup maple syrup
- 1 bag (12 oz - 340 g) of fresh red cranberries
- 1 teaspoon cinnamon

Directions:

1. In a small saucepan, add all the ingredients and let them boil. Reduce the temperature and simmer for 15 minutes or until the blueberries burst and the sauce begins to thicken.
2. Transfer it to a bowl and refrigerate it until it cools down, at least for an hour.

Nutrition: Calories: 240; Fat: 15 g; Carbs: 4 g; Fiber: 10 g; Proteins: 18 g.

Thick Mushroom Sauce

Preparation Time: 15 minutes
Cooking Time: 5 minutes
Servings: 4
Ingredients:

- 1 12 oz. (340 g) package of tender white or Portobello mushrooms
- 1 to 2 tablespoons low sodium soy sauce (use one without wheat if you are gluten sensitive)
- 2 tablespoons whole-grain wheat flour (use gluten-free flour if you are gluten sensitive)
- 1 to 2 cups of vegetable stock
- Salt or black pepper, to taste (optional)

Directions:

1. Clean and cut the mushrooms. Then skip them in water until they are soft (about 5 minutes).
2. Mix the flour with 1/4 cup of broth until it is lump-free (you can shake it in a small plastic container with a tight-fitting lid).
3. Add the remaining broth to the mushrooms, soy sauce, and about half of the flour mixture.
4. Let the thick sauce simmer for 3 to 5 minutes, stirring regularly.
5. If the sauce is not thick enough for your taste, add the remaining flour mixture and continue heating and stirring until it thickens.
6. Serve hot (and as soon as possible).

Nutrition: Calories: 200; Fat: 10 g; Carbs: 7 g; Fiber: 15 g; Proteins: 20 g.

Spiced Rhubarb Sauce

Preparation Time: 10 minutes
Cooking Time: 15 minutes **Servings:** 4
Ingredients:

- ½ cup water
- ½ cup sugar
- ¼ teaspoon grated nutmeg
- ¼ teaspoon ground ginger
- ¼ teaspoon ground cinnamon
- 1pound rhubarb, cut into ½- to 1-inch pieces

Directions:

1. In a large saucepan, bring the water, sugar, nutmeg, ginger, and cinnamon to boil.
2. Add the rhubarb and cook over medium-high heat, and stir frequently until the rhubarb is soft and saucy.
3. Chill for at least 30 minutes before serving.

Nutrition: Calories: 12; Fat: 0.7 g; Carbs: 1.5 g; Fiber: 0.4 g; Proteins: 0.3 g.

Alfredo Sauce

Preparation Time: 7 minutes
Cooking Time: 0 minutes
Servings: 4
Ingredients:

- 1 cup cashews, unsalted, soaked in warm water for 15 minutes
- 1 teaspoon minced garlic
- 1/4 teaspoon ground black pepper
- 1/3 teaspoon salt
- 1/4 cup nutritional yeast
- 2 tablespoons tamari
- 2 tablespoons olive oil
- 4 tablespoons water

Directions:

1. Drain the cashews and transfer them into a food processor. Add remaining ingredients in it and pulse for 3 minutes until thick sauce comes together.
2. Serve straight away.

Nutrition: Calories: 105.7; Fat: 5.3 g: Carbs: 11 g; Proteins: 4.7 g; Fiber: 2 g.

Avocado Pudding

Preparation Time: 10 minutes
Cooking Time: 0 minutes
Servings: 8
Ingredients:

- 2 ripe avocados, peeled, pitted and cut into pieces
- 1 tablespoon fresh lime juice
- 14 oz can coconut milk
- 80 drops of liquid stevia
- 2 teaspoons vanilla extract

Directions:
1. Add all ingredients into the blender and blend until smooth.
2. Serve and enjoy.

Nutrition: Calories: 105.7; Fat: 5.3 g: Carbs: 11 g; Proteins: 4.7 g; Fiber: 2 g.

Cheese Sauce

Preparation Time: 15 minutes
Cooking Time: 25 minutes
Servings: 6
Ingredients:

- Pinch of salt
- Pinch of black, ground pepper
- ½ teaspoon of onion powder
- ½ teaspoon of garlic powder
- ½ cup of yeast, nutritional
- 1/3 cup of extra-virgin olive oil
- ½ cup of water
- 1 tablespoon of freshly squeezed lemon juice
- 1 cup of carrots, washed, peeled and diced
- 2 cups of potatoes, washed, peeled and diced

Directions:
1. In a medium saucepan over medium heat, boil the carrots and potatoes until they have cooked soft. Drain and add these items to the blender.
2. Add in the remainder of the ingredients to the blender and pulse until smooth.
3. Serve warm along with tortilla chips or over whole-wheat pasta.

Tips:
1. Seal and store in the refrigerator for up to four days, or you can freeze it too. Let thaw, add a dash of water, give it a good stir and serve.

Nutrition: Calories: 12; Fat: 0.7 g; Carbs: 1.5 g; Fiber: 0.4 g; Proteins: 0.3 g.

Coriander Tahini Sauce

Preparation Time: 10 minutes
Cooking Time: 10 minutes
Servings: 6
Ingredients:

- 1/4 cup cashews, soaked overnight and drained
- 1/4 cup water
- 4 tablespoons tahini
- 1/4 cup fresh coriander leaves, roughly chopped
- 1 clove garlic, minced
- Kosher salt and cayenne pepper, to taste

Directions:
1. Process the cashews and water in your blender until creamy and uniform.
2. Add in the remaining ingredients and continue to blend until everything is well incorporated.
3. Keep in your refrigerator for up to a week. Bon appétit!

Nutrition: Calories: 91; Fat: 7.5 g; Carbs: 4.5 g; Proteins: 2.9 g.

Miso Sauce

Preparation Time: 10 minutes
Cooking Time: 8 minutes
Servings: 2
Ingredients:

- Pinch of salt
- Pinch of black, ground pepper
- 2 tablespoons extra-virgin olive oil
- 1 ½ cups orange juice
- ½ cup sweet white miso
- 2 cloves garlic, minced
- 2 tablespoons ginger, minced
- 1 teaspoon sesame oil
- 2 tablespoons tamari
- 2 tablespoons fresh mint
- 2 tablespoons fresh basil
- 3 tablespoons fresh cilantro
- ½ a chili, minced
- 1 ½ tablespoons ginger, minced

Directions:
1. In a bowl, combine all ingredients, whisk gently for one minute and serve.

Tips: Enhance the flavors in a salad or serve with a side or main meal.

Nutrition: Calories: 191; Fat: 20.2 g; Carbs: 0.8 g; Proteins: 0.5 g.

Classic Ranch Dressing

Preparation time: 15 minutes
Cooking Time: 10 minutes
Servings: 8
Ingredients:

- 1 cup vegan mayonnaise
- 1/4 almond milk, unsweetened
- 1 teaspoon sherry vinegar
- 1/2 teaspoons kosher salt
- 1/4 teaspoon black pepper
- 2 cloves garlic, minced
- 1/2 teaspoons dried chives
- 1/2 teaspoons dried dill weed
- 1 teaspoon dried parsley flakes
- 1/2 teaspoons onion powder
- 1/3 teaspoon paprika

Directions:

1. Using a wire whisk, thoroughly combine all the ingredients in a bowl.
2. Cover and place in your refrigerator until ready to serve.
3. Bon appétit!

Nutrition: Calories: 191; Fat: 20.2 g; Carbs: 0.8 g; Proteins: 0.5 g.

Easy Tofu Hollandaise

Preparation time: 15 minutes
Cooking Time: 15 minutes
Servings: 12
Ingredients:

- 1/4 cup vegan butter, at room temperature
- 1 cup silken tofu
- 1 cup unsweetened rice milk
- Sea salt and ground black pepper, to taste
- 1/4 cup nutritional yeast
- 1/2 teaspoons turmeric powder
- 2 tablespoons fresh lime juice

Directions:

1. Puree all the ingredients in a high-speed blender or food processor.
2. Then, heat the mixture in a small saucepan over low-medium heat; cook, stirring occasionally, until the sauce has reduced and thickened.
3. Bon appétit!

Nutrition: Calories: 82; Fat: 4.9 g; Carbs: 6.4 g; Proteins: 2.9 g.

Saffron Pistachio Beverage

Preparation Time: 5 minutes
Cooking Time: 0 minutes
Servings: 2
Ingredients:

- 8 strands of saffron
- 1 tablespoon cashews
- 1/4 teaspoon ground ginger
- 2 tablespoons pistachio
- 1/8 teaspoon cloves
- 1/4 teaspoon ground black pepper
- 1/4 teaspoon cardamom powder
- 3 tablespoons coconut sugar
- 1/4 teaspoon cinnamon
- 1/8 teaspoon fennel seeds
- 1/4 teaspoon poppy seeds

Directions:

1. Place all the ingredients in the order in a food processor or blender and then pulse for 2 to 3 minutes at high speed until smooth.
2. Pour the smoothie into two glasses and then serve.

Nutrition: Calories: 82; Fat: 4.9 g; Carbs: 6.4 g; Proteins: 2.9 g.

Garlic Alfredo Sauce

Preparation Time: 10 minutes
Cooking Time: 5 minutes
Servings: 4
Ingredients:

- 1 1/2 cups cashews, unsalted, soaked in warm water for 15 minutes
- 6 cloves of garlic, peeled, minced
- 1/2 medium sweet onion, peeled, chopped
- 1 teaspoon salt
- 1/4 cup nutritional yeast
- 1 tablespoon lemon juice
- 2 tablespoons olive oil
- 2 cups almond milk, unsweetened
- 12 ounces fettuccine pasta, cooked, for serving

Directions:

1. Take a small saucepan, place it over medium heat, add oil, and when hot, add onion and garlic, and cook for 5 minutes until sauté.
2. Meanwhile, drain the cashews, transfer them into a food processor, add remaining ingredients, including the onion mixture, except for pasta, and pulse for 3 minutes until very smooth.
3. Pour the prepared sauce over pasta, toss until coated and serve.

Nutrition: Calories: 439; Fat: 20 g: Carbs: 52 g; Proteins: 15 g; Fiber: 4 g.

Favorite Cranberry Sauce

Preparation Time: 10 minutes
Cooking Time: 15 minutes
Servings: 8
Ingredients:

- 1/2 cup brown sugar
- 1/2 cup water
- 8 ounces cranberries, fresh or frozen
- A pinch of allspice
- A pinch of sea salt
- 1 tablespoon crystallized ginger

Directions:

1. In a heavy-bottomed saucepan, bring the sugar and water to a rolling boil.
2. Stir until the sugar has dissolved.
3. Add in the cranberries, followed by the remaining ingredients. Turn the heat to a simmer and continue cooking for 10 to 12 minutes or until the cranberries burst.
4. Let it cool at room temperature. Store in a glass jar in your refrigerator. Bon appétit!

Nutrition: Calories: 62; Fat: 0.6 g; Carbs: 16 g; Proteins: 0.2 g.

CHAPTER 20:

DESSERTS

Banana Walnut Bread

Preparation Time: 5 minutes
Cooking Time: 50 minutes
Servings: 1
Ingredients:
- 1/2 cups whole wheat flour
- ¾ teaspoon baking soda
- 1 very ripe banana, mashed
- ½ cup maple syrup
- ¼ cup unsweetened applesauce
- 2 tablespoons aquafaba (the liquid from a can of chickpeas)
- 1 teaspoon vanilla extract
- 1 teaspoon pink Himalayan salt
- ¾ cup chopped walnuts

Directions:
1. Preheat the oven to 180° C or 350° F.
2. Line the pan using parchment paper or a silicone liner.
3. In a mixing bowl, sift the flour and baking soda together.
4. In a separate container, combine the mashed bananas, maple syrup, applesauce, aquafaba, vanilla, and salt. Mix well. Stir in the flour mixture and mix well. Gently stir the walnuts.
5. Transfer the combination into the arranged pan. Bake it for 40 to 50 minutes, until brown on the top and edges. Enjoy right after it cools or store it in a reusable container at room temperature for up to 5 days.

Nutrition: Calories: 541; Fat: 17 g; Carbs: 96 g; Proteins: 12 g; Fibers: 11 g.

Cashew Chickpea Bars

Preparation Time: 5 minutes
Cooking Time: 15 minutes
Servings: 1
Ingredients:
- 1 Medjool dates, pitted
- 1/4 cup cashews
- 1/4 cup cooked chickpeas (drained and rinsed, if canned)
- 1 tablespoon sunflower seed
- 1 tablespoon pumpkin seed
- 1 teaspoon vanilla extract
- 8 ounces (227 g) vegan dark mini chocolate chips

Directions:
1. Line a baking sheet with parchment paper or a silicone liner.
2. In a food processor, combine the dates, cashews, chickpeas, sunflower seeds, pumpkin seeds, and vanilla. Blend, but leave the mixture a little chunky.
3. Shape the mixture into bars and place them on the prepared baking sheet.
4. Bake for 15 minutes or until the edges become lightly browned. Remove from the oven and let cool for 10 minutes.
5. In a small saucepan over low heat, stir the chocolate chips until melted. Coat the top of the bars with the melted chocolate and let cool to room temperature.

Nutrition: Calories: 299; Fat: 15 g; Carbs: 42 g; Proteins: 5 g; Fibers: 5 g.

Chocolate Avocado Pudding

Preparation Time: 5 minutes
Cooking Time: 0 minutes
Servings: 1
Ingredients:
- 2 ripe avocados, pitted and peeled
- ¼ cup unsweetened plant-based milk
- 1/3 cup coconut sugar
- 1/3 cup cocoa powder
- 1 teaspoon vanilla extract

Directions:
1. In a food processor, combine all the ingredients and blend until you achieve a smooth pudding consistency. Serve immediately.

Nutrition: Calories: 457; Fat: 29 g; Carbs: 56 g; Proteins: 6 g; Fibers: 17 g.

Cranberry and Almond Muffins

Preparation Time: 10 minutes
Cooking Time: 20 minutes
Servings: 1
Ingredients:

- 1/2 cups whole wheat flour (or gluten-free flour)
- 1 teaspoon baking soda
- 1 teaspoon baking powder
- ½ teaspoon pink Himalayan salt
- 1/4 cup unsweetened plant-based milk
- 1/8 cup dried cranberries, soaked in water for 1 hour to soften
- 1/8 cup maple syrup
- 1/8 cup chopped almonds
- 1/8 cup unsweetened applesauce
- 1 tablespoon freshly squeezed lemon juice
- 1 tablespoons aquafaba (the liquid from a can of chickpeas)
- ½ teaspoon vanilla extract

Directions:

1. Preheat the oven to 375ºF (190ºC). Insert silicone muffin cups into a muffin pan.
2. In a bowl, combine the flour, baking soda, baking powder, and salt. Mix well.
3. In a separate bowl, combine the milk, cranberries, maple syrup, almonds, applesauce, lemon juice, aquafaba, and vanilla. Mix well.
4. Combine the wet and dry ingredients and mix well.
5. Fill each muffin cup a little more than half full with batter. Bake for 20 minutes, or until lightly browned and a toothpick inserted into the center of a muffin comes out clean. Enjoy as soon as they cool or store in a reusable container at room temperature.

Nutrition: Calories: 143; Fat: 2 g; Carbs: 31 g; Proteins: 3 g; Fibers: 3 g

Chocolate Chip Cashew Bites

Preparation Time: 10 minutes
Cooking Time: 0 minutes
Servings: 1
Ingredients:

- ¼ cup rolled oats
- ½ cup cashews
- 3 tablespoons whole wheat flour (or gluten-free flour)
- ½ teaspoon ground flaxseed
- ¼ teaspoon Himalayan pink salt
- 2 tablespoons maple syrup

- 1 teaspoon vanilla extract
- 2 tablespoons vegan dark chocolate chips

Directions:

1. In a food processor, combine oats, cashews, flour, flaxseed, and salt.
2. When the dry ingredients are fully mixed, add the maple syrup and vanilla and continue to mix in the processor.
3. Add the chocolate chips and mix them in with a spoon. Using your hands, shape the mixture into 1-inch balls. Enjoy immediately or store in a reusable container in the refrigerator for up to 5 days.

Nutrition: Calories: 81; Fat: 4 g; Carbs: 10 g; Proteins: 2 g; Fibers: 1 g.

Banana Orange Nice Cream

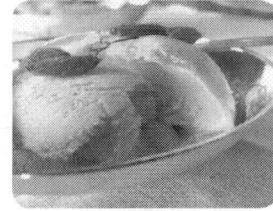

Preparation Time: 5 minutes
Cooking Time: 0 minutes
Servings: 1
Ingredients:

- 1 orange, peeled, separated into segments, and frozen
- 2 bananas, peeled, sliced, and frozen
- ½ teaspoon vanilla extract
- ¼ teaspoon hemp seeds

Directions:

1. In a food processor or blender, combine all the ingredients and blend until smooth and creamy. Enjoy immediately or store in a reusable container in the freezer for up to 1 month.

Nutrition: Calories: 283; Fat: 1 g; Carbs: 70 g; Proteins: 4 g; Fibers: 9 g.

Pineapple Coconut Macaroons

Preparation Time: 5 minutes
Cooking Time: 20 minutes **Servings:** 1
Ingredients:

- 1/3 cups unsweetened coconut shreds
- ½ cup chopped pineapple
- ½ cup coconut sugar - ½ banana
- 3 tablespoons wheat flour (or gluten-free flour)

Directions:

1. Preheat the oven to 350ºF (180ºC). Line a baking sheet with parchment paper or a silicone liner.
2. In a food processor, combine all the ingredients and process until almost smooth.
3. Use a tablespoon to make ten heaping macaroons. Space them evenly on the prepared baking sheet.
4. Bake for 20 minutes, or until the tops and bottoms are light browns.
5. Let cool on a wire rack for 10 minutes before serving. Store in a reusable container in the refrigerator for up to 5 days.

Nutrition: Calories: 90; Fat: 4 g; Carbs: 15 g; Proteins: 1 g; Fibers: 1 g.

Chocolate Bark

Preparation Time: 5 minutes
Cooking Time: 5 minutes **Servings:** 1
Ingredients:
- ¼ cup dried cranberries
- 3 tablespoons chopped pistachios
- 3 tablespoons chopped almonds
- 3 tablespoons pumpkin seeds
- 3 tablespoons sunflower seeds
- 1 (8-ounce / 227-g) bag vegan dark chocolate chips Pink Himalayan salt, to taste

Directions:
1. Line an 8-inch square baking pan with parchment paper. Spread out the cranberries, pistachios, almonds, pumpkin seeds, and sunflower seeds on the baking pan.
2. In a small nonstick saucepan on low heat, gently heat the chocolate chips, stirring continuously, until they are melted and smooth.
3. Pour the melted chocolate evenly over the nuts, seeds, and dried fruit in the baking pan. Let cool to room temperature. Sprinkle with salt. Break the bark into pieces and remove it from the baking pan.

Nutrition: Calories: 275; Fat: 18 g; Carbs: 30 g; Proteins: 4 g; Fibers: 4 g.

Vanilla Rice Pudding with Cherries

Preparation Time: 5 minutes
Cooking Time: 30 minutes
Servings: 1

Ingredients:
- 1/2 cup short-grain brown rice
- ¾ cups coconut milk, plus more as needed
- ½ cups water
- 1 tablespoon unrefined sugar or pure maple syrup, plus more as needed
- 1 teaspoon vanilla extract
- Salt, to taste
- ¼ cup dried cherries or ½ cup fresh or frozen pitted cherries

Directions:
1. Combine the rice, milk, water, sugar, vanilla, and salt in the Instant Pot.
2. Lock the lid. Select the Manual mode and set the cooking time for 30 minutes at High Pressure.
3. When the timer beeps, perform a natural pressure release for 20 minutes, then release any remaining pressure. Carefully remove the lid.
4. Stir in the cherries and rest the lid back on (no need to lock it), and let sit for about 10 minutes.
5. Serve with more milk or sugar, as needed.

Nutrition: Calories: 150; Fat: 8 g; Carbs: 17 g; Proteins: 5 g; Fibers: 5 g.

Chocolate Chip Banana Cookies

Preparation Time: 5 minutes
Cooking Time: 10 minutes
Servings: 1
Ingredients:
- 2 bananas
- 1 cup rolled oats
- 1 teaspoon ground flaxseed
- 1 teaspoon vanilla extract
- ¼ cup vegan mini chocolate chips
- ¼ cup chopped walnuts

Directions:
1. Preheat the oven to 350ºF (180ºC). Line a baking sheet with parchment paper or a silicone liner.
2. In a food processor, combine the bananas, oats, flaxseed, and vanilla and blend until very well combined. Use a wooden spoon to stir in the chocolate chips and walnuts.
3. Scoop the batter into nine cookies, spacing them out on the prepared baking sheet. Bake for 8 to 12 minutes, or until the bottoms are light brown. Enjoy right after they cool or store in a reusable container at room temperature.

Nutrition: Calories: 122; Fat: 5 g; Carbs: 17 g; Proteins: 2 g; Fibers: 2 g.

Cherry-Chocolate Ice Cream

Preparation Time: 15 minutes
Cooking Time: 0 minutes
Servings: 1
Ingredients:

- 1 frozen banana
- 1 teaspoon pure vanilla extract
- 1 tablespoons maple syrup
- 1 tablespoons coconut cream
- 1 tablespoon unsweetened almond milk (or any nut milk)
- 1/4 cup frozen dark sweet cherries
- 1/8 cup dairy-free dark chocolate chips

Directions:

1. In a food processor, combine the bananas, vanilla, maple syrup, coconut cream, and almond milk.
2. Blend until it reaches a batter-like consistency, occasionally stopping to scrape down the sides of the bowl.
3. Scoop out about 1 cup of the banana mixture and place in a freezer-safe container. Add the cherries to the food processor with the remaining banana mixture, and blend until the mixture is pink, but you can still see some chunks. Add the chocolate chips and blend again until just combined.
4. Transfer the mixture to the container with the plain banana ice cream and gently stir to create white and pink swirls. Cover and freeze until solid, about 1 hour.

Nutrition: Calories: 252; Fat: 10 g; Carbs: 38 g; Proteins: 2 g; Fibers: 2 g.

Raw Cacao Mint Cheesecake

Preparation Time: 10 minutes
Cooking Time: 0 minutes **Servings:** 1
Ingredients:
Almond Base:

- ½ cups raw almonds
- 1 Medjool dates, pitted
- 1 tablespoon cacao powder
- 1 tablespoon vegan butter, melted (or coconut oil)

Chocolate Layer:

- ½ cups raw cashews
- 3 tablespoons maple syrup
- 2 tablespoons cacao powder
- ¼ cup coconut oil, melted
- ¼ teaspoon peppermint extract
- ¼ cup cacao nibs (or dark chocolate chips)

Mint Layer:

- 1½ cups raw cashews
- 1 cup mint leaves
- ¼ cup maple syrup
- 2 tablespoons coconut oil, melted

Optional Garnish:

- Cacao nibs - Mint leaves

Directions:

1. Line the bottom of a springform pan with parchment paper. Place the cashews for the mint layer in a heatproof bowl and add boiling water to cover. Let soak 10 minutes and then drain. Set aside until ready to use.
2. In a food processor, combine all ingredients for the almond base and blend until creamy. Press the mixture down in the pan and smooth out the top with a spatula. Place in the freezer while you make the next layer.
3. Without rinsing the food processor, add all ingredients for the chocolate layer, except the cacao nibs. Blend until smooth, then use a spatula to stir in the cacao nibs. Take the pan out of the freezer and add this layer. Smooth it out evenly, and then return to the freezer while you make the top layer.
4. Rinse the food processor bowl and blade (this is to remove any chocolate residue and ensure that the top layer will be light green in color). Place all ingredients for the mint layer in the food processor and blend until smooth.
5. Add to the pan and smooth it out evenly. Return to the freezer until ready to serve. Take out to thaw 10 minutes before serving and garnish with cacao nibs and mint leaves, if desired.

Nutrition: Calories: 271; Fat: 19 g; Carbs: 19 g; Proteins: 6 g; Fibers: 2 g.

Watermelon Strawberry Ice Pops

Preparation Time: 5 minutes
Cooking Time: 0 minutes **Servings:** 1
Ingredients:

- 1 cup diced watermelon
- 1 strawberry, tops removed
- 1 tablespoon freshly squeezed lime juice

Directions:

1. In a blender, combine the watermelon, strawberries, and lime juice. Blend for 1 to 2 minutes, or until well combined.
2. Pour evenly into six ice-pop molds, insert ice-pop sticks, and freeze for at least 6 hours before serving.

Nutrition: Calories: 61; Fat: 0 g; Carbs: 15 g; Proteins: 1 g; Fiber: 1 g.

Peppermint Chocolate Nice Cream

Preparation Time: 5 minutes
Cooking Time: 0 minutes
Servings: 1
Ingredients:

- 3 frozen ripe bananas, broken into thirds
- 3 tablespoons plant-based milk
- 2 tablespoons cocoa powder
- 1/8 teaspoon peppermint extract

Directions:
1. In a food processor, combine the bananas, milk, cocoa powder, and peppermint.
2. Process on medium speed for 30 to 60 seconds, or until the bananas have been blended into smooth soft-consistency, and serve. (If you notice any banana pieces stuck toward the top and sides of the food processor, you may need to stop and scrape them down with a spatula, then pulse until smooth.)

Nutrition: Calories: 173; Fat: 2 g; Carbs: 43 g; Proteins: 3 g; Fibers: 6 g.

Apple Crisp with Oats

Preparation Time: 10 minutes
Cooking Time: 35 minutes
Servings: 1
Ingredients:

- 1 medium apples, cored and cut into ¼-inch pieces
- 1/8 cup apple juice
- 1/4 teaspoon vanilla extract
- 1/4 teaspoon ground cinnamon, divided
- 1/2 cups rolled oats
- 1/8 cup maple syrup

Directions:
1. Preheat the oven to 375°F (190°C).
2. In a large bowl, combine the apple slices, apple juice, vanilla, and ½ teaspoon of cinnamon. Mix well to thoroughly coat the apple slices.
3. Layer the apple slices on the bottom of a round or square baking dish. Take any leftover liquid and pour it over the apple slices.
4. In a large bowl, stir together the oats, maple syrup, and the remaining ½ teaspoon of cinnamon until the oats are completely coated.
5. Sprinkle the oat mixture over the apples, being sure to spread it out evenly so that none of the apple slices are visible.
6. Bake for 35 minutes, or until the oats begin to turn golden brown, and serve.

Nutrition: Calories: 213; Fat: 2 g; Carbs: 47 g; Proteins: 4 g; Fibers: 6 g.

Desserts Recipes Raspberry Muffins

Preparation Time: 10 minutes
Cooking Time: 25 minutes
Servings: 12
Ingredients:

- 1/2 cup and 2 tablespoons whole-wheat flour
- 1 (1/2) cup raspberries, fresh and more for decorating
- 1 cup white whole-wheat flour
- 1/8 teaspoon salt
- 3/4 cup of coconut sugar
- 2 teaspoons baking powder
- 1 teaspoon apple cider vinegar
- 1 1/4 cups water
- 1/2 cup olive oil

Directions:
1. Switch on the oven, then set it to 400°F and let it preheat.
2. Meanwhile, take a large bowl and place both flours in it. Add salt and baking powder. Stir until combined.
3. Take a medium bowl; add oil to it and then whisk in the sugar until dissolved.
4. Whisk in vinegar and water until blended, slowly stir in flour mixture until smooth batter comes together, and then fold in berries.
5. Take a 12-cups muffin pan and, grease it with oil. Fill evenly with the prepared mixture and then put a raspberry on top of each muffin.
6. Bake the muffins for 25 minutes until the top is golden brown. Then serve.

Nutrition: Calories: 109; Fat: 3.4 g; Proteins: 2.1 g; Carbs: 17.6 g; Fiber: 1 g.

Chocolate Chip Cake

Preparation Time: 10 minutes.
Cooking Time: 50 minutes.
Servings: 10
Ingredients:

- 2 cups white whole-wheat flour
- 1/4 teaspoon baking soda
- 1/3 cup coconut sugar
- 2 teaspoons baking powder
- 1/2 teaspoons salt
- 1/2 cup chocolate chips, vegan
- 1 teaspoon vanilla extract, unsweetened
- 1 tablespoon applesauce
- 1 teaspoon apple cider vinegar
- 1/4 cup melted coconut oil
- 1/2 teaspoons almond extract, unsweetened
- 1 cup almond milk, unsweetened

Directions:
1. Switch on the oven, then set it to 360°F and let it preheat.
2. Meanwhile, take a 9 x 5-inches loaf pan. Grease it with oil and then set aside until required.

3. Take a large bowl, add sugar to it, pour in oil, vanilla and almond extract, vinegar, applesauce and milk. Then whisk until well combined.
4. Take a large bowl, place flour in it, add salt, baking powder and soda. Stir until mixed.
5. Stir the flour mixture into the milk mixture until smooth batter comes together and then fold in 1/3 cup of chocolate chips.
6. Spoon the batter into the loaf pan, scatter the remaining chocolate chips on top and then bake for 50 minutes.
7. When done, let the bread cool for 10 minutes and then cut it into slices.
8. Serve straight away.

Nutrition: Calories: 218; Fat: 8 g; Proteins: 3.4 g; Carbs: 32 g; Fiber: 2 g.

Coffee Cake

Preparation Time: 10 minutes
Cooking Time: 45 minutes
Servings: 9
Ingredients:
For the cake:
- 1/3 cup coconut sugar
- 1 teaspoon vanilla extract, unsweetened
- 1/4 cup olive oil
- 1/8 teaspoon almond extract, unsweetened
- ¼ cup ground coffee
- 1 3/4 cup white whole-wheat flour
- 2 teaspoons baking powder
- 1/2 teaspoons salt
- 1/4 teaspoon baking soda
- 1 teaspoon apple cider vinegar
- 1 tablespoon applesauce
- 1 cup almond milk, unsweetened

For the Streusel bread:
- 1/2 cup white whole-wheat flour
- 2 teaspoons cinnamon
- 1/3 cup coconut sugar
- 1/2 teaspoons salt
- 2 tablespoons olive oil
- 1 tablespoon coconut butter

Directions:
1. Switch on the oven, then set it to 350°F and let it preheat.
2. Meanwhile, take a large bowl, pour in milk, coffee, add applesauce, vinegar, sugar, oil, vanilla and almond extract and then whisk until blended.
3. Take a medium bowl, place flour in it, add salt, baking powder and soda, and stir until mixed.
4. Stir the flour mixture into the milk mixture until smooth batter comes together, and then spoon the mixture into a loaf pan lined with parchment paper.
5. Prepare Streusel bread and for this, take a medium bowl, place flour in it, and add sugar, salt, and cinnamon.

6. Stir until mixed, and then mix butter and oil with fingers until the crumble mixture comes together.

7. Spread the prepared Streusel on top of the batter of the cake, and then bake for 45 minutes until the top turn golden brown and the cake have thoroughly cooked.
8. When done, let the cake rest in its pan for 10 minutes, remove it to cool completely, and then cut it into slices.
9. Serve straight away.

Nutrition: Calories: 259; Fat: 10 g; Proteins: 3 g; Carbs: 37 g; Fiber: 1 g.

Chocolate Marble Cake

Preparation Time: 15 minutes
Cooking Time: 50 minutes
Servings: 8
Ingredients:
- 1 (1/2) cup white whole-wheat flour
- 1 tablespoon flaxseed meal
- 2 (1/2) tablespoons cocoa powder
- 1/4 teaspoon salt
- 4 tablespoons chopped walnuts
- 1 teaspoon baking powder
- 2/3 cup coconut sugar
- 1/4 teaspoon baking soda
- 1 teaspoon vanilla extract, unsweetened
- 3 tablespoons peanut butter
- 1/4 cup olive oil
- 1 cup almond milk, unsweetened

Directions:
1. Switch on the oven, then set it to 350°F and let it preheat.
2. Meanwhile, take a medium bowl, place flour in it, add salt, baking powder, and soda. Then stir until mixed.
3. Take a large bowl, pour in milk, add sugar, flaxseed meal, oil and vanilla. Whisk until sugar has dissolved, and then whisk in flour mixture until smooth batter comes together.
4. Spoon half of the prepared batter in a medium bowl. Add cocoa powder, and stir until combined.
5. Add peanut butter into the other bowl and then stir until combined.
6. Take a loaf pan, line it with a parchment sheet, spoon half of the chocolate batter in it, and then spread it evenly.

7. Layer the chocolate batter with half of the peanut butter batter, cover with the remaining chocolate batter and then layer with the remaining peanut butter batter.
8. Make swirls into the batter with a toothpick, smooth the top with a spatula, sprinkle walnuts on top, and then bake for 50 minutes until done.

9. When done, let the cake rest in its pan for 10 minutes. Then remove it to cool completely and cut it into slices.
10. Serve straight away.

Nutrition: Calories: 299; Fat: 14 g; Proteins: 6 g; Carbs: 39 g; Fiber: 3 g.

Chocolate Chip Cookies

Preparation Time: 10 minutes
Cooking Time: 10 minutes
Servings: 11
Ingredients:

- 1 ¼ cup white whole-wheat flour
- 1 ½ tablespoon flax seed
- ½ teaspoon baking soda
- ½ cup of coconut sugar
- ¼ teaspoon of sea salt
- ¼ cup powdered coconut sugar
- 1 teaspoon baking powder
- 2 teaspoons vanilla extract, unsweetened
- 4 ½ tablespoons water
- ½ cup of coconut oil
- 1 cup chocolate chips, vegan

Directions:

1. Take a large bowl and place flax seeds in it. Stir in water and then let the mixture rest for 5 minutes until creamy.
2. Then add the remaining ingredients into the flax seed's mixture except for flour and chocolate chips. Beat until light batter comes together.
3. Beat in flour, ¼ cup at a time, until smooth batter comes together, and then fold in chocolate chips.
4. Use an ice cream scoop to scoop the batter onto a baking sheet lined with parchment sheet with some distance between cookies. Then bake for 10 minutes until cookies turn golden brown.
5. When done, let the cookies cool on the baking sheet for 3 minutes and cool completely on the wire rack for 5 minutes.
6. Serve straight away.

Nutrition: Calories: 141; Fat: 7 g; Proteins: 1 g; Carbs: 17 g; Fiber: 2 g.

Lemon Cake

Preparation Time: 10 minutes
Cooking Time: 50 minutes
Servings: 9
Ingredients:

- 1 (1/2) cup white whole-wheat flour
- 1 (1/2) teaspoon baking powder
- 2 tablespoons almond flour
- 1 lemon, zested
- 1/4 teaspoon baking soda
- 1/8 teaspoon turmeric powder
- 1/3 teaspoon salt
- 1/4 teaspoon vanilla extract, unsweetened
- 1/3 cup lemon juice

- 1/2 cup maple syrup
- 1/4 cup olive oil
- 1/4 cup of water

For the frosting:

- 1 tablespoon lemon juice
- 1/8 teaspoon salt
- 1/4 cup maple syrup
- 2 tablespoons powdered sugar
- 6 ounces vegan cream cheese, softened

Directions:

1. Switch on the oven, then set it to 350°F and let it preheat.
2. Take a large bowl, pour in water, lemon juice and oil. Add vanilla extract and maple syrup and whisk until blended.
3. Whisk in flour, ¼ cup at a time until smooth. Then whisk in almond flour, salt, turmeric, lemon zest, baking soda and powder until well combined.
4. Take a loaf pan. Grease it with oil, spoon the prepared batter in it and then bake for 50 minutes.
5. Meanwhile, prepare the frosting and for this, take a small bowl and place all the ingredients in it. Whisk until smooth and then let it chill until required.
6. When the cake has cooked, let it cool for 10 minutes in its pan and then let it cool completely on the wire rack.
7. Spread the prepared frosting on top of the cake. Slice the cake and then serve.

Nutrition: Calories: 275; Fat: 12 g; Proteins: 3 g; Carbs: 38 g; Fiber: 1 g.

Banana Muffins

Preparation Time: 10 minutes
Cooking Time: 30 minutes
Servings: 12
Ingredients:

- 1 (½) cup mashed banana
- 1 (½) cup and 2 tablespoons white whole-wheat flour, divided
- ¼ cup of coconut sugar
- ¾ cup rolled oats, divided
- 1 teaspoon ginger powder
- 1 tablespoon ground cinnamon, divided
- 2 teaspoons baking powder
- ½ teaspoon salt
- 1 teaspoon baking soda
- 1 tablespoon vanilla extract, unsweetened
- ½ cup maple syrup
- 1 tablespoon rum
- ½ cup of coconut oil

Directions:

1. Switch on the oven. Then set it to 350°F and let it preheat.
2. Meanwhile, take a medium bowl. Place 1 (½) cups flour in it, add ½ cup oats, ginger, baking powder, soda, salt, and 2 teaspoons cinnamon. Stir until mixed.

3. Place ¼ cup of coconut oil in a heatproof bowl. Melt it in the microwave oven and then whisk in maple syrup until combined.
4. Add mashed banana along with rum and vanilla. Stir until combined and then whisk this mixture into the flour mixture until the smooth batter comes together.
5. Take a separate medium bowl. Place the remaining oats and flour in it. Add cinnamon, coconut sugar and coconut oil.
6. Then stir with a fork until a crumbly mixture comes together.

7. Take a 12-cups muffin pan and fill evenly with prepared batter. Top with oats mixture, and then bake for 30 minutes until firm and the top turns golden brown.
8. When done, let the muffins cool for 5 minutes in their pan and then cool the muffins completely before serving.

Nutrition: Calories: 240; Fat: 9.3 g; Proteins: 2.6 g; Carbs: 35.4 g; Fiber: 2 g.

No-Bake Cookies

Preparation Time: 30 minutes.
Cooking Time: 0 minutes.
Servings: 9
Ingredients:
- 1 cup rolled oats
- 1/4 cup of cocoa powder
- 1/8 teaspoon salt
- 1 teaspoon vanilla extract, unsweetened
- 1/4 cup and 2 tablespoons peanut butter, divided
- 6 tablespoons coconut oil, divided
- 1/4 cup and 1 tablespoon maple syrup, divided

Directions:
1. Take a small saucepan, place it over low heat, add 5 tablespoons of coconut oil and then let it melt.
2. Whisk in 2 tablespoons peanut butter, salt, 1 teaspoon vanilla extract and ¼ cup each of cocoa powder and maple syrup. Whisk until well combined.
3. Remove the pan from heat. Stir in oats and then spoon the mixture evenly into 9 cups of a muffin pan.
4. Wipe clean the pan and return it over low heat. Add the remaining coconut oil, maple syrup, and peanut butter, stir until combined. Cook for 2 minutes until thoroughly warmed.
5. Drizzle the peanut butter sauce over the oat mixture in the muffin pan and then let it freeze for 20 minutes or more until set.
6. Serve straight away.

Nutrition: Calories: 213; Fat: 14.8 g; Proteins: 4 g; Carbs: 17.3 g; Fiber: 2.1 g.

Peanut Butter and Oats Bars

Preparation Time: 40 minutes
Cooking Time: 8 minutes
Servings: 8

Ingredients:
- 1 cup rolled oats
- 1/8 teaspoon salt
- 1/4 cup chocolate chips, vegan
- 1/4 cup maple syrup
- 1 cup peanut butter

Directions:
1. Take a medium saucepan and place it over medium heat. Add peanut butter, salt and maple syrup. Then whisk until combined and thickened; this will take 5 minutes.
2. Remove pan from heat and place oats in a bowl. Pour peanut butter mixture on it, and stir until well combined.
3. Take an 8 x 6-inch baking dish. Line it with a parchment sheet, spoon the oats mixture in it and then spread evenly, pressing the mixture into the dish.
4. Sprinkle the chocolate chips on top. Press them into the bar mixture and then let the mixture rest in the refrigerator for 30 minutes or more until set.
5. When ready to eat, cut the bar mixture into even size pieces and then serve.

Nutrition: Calories: 274; Fat: 17 g; Proteins: 10 g; Carbs: 19 g; Fiber: 3 g.

Baked Apples

Preparation Time: 5 minutes
Cooking Time: 20 minutes
Servings: 4
Ingredients:
- 6 medium apples, peeled, cut into chunks
- 1 teaspoon ground cinnamon
- 2 tablespoons melted coconut oil

Directions:
1. Switch on the oven, then set it to 350°F and let it preheat.
2. Take a medium baking dish and then spread apple pieces in it.
3. Take a small bowl, place coconut oil in it, stir in cinnamon, drizzle this mixture over apples and then toss until coated.
4. Place the baking dish into the oven and then bake for 20 minutes or more until apples turn soft, stirring halfway.
5. Serve straight away.

Nutrition: Calories: 170; Fat: 3.8 g; Proteins: 0.5 g; Carbs: 31 g; Fiber: 5.5 g.

Chocolate Strawberry Shake

Preparation Time: 5 minutes
Cooking Time: 0 minutes
Servings: 2
Ingredients:
- 2 cups almond milk, unsweetened
- 4 bananas, peeled, frozen
- 4 tablespoons cocoa powder
- 2 cups strawberries, frozen

Directions:
1. Place all the ingredients into the jar of a high-speed food processor or blender in the order stated in the ingredients list, and then cover it with the lid.
2. Pulse for 1 minute until smooth and then serve.

Nutrition: Calories: 208; Fat: 0.2 g; Proteins: 12.4 g; Carbs: 26.2 g; Fiber: 1.4 g.

Chocolate Clusters

Preparation Time: 15 minutes
Cooking Time: 0 minutes
Servings: 12
Ingredients:
*   1 cup chopped dark chocolate, vegan
*   1 cup cashews, roasted
*   1 teaspoon sea salt flakes

Directions:
1. Take a large baking sheet, line it with wax paper and then set aside until required.
2. Take a medium bowl, place chocolate in it, and then microwave for 1 minute.
3. Stir the chocolate and then continue microwaving it at 1-minute intervals until the chocolate melts completely, stirring at every interval.
4. When melted, stir the chocolate to bring it to 90°F and then stir in cashews.
5. Scoop the walnut-chocolate mixture on the prepared baking sheet, ½ tablespoon per cluster. Then sprinkle with sea salt.
6. Let the clusters stand at room temperature until harden and then serve.

Nutrition: Calories: 79.4; Fat: 6.6 g; Proteins: 1 g; Carbs: 5.8 g; Fiber: 1.1 g.

Banana Coconut Cookies

Preparation Time: 40 minutes
Cooking Time: 20 minutes
Servings: 8
Ingredients:
*   1 (½) cup shredded coconut, unsweetened
*   1 cup mashed banana

Directions:
1. Switch on the oven, then set it to 350°F and let it preheat.
2. Take a medium bowl, place the mashed banana in it, and stir in coconut until well combined.
3. Take a large baking sheet, line it with a parchment sheet, and then scoop the prepared mixture on it, 2 tablespoons of mixture per cookie.
4. Place the baking sheet into the refrigerator and then let it cool for 30 minutes or more until harden.
5. Serve straight away.

Nutrition: Calories: 51; Fat: 3 g; Proteins: 0.2 g; Carbs: 4 g; Fiber: 1 g.

Chocolate Pots

Preparation Time: 4 hours and 10 minutes.

Cooking Time: 3 minutes. **Servings:** 4
Ingredients:
*   6 ounces chocolate, unsweetened
*   1 cup Medjool dates, pitted
*   1 (¾) cup almond milk, unsweetened

Directions:
1. Cut the chocolate into small pieces, place them in a heatproof bowl and then microwave for 2 to 3 minutes until completely melted, stirring every minute.
2. Place dates in a blender, pour in the milk and then pulse until smooth.
3. Add chocolate into the blender and then pulse until combined.
4. Divide the mixture into the small mason jars, and then let them rest for 4 hours until set. Serve straight away.

Nutrition: Calories: 321; Fat: 19 g; Proteins: 6 g; Carbs: 34 g; Fiber: 4 g.

Maple Syrup and Tahini Fudge

Preparation Time: 2 hours
Cooking Time: 3 minutes
Servings: 15
Ingredients:
*   1 cup dark chocolate chips, vegan
*   ¼ cup maple syrup
*   ½ cup tahini

Directions:
1. Take a heatproof bowl, place chocolate chips in it and then microwave for 2 to 3 minutes until melt completely, stirring every minute.
2. When melted, remove the chocolate bowl from the microwave and then whisk in maple syrup and tahini until smooth.
3. Take a 4 x 8-inch baking dish and line it with wax paper. Spoon the chocolate mixture in it and then press it into the baking dish.
4. Cover another sheet with wax paper. Press it down until smooth, and let the fudge rest for 1 hour in the freezer until set.
5. Then cut the fudge into 15 squares and serve.

Nutrition: Calories: 110.7; Fat: 5.3 g; Proteins: 2.2 g; Carbs: 15.1 g; Fiber: 1.6 g.

Butter Carrots

Preparation Time: 10 minutes
Cooking Time: 10 minutes **Servings:** 4
Ingredients:
*   2 cups baby carrots
*   1 tablespoon brown sugar
*   ½ tablespoon vegan butter, melted
*   A pinch salt and black pepper

Directions:
1. Take a baking dish suitable to fit in your air fryer. Toss carrots with sugar, butter, salt and black pepper in the baking dish. Place the dish in the air fryer basket and seal the fryer. Cook the carrots for 10 minutes at 350° F on air fryer mode.

Nutrition: Calories: 270; Fat: 10 g; Carbs: 25 g; Proteins: 5 g; Fiber: 4 g.

Leeks with Butter

Preparation Time: 10 minutes
Cooking Time: 7 minutes
Servings: 4
Ingredients:

- 1 tablespoon vegan butter, melted
- 1 tablespoon lemon juice
- 4 leeks, washed and halved
- Salt and black pepper to taste

Directions:

1. Take a baking dish suitable to fit in your air fryer.
2. Toss the leeks with butter, salt, and black pepper in the dish. Place the dish in the air fryer basket.
3. Seal the fryer and cook the carrots for 7 minutes at 350° F on air fryer mode.
4. Add a drizzle of lemon juice.
5. Mix well, then serve.

Nutrition: Calories: 230; Fat: 9 g; Carbs: 20 g; Proteins: 6 g; Fiber: 8 g.

Juicy Brussel Sprouts

Preparation Time: 10 minutes
Cooking Time: 10 minutes **Servings:** 4
Ingredients:

- 1-pound Brussels sprouts, trimmed
- ¼ cup green onions, chopped
- 6 cherry tomatoes, halved
- 1 tablespoon olive oil
- Salt and black pepper to taste

Directions:

1. Take a baking dish suitable to fit in your air fryer. Toss Brussels sprouts with salt and black pepper in the dish. Place this dish in the air fryer and seal the fryer. Cook the sprouts for 10 minutes at 350° F on air fryer mode.
2. Toss these sprouts with green onions, tomatoes, olive oil, salt, and pepper in a salad bowl.

Nutrition: Calories: 120; Fat: 3 g; Carbs: 23 g; Proteins: 4 g; Fiber: 9 g.

Parsley Potatoes

Preparation Time: 10 minutes
Cooking Time: 10 minutes **Servings:** 4
Ingredients:

- 1-pound gold potatoes, sliced
- 2 tablespoons olive oil
- ¼ cup parsley leaves, chopped
- Juice from ½ lemon
- Salt and black pepper to taste

Directions:

1. Take a baking dish suitable to fit in your air fryer.
2. Place the potatoes and season them liberally with salt, pepper, olive oil, and lemon juice.
3. Place the baking dish in the air fryer basket and seal it.

4. Cook the potatoes for 10 minutes at 350° F on air fryer mode.
5. Serve warm with parsley garnishing.

Nutrition: Calories: 280; Fat: 5 g; Carbs: 36 g; Proteins: 4 g; Fiber3 g.

Fried Asparagus

Preparation Time: 10 minutes
Cooking Time: 8 minutes
Servings: 4
Ingredients:

- 2 pounds fresh asparagus, trimmed
- ½ teaspoon oregano, dried
- 4 ounces vegan feta cheese, crumbled
- 4 garlic cloves, minced
- 2 tablespoons parsley, chopped
- ¼ teaspoon red pepper flakes
- ¼ cup olive oil
- Salt and black pepper to the taste
- 1 teaspoon lemon zest
- 1 lemon, juiced

Directions:

1. Combine lemon zest with oregano, pepper flakes, garlic and oil in a large bowl.
2. Add asparagus, salt, pepper, and cheese to the bowl.
3. Toss well to coat, then place the asparagus in the air fryer basket.
4. Seal the fryer and cook them for 8 minutes at 350° F on Air fryer mode.
5. Garnish with parsley and lemon juice.
6. Enjoy warm.

Nutrition: Calories: 310; Fat: 10 g; Carbs: 32 g; Proteins: 6 g; Fiber: 9 g.

Balsamic Artichokes

Preparation Time: 10 minutes
Cooking Time: 7 minutes
Servings: 4
Ingredients:

- 4 big artichokes, trimmed
- ¼ cup olive oil
- 2 garlic cloves, minced
- 2 tablespoons lemon juice
- 2 teaspoons balsamic vinegar
- 1 teaspoon oregano, dried
- Salt and black pepper to taste

Directions:

1. Season artichokes liberally with salt and pepper, then rub them with half of the lemon juice and oil.

2. Add the artichokes to a baking dish suitable to fit in the air fryer.
3. Place the artichoke dish in the air fryer basket and seal it.
4. Cook them for 7 minutes at 360º F on air fryer mode.
5. Whisk remaining lemon juice, oil, vinegar, oregano, garlic, salt and pepper in a bowl.
6. Pour this mixture over the artichokes and mix them well. Enjoy.

Nutrition: Calories: 310; Fat: 10 g; Carbs: 25 g; Proteins: 4 g; Fiber: 9 g.

Tomato Kebabs

Preparation Time: 10 minutes
Cooking Time: 6 minutes
Servings: 4
Ingredients:

- 3 tablespoons balsamic vinegar
- 24 cherry tomatoes
- 2 cups vegan feta cheese, sliced
- 2 tablespoons olive oil
- 3 garlic cloves, minced
- 1 tablespoon thyme, chopped
- Salt and black pepper to taste

For the Dressing:

- 2 tablespoons balsamic vinegar
- 4 tablespoons olive oil
- Salt and black pepper to taste

Directions:

1. In a medium bowl, combine oil, garlic cloves, thyme, salt, vinegar, and black pepper.
2. Mix well, then add the tomatoes and coat them liberally.
3. Thread 6 tomatoes and cheese slices on each skewer alternatively.
4. Place these skewers in the air fryer basket and seal them.
5. Cook them for 6 minutes on air fryer mode at 360º F.
6. Meanwhile, whisk together the dressing ingredients.
7. Place the cooked skewers on the serving plates.
8. Pour the vinegar dressing over them.
9. Enjoy.

Nutrition: Calories: 190; Fat: 6 g; Carbs: 18 g; Proteins: 8 g; Fiber: 6 g.

Eggplant and Zucchini Snack

Preparation Time: 10 minutes
Cooking Time: 8 minutes
Servings: 4
Ingredients:

- 1 eggplant, cubed
- 3 zucchinis, cubed
- 2 tablespoons lemon juice
- 1 teaspoon oregano, dried

- 3 tablespoons olive oil
- 1 teaspoon thyme, dried
- Salt and black pepper to taste

Directions:

1. Take a baking dish suitable to fit in your air fryer.
2. Combine all ingredients in the baking dish.
3. Place the eggplant dish in the air fryer basket and seal it.
4. Cook them for 8 minutes at 360º F on air fryer mode.
5. Enjoy warm.

Nutrition: Calories: 210; Fat: 4 g; Carbs: 16 g; Proteins: 3 g; Fiber: 9 g.

Artichokes with Mayo Sauce

Preparation Time: 10 minutes
Cooking Time: 6 minutes **Servings:** 4
Ingredients:

- 2 artichokes, trimmed
- 1 tablespoon lemon juice
- 2 garlic cloves, minced
- A drizzle of olive oil

For the Sauce:

- 1 cup vegan mayonnaise
- ¼ cup olive oil
- ¼ cup coconut oil
- 3 garlic cloves

Directions:

1. Toss artichokes with lemon juice, oil and 2 garlic cloves in a large bowl.
2. Place the seasoned artichokes in the air fryer basket and seal it.
3. Cook the artichokes for 6 minutes at 350º on air fryer mode.
4. Blend coconut oil with olive oil, mayonnaise and 3 garlic cloves in a food processor.
5. Place the artichokes on the serving plates.
6. Pour the mayonnaise mixture over the artichokes.
7. Enjoy fresh.

Nutrition: Calories: 230; Fat: 11 g; Carbs: 24 g; Proteins: 6 g; Fiber: 11 g.

Fried Mustard Greens

Preparation Time: 10 minutes
Cooking Time: 11 minutes
Servings: 4
Ingredients:

- 2 garlic cloves, minced
- 1 tablespoon olive oil
- ½ cup yellow onion, sliced
- 3 tablespoons vegetable stock
- ¼ teaspoon dark sesame oil
- 1-pound mustard greens, torn
- Salt and black pepper to taste

Directions:

1. Take a baking dish suitable to fit in your air fryer.
2. Add oil and place it over medium heat and sauté onions in it for 5 minutes.

3. Stir in garlic, greens, salt, pepper, and stock.
4. Mix well, then place the dish in the air fryer basket.
5. Seal it and cook them for 6 minutes at 350º F on air fryer mode.
6. Drizzle sesame oil over the greens.

Nutrition: Calories: 210; Fat: 8 g; Carbs: 24 g; Proteins: 4 g; Fiber: 10 g.

Cheese Brussels Sprouts

Preparation Time: 10 minutes
Cooking Time: 8 minutes
Servings: 4
Ingredients:

- 1-pound Brussels sprouts washed
- 3 tablespoons vegan parmesan, grated
- Juice from 1 lemon
- 2 tablespoons vegan butter
- Salt and black pepper to taste

Directions:

1. Spread the Brussels sprouts in the air fryer basket.
2. Seal it and cook them for 8 minutes at 350º F on air fryer mode.
3. Place a nonstick pan over medium-high heat and add butter to melt.
4. Stir in pepper, salt, lemon juice, and Brussels sprouts.
5. Mix well, then add parmesan.
6. Serve warm.

Nutrition: Calories: 160; Fat: 7 g; Carbs: 18 g; Proteins: 5 g; Fiber: 12 g.

Mushroom Stuffed Poblano

Preparation Time: 10 minutes
Cooking Time: 20 minutes
Servings: 10
Ingredients:

- 10 Poblano peppers, tops cut off and seeds removed
- 2 teaspoons garlic, minced
- 8 ounces mushrooms, chopped
- ½ cup cilantro, chopped
- 1 white onion, chopped
- 1 tablespoon olive oil
- Salt and black pepper to taste

Directions:

1. Place a nonstick pan over medium heat and add oil.
2. Stir in mushrooms and onion, sauté for 5 minutes.
3. Add salt, black pepper, cilantro and garlic.
4. Stir while cooking for 2 additional minutes, then take it off the heat.
5. Divide this mixture into the Poblano peppers and stuff them neatly.
6. Place the peppers in the air fryer basket and seal it.
7. Cook them for 15 minutes at 350º F on air fryer mode. Enjoy.

Nutrition: Calories: 220; Fat: 2 g; Carbs: 20 g; Proteins: 4 g; Fiber: 6 g.

Mushroom Stuffed Tomatoes

Preparation Time: 10 minutes
Cooking Time: 15 minutes
Servings: 4
Ingredients:

- 4 tomatoes, tops removed and pulp removed (reserve for filling)
- 1 yellow onion, chopped
- ½ cup mushrooms, chopped
- 1 tablespoon bread crumbs
- 1 tablespoon vegan butter
- ¼ teaspoon caraway seeds
- 1 tablespoon parsley, chopped
- 2 tablespoons celery, chopped
- 1 cup vegan cheese, shredded
- Salt and black pepper to the taste

Directions:

1. Place a pan over medium heat, add butter.
2. When it melts, add onion and celery to the sauté for 3 minutes.
3. Stir in mushrooms and tomato pulp. Cook for 1 minute, then add crumbled bread, pepper, salt, cheese, parsley, and caraway seeds.
4. Cook while stirring for 4 minutes, then remove from the heat. After cooling the mixture, stuff it equally in the tomatoes.
5. Place the tomatoes in the air fryer basket and seal it. Cook them for 8 minutes at 350º F on air fryer mode. Enjoy.

Nutrition: Calories: 280; Fat: 9 g; Carbs: 35 g; Proteins: 11 g; Fiber: 11 g.

Banana Cinnamon Muffins

Preparation Time: 10 minutes
Cooking Time: 22 minutes
Servings: 12
Ingredients:

- 3 very ripe bananas, mashed
- ½ cup vanilla almond milk
- 1 cup sugar
- 2 cups flour
- 1 teaspoon baking soda
- ½ teaspoon cinnamon
- ¼ teaspoon salt

Directions:

1. Preheat your oven to 350º F.
2. Separately, whisk together the dry ingredients in one bowl and the wet ingredients in another bowl.
3. Beat the two mixtures together until smooth.
4. Line a muffin tray with muffin cups and evenly divide the muffin batter among the cups.

5. Bake for 22 minutes and serve.
Nutrition: Calories: 320; Fat: 4 g; Carbs: 55 g; Proteins: 8 g; Fiber: 4.

Cashew Oat Muffins
Preparation Time: 10 minutes
Cooking Time: 22 minutes **Servings:** 12
Ingredients:
- 3 cups rolled oats
- ¾ cup raw cashews
- ¼ cup maple syrup
- ¼ cup sugar
- 1 teaspoon vanilla extract
- ½ teaspoon salt
- 1½ teaspoon baking soda
- 2 cups water

Directions:
1. Preheat your oven to 375° F.
2. Separately, whisk together the dry ingredients in one bowl and the wet ingredients in another bowl.
3. Beat the two mixtures together until smooth.
4. Fold in cashews and give it a gentle stir.
5. Line a muffin tray with muffin cups and evenly divide the muffin batter among the cups.
6. Bake for 22 minutes and serve.

Nutrition: Calories: 520; Fat: 4 g; Carbs: 54 g; Proteins: 9 g; Fiber: 8.

Banana Walnut Muffins
Preparation Time: 10 minutes
Cooking Time: 18 minutes **Servings:** 12
Ingredients:
- 4 large pitted dates, boiled
- 1 cup almond milk
- 2 tablespoons lemon juice
- 2½ cups rolled oats
- 1 teaspoon baking powder
- 1 teaspoon baking soda
- 1 teaspoon cinnamon
- ¼ teaspoon nutmeg
- 1/8 teaspoon salt
- 1½ cups mashed banana
- ¼ cup maple syrup
- 1 tablespoon vanilla extract
- 1 cup walnuts, chopped

Directions:
1. Preheat your oven to 350° F.
2. Separately, whisk together the dry ingredients in one bowl and the wet ingredients in another bowl.
3. Beat the two mixtures together until smooth. Fold in walnuts and give it a gentle stir.
4. Line a muffin tray with muffin cups and evenly divide the muffin batter among the cups.
5. Bake for 18 minutes and serve.

Nutrition: Calories: 330; Fat: 4 g; Carbs: 55 g; Proteins: 6 g; Fiber: 4.

Carrot Flaxseed Muffins
Preparation Time: 10 minutes
Cooking Time: 20 minutes
Servings: 12
Ingredients:
- 2 tablespoons ground flax
- 5 tablespoons water
- ¾ cup almond milk
- ¾ cup applesauce
- ½ cup maple syrup
- 1 teaspoon vanilla extract
- 1½ cups whole wheat flour
- ½ cup rolled oats
- 1 cup grated carrot

Directions:
1. Whisk flaxseed with water in a bowl and leave it for 10 minutes. Separately, whisk together the dry ingredients in one bowl and the wet ingredients in another bowl.
2. Beat the two mixtures together until smooth. Fold in flaxseed and carrots, give it a gentle stir.
3. Line a muffin tray with muffin cups and evenly divide the muffin batter among the cups.
4. Bake for 20 minutes and serve.

Nutrition: Calories: 320; Fat: 4 g; Carbs: 50 g; Proteins: 4 g; Fiber: 6 g.

Chocolate Peanut Fat Bombs
Preparation Time: 10 minutes
Cooking Time: 1 hour 1 minute
Servings: 12
Ingredients:
- ½ cup coconut butter
- 1 cup plus 2 tablespoons peanut butter
- 5 tablespoons cocoa powder
- 2 teaspoons maple syrup

Directions:
1. In a bowl, combine all the ingredients. Melt them in the microwave for 1minute.
2. Mix well, then divide the mixture into silicone molds. Freeze them for 1 hour to set.

Nutrition: Calories: 350; Fat: 15 g; Carbs: 45 g; Proteins: 8 g; Fiber: 4 g.

Protein Fat Bombs
Preparation Time: 10 minutes
Cooking Time: 1 hour
Servings: 12
Ingredients:
- 1 cup coconut oil
- 1 cup peanut butter, melted
- ½ cup cocoa powder
- ¼ cup plant-based protein powder
- 1 pinch of salt
- 2 cups unsweetened shredded coconut

Directions:

1. In a bowl, add all the ingredients except coconut shreds.
2. Mix well, then make small balls out of this mixture and place them into silicone molds.
3. Freeze for 1 hour to set. Roll the balls in the coconut shreds. Serve.

Nutritional: Calories: 340; Fat: 14 g; Carbs: 35 g; Proteins: 12 g; Fiber: 3 g.

Mojito Fat Bombs

Preparation Time: 10 minutes
Cooking Time: 1 hour and 1 minute
Servings: 12
Ingredients:

- ¾ cup hulled hemp seeds
- ½ cup coconut oil
- 1 cup fresh mint
- ½ teaspoon mint extract
- Juice & zest of two limes
- ¼ teaspoon stevia

Directions:

1. In a bowl, combine all the ingredients. Melt in the microwave for 1 minute.
2. Mix well, then divide the mixture into silicone molds. Freeze them for 1 hour to set. Serve.

Nutrition: Calories: 290; Fat: 12 g; Carbs: 35 g; Proteins: 6 g; Fiber: 2 g.

Key Lime Pie

Preparation Time: 15 minutes
Cooking Time: 3 hours
Servings: 12
Ingredients:
For the Crust:

- ¾ cup coconut flakes, unsweetened
- 1 cup dates, soaked in warm water for 10 minutes in water, drained

For the Filling:

- ¾ cup of coconut meat
- 1 ½ avocado, peeled, pitted
- 2 tablespoons key lime juice
- ¼ cup agave

Directions:

1. Prepare the crust. For this, place all its ingredients in a food processor and pulse for 3 to 5 minutes until the thick paste comes together.
2. Take an 8-inch pie pan, grease it with oil, pour crust mixture in it and spread and press the mixture evenly in the bottom and along the sides. Freeze until required.
3. Prepare the filling: place all its ingredients in a food processor, and pulse for 2 minutes until smooth.
4. Pour the filling into the prepared pan. Smooth the top, and freeze for 3 hours until set.
5. Cut pie into slices and then serve.

Nutrition: Calories: 310; Fat: 9 g; Carbs: 45 g; Proteins: 4 g; Fiber: 2 g.

Chocolate Mint Grasshopper Pie

Preparation Time: 4 hours
Cooking time: 15 minutes
Servings: 4
Ingredients:
For the Crust:

- 1 cup dates, soaked in warm water for 10 minutes in water, drained
- 1/8 teaspoons salt
- 1/2 cup pecans
- 1 teaspoons cinnamon
- 1/2 cup walnuts

For the Filling:

- ½ cup mint leaves
- 2 cups of cashews, soaked in warm water for 10 minutes in water, drained
- 2 tablespoons coconut oil
- 1/4 cup and 2 tablespoons of agave
- 1/4 teaspoons spirulina
- 1/4 cup water

Directions:

1. Prepare the crust: place all its ingredients in a food processor and pulse for 3 to 5 minutes until the thick paste comes together.
2. Take a 6-inch springform pan and grease it with oil. Place crust mixture in it, spread and press the mixture evenly in the bottom and along the sides. Freeze until required.
3. Prepare the filling: place all its ingredients in a food processor, and pulse for 2 minutes until smooth.
4. Pour the filling into the prepared pan, smooth the top, and freeze for 4 hours until set.
5. Cut pie into slices and then serve.

Nutrition: Calories: 340; Fat: 9 g; Carbs: 45 g; Proteins: 4 g; Fiber: 3 g.

Chocolate Raspberry Brownies

Preparation Time: 15 minutes + 8 hours
Cooking time: 15 minutes **Servings:** 4
Ingredients:
For the Chocolate Brownie Base:

- 12 Medjool Dates, pitted
- 3/4 cup oat flour
- 3/4 cup almond meal
- 3 tablespoons cacao
- 1 teaspoon vanilla extract, unsweetened
- 1/8 teaspoon sea salt
- 3 tablespoons water
- 1/2 cup pecans, chopped

For the Raspberry Cheesecake:

- 3/4 cup cashews, soaked, drained
- 6 tablespoons agave nectar
- 1/2 cup raspberries

- 1 teaspoon vanilla extract, unsweetened
- 1 lemon, juiced
- 6 tablespoons liquid coconut oil

For the Chocolate Coating:
- 2 1/2 tablespoons cacao powder
- 3 3/4 tablespoons coconut Oil
- 2 tablespoons maple syrup
- 1/8 teaspoon sea salt

Directions:
1. Prepare the crust: place all its ingredients in a food processor and pulse for 3 to 5 minutes until the thick paste comes together.
2. Take a 6-inch springform pan and grease it with oil. Place crust mixture in it, spread and press the mixture evenly in the bottom and along the sides. Freeze until required.
3. Prepare the cheesecake topping: place all its ingredients in a food processor and pulse for 2 minutes until smooth.
4. Pour the filling into the prepared pan. Smooth the top, and freeze for 8 hours until solid.
5. Prepare the chocolate coating: whisk together all its ingredients until smooth, drizzle on top of the cake and then serve.

Nutritional: Calories: 340; Fat: 7 g; Carbs: 50 g; Proteins: 4 g; Fiber: 4 g.

Banana Shake Bowls

Preparation Time: 5 minutes
Cooking Time: 0 minutes
Servings: 4
Ingredients:
- 4 medium bananas, peeled
- 1 avocado, peeled, pitted and mashed
- ¾ cup almond milk
- ½ teaspoon vanilla extract

Directions:
1. In a blender, combine the bananas with the avocado and the other ingredients. Pulse, divide into bowls and keep in the fridge until serving.

Nutrition: Calories: 185; Fat: 4.3 g; Fiber: 4 g; Carbs: 6 g; Protein 6.45 g.

Cold Lemon Squares

Preparation Time: 30 minutes
Cooking Time: 0 minutes
Servings: 4
Ingredients:
- 1 cup avocado oil+ a drizzle
- 2 bananas, peeled and chopped
- 1 tablespoon honey ¼ cup lemon juice
- A pinch of lemon zest, grated

Directions:
1. In your food processor, mix the bananas with the rest of the ingredients. Pulse well and spread on the bottom of a pan greased with a drizzle of oil.

2. Introduce in the fridge for 30 minutes, slice into squares and serve.

Nutrition: Calories: 136; Fat: 11.2 g; Fiber: 0.2 g; Carbs: 7 g; Proteins: 1.1 g.

Blackberry and Apples Cobbler

Preparation Time: 10 minutes
Cooking Time: 30 minutes
Servings: 6
Ingredients:
- ¾ cup stevia
- 6 cups blackberries
- ¼ cup apples, cored and cubed
- ¼ teaspoon baking powder
- 1 tablespoon lime juice
- ½ cup almond flour
- ½ cup water
- 3 and ½ tablespoon avocado oil
- Cooking spray

Directions:
1. In a bowl, mix the berries with half of the stevia and lemon juice. Sprinkle some flour all over, whisk and pour into a baking dish greased with cooking spray.
2. In another bowl, mix flour with the rest of the sugar, baking powder, water and oil. Stir the whole mixture with your hands.
3. Spread over the berries, introduce in the oven at 375° F, and bake for 30 minutes. Serve warm.

Nutrition: Calories: 221; Fat: 6.3 g; Fiber: 3.3 g; Carbs: 6 g; Proteins: 9 g.

Black Tea Cake

Preparation Time: 10 minutes
Cooking Time: 35 minutes
Servings: 8
Ingredients:
- 6 tablespoons black tea powder
- 2 cups almond milk, warmed up
- 1 cup avocado oil
- 2 cups stevia
- 4 eggs
- 2 teaspoons vanilla extract
- 3 and ½ cups almond flour
- 1 teaspoon baking soda
- 3 teaspoons baking powder

Directions:
1. In a bowl, combine the almond milk with the oil, stevia and the rest of the ingredients. Whisk well.

2. Pour this into a cake pan lined with parchment paper. Introduce it in the oven at 350° F and bake for 35 minutes.
3. Leave the cake to cool down, slice, and serve.

Nutrition: Calories: 200; Fat: 6.4 g; Fiber: 4 g; Carbs: 6.5 g; Proteins: 5.4 g.

Green Tea and Vanilla Cream

Preparation Time: 2 hours
Cooking Time: 0 minutes
Servings: 4
Ingredients:
- 14 ounces almond milk, hot
- 2 tablespoons green tea powder
- 14 ounces heavy cream
- 3 tablespoons stevia
- 1 teaspoon vanilla extract
- 1 teaspoon gelatin powder

Directions:
1. In a bowl, combine the almond milk with the green tea powder and the rest of the ingredients. Whisk well, cool down and divide into cups. Keep in the fridge for 2 hours before serving.

Nutrition: Calories: 120; Fat: 3 g; Fiber: 3 g; Carbs: 7 g; Proteins: 4 g.

Figs Pie

Preparation Time: 10 minutes
Cooking Time: 1 hour
Servings: 8
Ingredients:
- ½ cup stevia
- 6 figs, cut into quarters
- ½ teaspoon vanilla extract
- 1 cup almond flour
- 4 eggs, whisked

Directions:
1. Spread the figs on the bottom of a springform pan lined with parchment paper.
2. In a bowl, combine the other ingredients, whisk and pour over the figs.
3. Bake at 375 digress F for 1 hour. Flip the pie upside down when it's done and serve.

Nutrition: Calories: 200; Fat: 4.4 g; Fiber: 3 g; Carbs: 7.6 g; Proteins: 8 g.

Cherry Cream

Preparation Time: 2 hours
Cooking Time: 0 minutes
Servings: 4
Ingredients:
- 2 cups cherries, pitted and chopped
- 1 cup almond milk
- ½ cup whipping cream

- 3 eggs, whisked
- 1/3 cup stevia
- 1 teaspoon lemon juice
- ½ teaspoon vanilla extract

Directions:
1. In your food processor, combine the cherries with the milk and the rest of the ingredients. Pulse well; divide into cups and keep in the fridge for 2 hours before serving.

Nutrition: Calories: 200; Fat: 4.5 g; Fiber: 3.3 g; Carbs: 5.6 g; Proteins: 3.4 g.

Strawberries Cream

Preparation Time: 10 minutes
Cooking Time: 20 minutes
Servings: 4
Ingredients:
- ½ cup stevia
- 2 pounds strawberries, chopped
- 1 cup almond milk
- Zest of 1 lemon, grated
- ½ cup heavy cream
- 3 egg yolks, whisked

Directions:
1. Heat up a pan with the milk over medium-high heat. Add the stevia and the rest of the ingredients.
2. Whisk well and simmer for 20 minutes.
3. Divide into cups and serve cold.

Nutrition: Calories: 152; Fat: 4.4 g; Fiber: 5.5 g; Carbs: 5.1 g; Proteins: 0.8 g.

Apples and Plum Cake

Preparation Time: 10 minutes
Cooking Time: 40 minutes
Servings: 4
Ingredients:
- 7 ounces almond flour
- 1 egg, whisked
- 5 tablespoons stevia
- 3 ounces warm almond milk
- 2 pounds plums, pitted and cut into quarters
- 2 apples, cored and chopped
- Zest of 1 lemon, grated
- 1 teaspoon baking powder

Directions:
1. In a bowl, mix the almond milk with the egg, stevia, and the rest of the ingredients. Whisk well.
2. Grease a cake pan with the oil and pour the cake mix inside. Introduce it in the oven and bake at 350° F for 40 minutes.
3. Cool down, slice and serve.

Nutrition: Calories: 209; Fat: 6.4 g; Fiber: 6 g; Carbs: 8 g; Proteins: 6.6 g.

Cinnamon Chickpeas Cookies

Preparation Time: 10 minutes
Cooking Time: 20 minutes **Servings:** 12
Ingredients:

- 1 cup canned chickpeas, drained, rinsed and mashed
- 2 cups almond flour
- 1 teaspoon cinnamon powder
- 1 teaspoon baking powder
- 1 cup avocado oil
- ½ cup stevia
- 1 egg, whisked
- 2 teaspoons almond extract
- 1 cup raisins
- 1 cup coconut, unsweetened and shredded

Directions:

1. In a bowl, combine the chickpeas with the flour, cinnamon and the other ingredients. Whisk well until you obtain a dough.
2. Scoop tablespoons of dough on a baking sheet lined with parchment paper. Introduce them in the oven at 350° F and bake for 20 minutes.
3. Leave them to cool down for a few minutes and serve.

Nutrition: Calories: 200; Fat: 4.5 g; Fiber: 3.4 g; Carbs: 9.5 g; Proteins: 2.4 g.

CHAPTER 21:

RAW RECIPES

Raw Collard Wraps

Preparation Time: 15 minutes.
Cooking Time: 0 minutes. **Servings:** 3
Ingredients:

- 4 large collard leaves
- 1 red bell pepper, julienned
- 1 avocado
- 3 ounces alfalfa sprouts
- ½ lime, juiced
- 1 cup raw pecans, chopped
- 1 tablespoon tamari
- ½ teaspoon garlic, minced
- ½ teaspoon ginger, grated
- 1 teaspoon olive oil

Directions:

1. Soak the leaves in warm water for 10 minutes, then drain.
2. Puree cumin with olive oil, tamari and pecans in a blender.
3. Spread the collard leaf on the working surface and top them with the pecan's mixture.
4. Divide the avocado slices, red pepper slices and alfalfa sprouts on top.
5. Drizzle the lime juice on top and roll the leaves.
6. Cut the roll in half and serve.

Serving Suggestion: Serve the wraps with vegan spinach dip.
Variation Tip: Add grilled tofu to the wraps.
Nutrition: Calories: 332; Fat: 10 g; Sodium: 994 mg; Carbs: 21 g; Fiber: 0.4 g; Sugar: 3 g; Proteins: 8 g.

Avocado Chickpea Lettuce Cups

Preparation Time: 10 minutes.
Cooking Time: 0 minutes.
Servings: 6
Ingredients:

- 1 tablespoon Dijon mustard
- 1 tablespoon shallots, minced
- 1 lime, juiced
- 2 tablespoons fresh cilantro, chopped
- 1 tablespoon apple cider vinegar
- 2½ tablespoons olive oil
- 1 can chickpeas, drained
- 8 ounces jarred hearts of palm, drained
- ½ cup fresh cucumber, diced

- 2 small avocados, peeled, seeded and diced
- 4 handfuls of mixed greens
- Salt and black pepper to taste

Directions:

1. Mix shallots with apple cider vinegar, cilantro, lime zest and juice in a bowl.
2. Stir in oil, black pepper and salt; then mix well.
3. Add cucumber, the heart of palm and chickpeas; mix well.
4. Fold in avocados and greens; then mix again.
5. Serve.

Serving Suggestion: Serve the lettuce cups with mashed cauliflower.
Variation Tip: Add crumbled tofu to the filling.
Nutrition: Calories: 285; Fat: 8 g; Sodium: 146 mg; Carbs: 35 g; Fiber: 0.1 g; Sugar: 0.4 g; Proteins: 1 g.

Watermelon Salad

Preparation Time: 10 minutes
Cooking Time: 0 minutes
Servings: 2
Ingredients:

- ½ teaspoon agave nectar
- 2 tablespoons lemon juice
- 1 tablespoon extra-virgin olive oil
- 1 jalapeno, seeded and chopped
- 12 ounces watermelon, chopped
- 1 red onion, thinly sliced
- ½ cup chopped basil leaves
- 2 cups baby arugula

Directions:

1. In a bowl, toss together the watermelon with the jalapeno, onion, basil, arugula, oil, agave nectar, lemon juice and oil.
2. Serve for breakfast.

Nutrition: Calories: 128; Fat: 8 g; Fiber: 2 g; Carbs: 16 g; Proteins: 2 g.

Chickpea Salad

Preparation Time: 10 minutes
Cooking Time: 0 minutes
Servings: 6
Ingredients:

- 3 cups cooked garbanzo beans
- 1 red bell pepper, diced

- 1 yellow bell pepper, diced
- 1 cup vine tomatoes, chopped
- 1 cup cucumber, chopped
- 5 scallions, sliced
- 1 cup fresh mint, chopped
- 1 cup Italian parsley, chopped
- 1 garlic clove, minced
- Salt and black pepper, to taste
- ½ cup olive oil
- Zest of 1 lemon
- ¼ cup lemon juice
- 1 teaspoon sumac
- ½ teaspoon cayenne chili flakes

Directions:
1. Mix beans with bell pepper, cucumber and the rest of the ingredients in a salad bowl.
2. Serve.

Serving Suggestion: Serve the salad with cauliflower fried rice.
Variation Tip: Add crushed nuts or corns to the salad.
Nutrition: Calories: 240; Fat: 14 g; Sodium: 220 mg; Carbs: 12 g; Fiber: 0.2 g; Sugar: 1 g; Proteins: 7 g.

Cabbage Mango Slaw

Preparation Time: 10 minutes
Cooking Time: 0 minutes
Servings: 6
Ingredients:

- 3 cups cabbage, shredded
- 1 large mango, pitted and cubed
- ½ cup cilantro, chopped
- ¼ cup red onion, diced
- 1 jalapeño, chopped
- 2 teaspoons olive oil
- 1 orange, zest and juice
- 1 lime juice - ½ teaspoon salt

Directions:
1. Mix shredded cabbage with mango and the rest of the ingredients in a salad bowl.
2. Serve.

Serving Suggestion: Serve the salad with grilled tofu steaks.
Variation Tip: Add crushed nuts to the salad.
Nutrition: Calories: 280; Fat: 8 g; Sodium: 339 mg; Carbs: 26 g; Fiber: 1 g; Sugar: 2 g; Proteins: 2 g.

Quinoa Crunch Salad

Preparation Time: 10 minutes
Cooking Time: 0 minutes **Servings:** 6
Ingredients:

- 4 cups cooked quinoa
- 1 cup pomegranate seeds
- 4 scallions, chopped
- 1 cup Italian parsley, chopped
- ½ cup toasted almonds, sliced
- ½ orange, zest and juice
- 1/3 cup olive oil

- ½ teaspoon salt
- ¼ teaspoon cracked black pepper
- ¼ teaspoon cinnamon
- ¼ teaspoon allspice
- 2 apples, sliced

Preparation:
1. Mix quinoa with scallions, almonds and the rest of the ingredients in a salad bowl.
2. Serve fresh.

Serving Suggestion: Serve the salad with tomato soup
Variation Tip: Add chopped berries to the salad.
Nutritional Information Per Servings: Calories: 261; Fat: 16 g; Sodium: 189 mg; Carbs: 23 g; Fiber: 0.3 g; Sugar: 18.2 g; Proteins: 3.3 g.

Fennel Salad with Cucumber

Preparation Time: 15 minutes
Cooking Time: 0 minutes **Servings:** 6
Ingredients:

- 2 fennel bulbs, cored and sliced
- 3 Persian cucumbers
- ½ cup fresh dill, chopped
- ¼ cup white onion, sliced
- 1/3 cup olive oil
- 3 tablespoons lemon juice
- Salt to taste
- Black pepper to taste

Directions:
1. Mix fennel with the rest of the ingredients in a salad bowl.
2. Cover and refrigerate this salad for 15 minutes.
3. Serve

Serving Suggestion: Serve the salad with white bean soup.
Variation Tip: Add crushed nuts or chopped cranberries to the salad.
Nutritional Information Per Servings: Calories: 205; Fat: 20 g; Sodium: 941 mg; Carbs: 6.1 g; Fiber: 0.9 g; Sugar: 0.9 g; Proteins: 5.2 g.

Kohlrabi Slaw with Cilantro

Preparation Time: 10 minutes
Cooking Time: 0 minutes
Servings: 6
Ingredients:

- 6 cups kohlrabi, cut into matchsticks
- ½ cup cilantro, chopped
- ½ jalapeño, minced
- ¼ cup scallion, chopped
- Zest from 1 orange
- Juice from 1 orange
- Zest and juice from 1 lime
- Citrus Dressing:
- ¼ cup olive oil
- ¼ cup orange juice
- 1/8 cup lime juice
- ¼ cup honey

- ½ teaspoon kosher salt
- 1 tablespoon rice wine vinegar

Directions:
1. Mix all the citrus dressing ingredients in a salad bowl.
2. Toss in kohlrabi and the rest of the ingredients; then mix well.
3. Serve.

Serving Suggestion: Serve the salad with cauliflower soup.

Variation Tip: Add crushed nuts or chopped berries to the salad.

Nutrition: Calories: 334; Fat: 16 g; Sodium: 462 mg; Carbs: 3 g; Fiber: 0.4 g; Sugar: 3 g; Proteins: 3.3 g.

Pumpkin Spice Granola Bites

Preparation Time: 2 hours
Cooking Time: 0 minutes
Servings:
Ingredients:
- .50 teaspoon Pumpkin Pie Spice
- .75 cup Old-fashioned Rolled Oats
- 15 Medjool dates
- .33 cup pumpkin puree
- .50 cup granola

Directions:
1. To start, place the oats into a food processor and process until it becomes flour. Once this is done, you should add in the spice, pumpkin, and dates. Puree everything again until you get a dough.
2. From this dough, use your hands to take small bits and roll them into ten balls.
3. Place the balls into the fridge for two hours and allow to firm up.
4. Finally, roll the balls in your favorite granola and then enjoy.

Nutrition: Calories: 100; Proteins: 10 g; Carbs: 25 g; Fat: 10 g.

Grapes, Avocado and Spinach Salad

Preparation Time: 10 minutes
Cooking Time: 0 minutes
Servings: 4
Ingredients:
- 1 cup green grapes, halved
- 2 cups baby spinach
- 1 avocado, pitted, peeled and cubed
- Salt and black pepper to the taste
- 2 tablespoons olive oil
- 1 tablespoon thyme, chopped
- 1 tablespoon rosemary, chopped
- 1 tablespoon lime juice
- 1 garlic clove, minced

Directions:
1. In a salad bowl, combine the grapes with the spinach and the other ingredients, toss, and serve for lunch.

Nutrition: Calories: 190; Fat: 17.1 g; Fiber: 4.6 g; Carbs: 10.9 g, Proteins: 1.7 g.

Arugula and Artichokes Bowls

Preparation Time: 5 minutes
Cooking Time: 0 minutes
Servings: 4
Ingredients:
- 2 cups baby arugula
- ¼ cup walnuts, chopped
- 1 cup canned artichoke hearts, drained and quartered
- 1 tablespoon balsamic vinegar
- 2 tablespoons cilantro, chopped
- 2 tablespoons olive oil
- Salt and black pepper to the taste
- 1 tablespoon lemon juice

Directions:
1. In a bowl, combine the artichokes with the arugula, walnuts and the other ingredients. Toss, divide into smaller bowls and serve for lunch.

Nutrition: Calories: 200; Fat: 2 g; Fiber: 1 g; Carbs: 5 g; Proteins: 7 g.

Spicy Southwestern Hummus Wraps

Preparation Time: 15 minutes
Cooking Time: 0 minutes **Servings:** 1
Ingredients:
- 1 whole-wheat wrap
- 1 cup lettuce, shredded
- 1 tablespoon tomato, diced
- 4 tablespoons hummus
- 2 tablespoons avocado, diced
- 2 tablespoons corn
- 2 tablespoons black beans

Directions:
1. For a quick lunch, simply lay out your wrap and spread the hummus over the surface.
2. Once the hummus is in place, layer the rest of the ingredients and then roll the wrap up before eating.

Nutrition: Calories: 400; Proteins: 15 g; Carbs: 50 g; Fat: 15 g.

Almond Chia Pudding

Preparation Time: 10 minutes
Cooking Time: 0 minutes
Servings: 2
Ingredients:
- 3 tablespoons almond butter
- 2 tablespoons maple syrup
- 1 cup almond milk
- ¼ cup plus 1 tablespoon chia seeds

Directions:
1. In a sealable container, add everything and mix well.
2. Seal the container and refrigerate overnight.
3. Serve with a splash of almond milk.

Nutrition: Calories: 212; Total Fat: 11.8 g; Saturated Fat: 2.2 g; Cholesterol: 23 mg; Sodium: 321 mg; Total Carbs: 14.6 g; Fibers 4.4 g; Sugar: 8 g; Proteins: 7.3 g.

Creaseless

Preparation Time: 5 minutes.
Cooking Time: 0 minutes.
Servings: 5
Ingredients:

- 3 tablespoons agave syrup
- 1 cup coconut milk, unsweetened
- ½ teaspoon vanilla extract, unsweetened
- 1 cup of orange juice

Directions:

1. Place all the ingredients in a food processor or blender and then pulse until combined.
2. Pour the mixture into five molds of Popsicle pan, insert a stick into each mold and then let it freeze for a minimum of 4 hours until hard.
3. Serve when ready.

Nutrition: Calories: 152; Fat: 10 g; Proteins: 1 g; Carbs: 16 g; Fiber: 1 g.

Peanut Butter, Nut and Fruit Cookies

Preparation Time: 30 minutes.
Cooking Time: 0 minutes.
Servings: 25
Ingredients:

- ¾ cup rolled oats
- ¼ cup chopped peanuts
- ½ cup coconut flakes, unsweetened
- ¼ cup and 2 tablespoons chopped cranberries, dried
- ¼ cup sliced almonds
- ¼ cup and 2 tablespoons raisins
- ¼ cup maple syrup
- ¾ cup peanut butter

Directions:

1. Take a baking sheet, line it with wax paper and then set it aside until required.
2. Take a large bowl, place oats, peanuts, almonds and coconut flakes in it, add ¼ cup of each of cranberries and raisins, and then stir until combined.
3. Add maple syrup and peanut butter, stir until well combined and then scoop the mixture on the prepared baking sheet with some distance between them.
4. Flatten each scoop of cookie mixture slightly, press the remaining cranberries and raisins into each cookie and then let it chill for 20 minutes until firm.
5. Serve straight away.

Nutrition: Calories: 140; Fat: 7 g; Proteins: 3 g; Carbs: 18 g; Fiber: 5 g.

CHAPTER 22:

ETHNIC RECIPES

Spinach and Mushroom Soup
Preparation Time: 5 minutes
Cooking Time: 15 minutes
Servings: 4-5
Ingredients:
- 1 small onion, finely cut
- 1 small carrot, chopped
- 1 small zucchini, peeled and diced
- 1 medium potato, peeled and diced
- 6-7 white button mushrooms, chopped
- 2 cups chopped fresh spinach
- 4 cups vegetable broth or water
- 4 tablespoons olive oil

Directions:
1. Heat olive oil in a large soup pot over medium heat. Add in potato, onion and mushroom and cook until vegetables are soft but not mushy.
2. Add chopped fresh spinach, zucchini and vegetable broth and simmer for about 15 minutes.

Nutrition: Calories: 200; Fat: 9 g; Carbs: 25 g; Proteins: 10 g; Fiber: 12 g.

Beetroot and Carrot Soup
Preparation Time: 5 minutes
Cooking Time: 20 minutes
Servings: 5-6
Ingredients:
- 4 beets, washed and peeled
- 2 carrots, peeled, chopped
- 2 potatoes, peeled, chopped
- 1 small onion, chopped
- 2 cups vegetable broth
- 2 cups water
- 3 tablespoons olive oil
- 1 cup finely cut green onions, to serve

Directions:
1. Heat olive oil in a deep saucepan over medium-high heat. Sauté the onion and carrot until tender. Add in beets, potatoes, broth and water.
2. Set aside to cool, then blend in batches until smooth.
3. Return soup to saucepan and cook, stirring, for 4-5 minutes, or until heated through. Season with salt and pepper and serve sprinkled with green onions.

Nutrition: Calories: 210; Fat: 6 g; Carbs: 25 g; Proteins: 8 g; Fiber: 10 g.

Creamy Potato Soup
Preparation Time: 5 minutes
Cooking Time: 15 minutes
Servings: 6-7
Ingredients:
- 4-5 medium potatoes, peeled and diced
- 2 carrots, chopped
- 1 zucchini, chopped
- 1 celery rib, chopped
- 5 cups water
- 3 tablespoons olive oil
- ½ tsp dried rosemary
- Salt and black pepper, to taste
- 1/2 cup fresh parsley, finely cut

Directions:
1. In a deep soup pot, heat olive oil over medium heat and sauté the vegetables and rosemary for 2-3 minutes. Add in 4 cups of water and bring the soup to a boil; then lower heat and simmer until all the vegetables are tender.
2. Blend soup in a blender until smooth. Serve warm, seasoned with black pepper and fresh parsley sprinkled over each serving.

Nutrition: Calories: 260; Fat: 8 g; Carbs: 35 g; Proteins: 9 g; Fiber: 9 g.

Spinach, Leek and Quinoa Soup
Preparation Time: 5 minutes
Cooking Time: 25 minutes
Servings: 4-5
Ingredients:
- ½ cup quinoa, very well washed
- 2 leeks halved lengthwise and sliced
- 1 onion, chopped
- 2 garlic cloves, chopped
- 1 can diced tomatoes (15 oz), undrained
- 2 cups fresh spinach, cut
- 4 cups vegetable broth
- 2 tablespoons olive oil
- Salt and pepper, to taste

Directions:

1. Heat olive oil in a large soup pot over medium heat and sauté onion for 2 minutes, stirring.
2. Add in leeks and cook for another 2-3 minutes. Stir in garlic, salt and black pepper to taste.
3. Add the vegetable broth, canned tomatoes and quinoa.

Nutrition: Calories: 310; Fat: 5 g; Carbs: 26 g; Proteins: 9 g; Fiber: 15 g.

Grilled Eggplant Roll-Ups

Preparation Time: 5 minutes
Cooking Time: 8 minutes
Servings: 8
Ingredients:

- 2 tablespoons olive oil
- 2 tablespoons basil, fresh, chopped
- 1 1/2 onion, sliced paper-thin
- 1 1/2 bell pepper, sliced paper-thin
- 1 large tomato
- 1 medium eggplant

Directions:

1. After cutting off both of the ends of the eggplant, slice it into strips, about a quarter-inch thick. Slice the onion, bell pepper, and tomato very thinly and set to the side.
2. Brush the olive oil onto the slices of eggplant and grill them in a skillet for three minutes on each side. When both sides are grilled, lay the slices of eggplant on a plate and lay a slice each of tomato, onion, and bell pepper on each zucchini slice.
3. Sprinkle all with the black pepper and the basil.
4. Carefully roll each slice as far as it will roll.

Nutrition: Calories: 180; Fat: 3 g; Carbs: 28 g; Proteins: 4 g; Fiber: 12 g.

Veggie Stuffed Peppers

Preparation Time: 30 minutes
Cooking Time: 30 minutes
Servings: 6
Ingredients:

- 2 tablespoons balsamic vinegar
- 1/4 cup parsley, fresh, chopped
- 1 bunch scallions, cleaned and sliced
- 1 half cucumber, peeled and diced
- 4 stalks celery, washed and diced
- 1 cup cherry tomatoes cut in quarters
- 3 green bell peppers, cleaned and cut in half across the middle
- 1/2 teaspoon salt
- 3 tablespoons Dijon mustard
- 1 teaspoon black pepper

Directions:

1. In one bowl, mix together the mustard, rice wine vinegar, salt, and pepper.
2. Add in the tomatoes, cucumbers, scallions, and celery and mix gently but well. Use a spoon to stuff this mix into the pepper halves.

Nutrition: Calories: 200; Fat: 6 g; Carbs: 15 g; Proteins: 6 g; Fiber: 18 g.

Sprout Wraps

Preparation Time: 15 minutes
Cooking Time: 0 minutes
Servings: 2
Ingredients:

- 2 large tortillas, whole-wheat
- 1/2 cup parsley, chopped
- 2 stalks onion, green
- 1 teaspoon black pepper
- 1 sliced thin cucumber
- 1 cup bean sprouts
- 1/2 teaspoon salt
- 1 tablespoon lemon juice
- 1 tablespoon olive oil

Directions:

1. Lay out each of the tortilla wraps on a plate. Divide all of the ingredients evenly between the two tortillas, leaving about two inches on either side to roll the tortilla up.
2. When you have added all of the ingredients on the tortilla, then fold in the sides and roll the tortilla up into a cylinder shape.

Nutrition: Calories: 220; Fat: 3 g; Carbs: 20 g; Proteins: 9 g; Fiber: 15 g.

Collard Wraps

Preparation Time: 20 minutes
Cooking Time: 0 minutes
Servings: 4
Ingredients:
For the Wrap:

- 4 cherry tomatoes, cut in half
- 1 quarter cup black olives, sliced
- 1/2 cup purple onion, diced fine
- 1/2 red bell pepper, cut in julienne strips
- 1 medium-sized cucumber, cut in julienne strips
- 4 large green collard leaves

For the Sauce:

- 1 teaspoon black pepper
- 1/2 teaspoon salt
- 2 tablespoons dill, fresh, minced
- 1/4 cup cucumber, seeded and grated
- 2 tablespoons olive oil
- 1 tablespoon white vinegar
- 1 teaspoon garlic powder

Directions:

1. Place all of the ingredients on the list for the sauce in a mixing bowl and mix well. Store the dressing in the refrigerator. Wash off the collard leaves and dry them; then cut off the stem from each leaf. Cover each leaf with two tablespoons of the sauce you just made.

2. In the middle of the collard leaf, layer all of the other ingredients. Fold the leaf up like a burrito by first folding the ends in and then rolling the leaf until it is all rolled. Cut into slices and serve with more dressing for dipping.

Nutrition: Calories: 170; Fat: 3 g; Carbs: 18 g; Proteins: 6 g; Fiber: 18 g.

Grape Tomatoes and Spiral Zucchini

Preparation Time: 5 minutes
Cooking Time: 10 minutes
Servings: 2
Ingredients:

- 1 large zucchini, cut in spirals
- 1 tablespoon basil, fresh, chopped
- 1 teaspoon black pepper
- 1 teaspoon rosemary
- 1/2 teaspoon salt
- 1 tablespoon lemon juice
- 1/4 teaspoon crushed red pepper flakes
- 1 cup grape tomatoes, cut in half
- 2 tablespoons garlic, minced
- 1 tablespoon olive oil

Directions:

1. Fry the minced garlic in olive oil for one minute. Pour in the pepper, salt, red pepper flakes, and tomatoes. Mix well; then turn the heat lower.
2. Simmer this mix for fifteen minutes.
3. Add in the basil, rosemary, and zucchini spiral noodles. Turn the heat back up, and cook for two minutes, stirring constantly.
4. Drizzle the lemon juice over all of it and serve.

Nutrition: Calories: 330; Fat: 14 g; Carbs: 25 g; Proteins: 4 g; Fiber: 10 g.

Cauliflower Fried Rice

Preparation Time: 5 minutes
Cooking Time: 10 minutes
Servings: 4
Ingredients:

- 12 ounces riced cauliflower, frozen or fresh
- 1 tablespoon sesame oil
- 2 tablespoons soy sauce
- 1/4 cup carrot, chopped fine
- Tofu, firm, cut into crumbles
- 2 tablespoons garlic, minced
- 1/4 cup green onion

Directions:

1. Cook the carrots and the riced cauliflower in the sesame oil for about five minutes, stirring sometimes.
2. Stir in this mix the chopped green onion and the garlic and cook for one minute.
3. Add the tofu to the rice mix and stir for about two to three minutes.
4. Just before serving, mix in the soy sauce.

Nutrition: Calories: 430; Fat: 12 g; Carbs: 50 g; Proteins: 6 g; Fiber: 18 g.

Mediterranean Style Pasta

Preparation Time: 10 minutes
Cooking Time: 15 minutes
Servings: 4
Ingredients:

- 12 ounces whole-wheat pasta, cooked
- 1/4 cup nutritional yeast
- 10 kalamata olives, cut in half
- 2 tablespoons parsley, chopped
- 2 tablespoons capers
- 1/2 cup tomatoes, diced
- 1 half teaspoon salt
- 1 teaspoon black pepper
- 2 tablespoons garlic, minced
- 2 tablespoons olive oil
- 1 cup spinach, packed

Directions:

1. Fry together in the olive oil, salt, spinach, and pepper for ten minutes until the spinach wilts.
2. Add in the capers, parsley, olives, and tomatoes. Mix well, cooking for another five minutes.
3. Blend in the whole-wheat pasta. Sprinkle on the nutritional yeast, and serve immediately.

Nutrition: Calories: 410; Fat: 9 g; Carbs: 45 g; Proteins: 8 g; Fiber: 8 g.

Squash and Sweet Potato Patties

Preparation Time: 15 minutes
Cooking Time: 10 minutes
Servings: 2
Ingredients:

- 2 tablespoons olive oil
- 1/2 teaspoon salt
- 1 teaspoon black pepper
- 1 quarter teaspoon parsley, dried
- 1/4 teaspoon cumin, ground
- 1/2 teaspoon garlic powder
- 2 cups sweet potato, cooked and mashed
- 1 cup squash, shredded

Directions:

1. Mix the sweet potato and squash in a mixing bowl. Add in all of the spices and mix these ingredients well.
2. Heat the oil in a skillet and separate the mix into four equal portions. Drop the portions into the oil and flatten slightly with a fork.
3. Fry each of the patties for five minutes on each side and serve.

Nutrition: Calories: 80; Fat: 3 g; Carbs: 12 g; Proteins: 2 g; Fiber: 5 g.

Stuffed Artichokes

Preparation Time: 40 minutes

Cooking Time: 30 minutes
Servings: 6
Ingredients:

- 3 artichokes
- 1/2 teaspoon celery salt
- 1/2 cup mushroom, chopped
- 1/2 teaspoon salt
- 1 teaspoon black pepper
- 2 tablespoons onion, minced
- 2 tablespoons lemon juice
- 2 tablespoon parsley, chopped

Directions:

1. Heat oven to 375º F. Tear off and discard the outside leaves of the artichokes.
2. Cut the inside of the artichokes in half across the middle. Drop the halves into already boiling water and cook them for twenty minutes.
3. Mix together the seasonings, onions, mushrooms, lemon juice, chili sauce, and parsley. Spoon this mixture into the boiled artichoke hearts. Place the filled hearts into a baking pan and bake for thirty minutes.

Nutrition: Calories: 230; Fat: 4 g; Carbs: 20 g; Proteins: 9 g; Fiber: 16 g.

Lima Bean Casserole

Preparation Time: 15 minutes
Cooking Time: 30 minutes
Servings: 5
Ingredients:

- 2 cups lima beans, canned
- 2 teaspoons lemon juice
- 1/2 teaspoon thyme
- 1 teaspoon black pepper
- 1/2 cup nutritional yeast
- 2 tablespoons olive oil
- 2 teaspoons dry mustard
- 1/2 teaspoon salt
- 2 teaspoon cumin

Directions:

1. Heat oven to 375º F.
2. Drain the beans and save the liquid. Dump the drained beans into an 8x8 inch baking pan.
3. Add the olive oil with the bean liquid to a skillet and heat until warm.
4. Add the pepper, salt, cumin, thyme, dry mustard, and lemon juice and stir together well.
5. Pour this mix over the beans in the baking pan and cover with the nutritional yeast.
6. Bake for thirty minutes.

Nutrition: Calories: 290; Fat: 9 g; Carbs: 34 g; Proteins: 18 g; Fiber: 12 g.

Corn and Okra Casserole

Preparation Time: 20 minutes
Cooking Time: 30 minutes **Servings:** 6
Ingredients:

- 1 pound okra
- 1 clove garlic, sliced
- 1 tablespoon parsley, chopped
- 3 tablespoons olive oil
- 2 large tomatoes, diced
- 1 green bell pepper, cleaned and sliced
- 1 can corn, whole kernel
- 1 small onion, sliced

Directions:

1. Heat oven to 375º F.
2. Cut the okra into bite-sized chunks.
3. Cook the garlic, onion, okra, and green pepper in the olive oil for ten minutes.
4. Stir in the parsley and the tomatoes and cook for an additional ten minutes.
5. Pour in the corn and dump the entire mixture into a nine by nine-inch baking pan and bake, not covered, for thirty minutes.

Nutrition: Calories: 310; Fat: 9 g; Carbs: 45 g; Proteins: 11 g; Fiber: 14 g.

Cucumber Tomato Toast

Preparation Time: 5 minutes
Cooking Time: 0 minutes
Servings: 1
Ingredients:

- 1 teaspoon balsamic vinegar
- 1/2 teaspoon oregano, dried
- 1/2 cucumber, diced
- 1/2 tomato, diced
- 2 slices whole-grain flatbread
- 1/2 teaspoon salt
- 1/4 teaspoon thyme
- 1/2 teaspoon black pepper
- 1 teaspoon olive oil

Directions:

1. Mix well the pepper, salt, olive oil, oregano, thyme, dill, tomato, and cucumber.
2. Top the flatbread with the mix.
3. Drizzle on vinegar to taste.

Nutrition: Calories: 190; Fat: 9 g; Carbs: 22 g; Proteins: 4 g; Fiber: 8 g.

Pasta Pomodoro with Olives and White Beans

Preparation Time: 30 minutes
Cooking time: 15 minutes **Servings:** 2
Ingredients:

- 4 ounces ziti or rigatoni, whole-wheat
- 1/2 cup nutritional yeast

- 1 15-ounce can cannellini beans, drain and rinse - 1/2 teaspoon black pepper
- 1/4 cup basil, ground
- 2 tablespoons black olives, chopped
- 2 medium-sized tomatoes, diced
- 2 tablespoons garlic, minced
- 1 tablespoon olive oil

Directions:
1. Cook the pasta per the package instructions.
2. Cook the beans and garlic in the hot oil for five minutes.
3. Take the pan from the heat. Add in the olives, pepper, basil, and tomatoes and mix well. Place the pasta on two plates, evenly divided and top with the tomato bean mix.
4. Sprinkle on the nutritional yeast and serve.

Nutrition: Calories: 340; Fat: 8 g; Carbs: 55 g; Proteins: 10 g; Fiber: 12 g.

Bean Bolognese

Preparation Time: 40 minutes
Cooking Time: 20 minutes
Servings: 4
Ingredients:
- 1 14-ounce can white beans, drain and rinse
- 8 ounces fettuccini, whole-wheat
- 1 small onion, chop
- 2 tablespoons olive oil
- 1/4 cup parsley, fresh, chopped, divided
- 1 14-ounce can tomatoes, diced
- 1/2 cup balsamic vinegar
- 1/4 cup celery, chop
- 1/2 cup carrot, chop
- 1 bay leaf
- 2 tablespoons garlic, minced
- 1/2 teaspoon salt

Directions:
1. Cook the pasta per the package directions.
2. Cook carrot, onion, celery, and garlic in the oil for 10 minutes. Add in the bay leaf and salt and stir for 1 minute. Throw away the bay leaf. Pour in the balsamic vinegar and boil for five minutes. Add in the beans, tomatoes, and two tablespoons of the parsley to the skillet and simmer for five minutes, stirring often.
3. Spoon the pasta into four bowls. Top the pasta with the sauce mix from the skillet. Sprinkle on the remainder of the parsley and serve.

Nutrition: Calories: 350; Fat: 9 g; Carbs: 38 g; Proteins: 6 g; Fiber: 12 g.

Fusilli with Tomatoes and Squash

Preparation Time: 25 minutes
Cooking Time: 10 minutes
Servings: 6
Ingredients:
- 12-ounces fusilli pasta
- 2 cups grape tomatoes, sliced in half

- 1/2 teaspoon black pepper
- 1/2 teaspoon rosemary
- 1-pound squash, yellow
- 1 onion, yellow, thin slice
- 1/2 teaspoon salt
- 1 tablespoon thyme, chop
- 2 tablespoons olive oil

Directions:
1. Cook the pasta per the package directions. Cut the neck off the squash.
2. Cut the squash into quarters longwise and slice thin.
3. Cook onion, pepper, squash, thyme, and salt in the hot olive oil for ten minutes, stirring often.
4. Pour in the tomatoes and cook for 5 more minutes.
5. Add in the cooked pasta and mix well.

Nutrition: Calories: 410; Fat: 8 g; Carbs: 45 g; Proteins: 8 g; Fiber: 15 g.

Tofu & Asparagus Stir Fry

Preparation Time: 20 minutes
Cooking Time: 10 minutes
Servings: 3
Ingredients:
- 1 tablespoon ginger, peeled and grated
- 8 ounces firm tofu, chopped into slices
- 4 green onions, sliced thin
- Toasted sesame oil to taste
- 1 bunch asparagus, trimmed and chopped
- 1 handful cashew nuts, chopped and toasted
- 2 tablespoons hoisin sauce
- 1 lime, juiced and zested
- 1 handful mint, fresh and chopped
- 1 handful basil, fresh and chopped
- 3 cloves garlic, chopped
- 3 handfuls spinach, chopped
- Pinch sea salt

Directions:
1. Get out a wok and heat up your oil. Add in your tofu, cooking for a few minutes.
2. Put your tofu to the side, and then sauté your red pepper flakes, ginger, salt, onions and asparagus for a minute.
3. Mix in your spinach, garlic, and cashews, cooking for another two minutes.
4. Add your tofu back in, and then drizzle in your lime juice, lime zest, hoisin sauce, cooking for another half a minute.
5. Remove it from heat, adding in your mint and basil.

Nutrition: Calories: 280; Fat: 8 g; Carbs: 24 g; Proteins: 22 g; Fiber: 14 g.

Cauliflower Steaks

Preparation Time: 10 minutes
Cooking Time: 20/25 minutes
Servings: 4
Ingredients:

- ¼ teaspoon black pepper
- ½ teaspoon sea salt, fine
- 1 tablespoon olive oil
- 1 head cauliflower, large
- ¼ cup creamy hummus
- 2 tablespoons lemon sauce
- ½ cup peanuts, crushed (optional)

Directions:

1. Start by heating your oven to 425° F.
2. Cut your cauliflower stems, and then remove the leaves.
3. Put the cut side down, and then slice half down the middle.
4. Cut into ¾ inch steaks. If you cut them thinner, they could fall apart.
5. Arrange them in a single layer on a baking sheet, drizzling with oil.
6. Season with salt and pepper, and bake for twenty to twenty-five minutes.
7. They should be lightly browned and tender.
8. Spread your hummus on the steaks, drizzling with your lemon sauce.
9. Top with peanuts if you're using it.

Nutrition: Calories: 160; Fat: 5 g; Carbs: 19 g; Proteins: 6 g; Fiber: 20 g.

Tofu Poke

Preparation Time: 30 minutes
Cooking Time: 0 minutes
Servings: 4
Ingredients:

- ¾ cup scallions, sliced thin
- 1 ½ tablespoons mirin
- ¼ cup tamari
- 1 ½ tablespoon dark sesame oil, toasted
- 1 tablespoon sesame seeds, toasted (optional)
- 2 teaspoons ginger, fresh and grated
- ½ teaspoon red pepper, crushed
- 12 ounces extra-firm tofu, drained and cut into ½ inch pieces
- 4 cups zucchini noodles
- 2 tablespoons rice vinegar
- 2 cups carrots, shredded
- 2 cups pea shoots
- ¼ cup basil, fresh and chopped
- ¼ cup peanuts, toasted and chopped (optional)

Directions:

1. Whisk your tamari, mirin, sesame seeds, oil, ginger, red pepper, and scallion greens in a bowl. Set two tablespoons of this sauce aside, and add the tofu to the remaining sauce. Toss to coat.
2. Combine your vinegar and zucchini noodles in a bowl.
3. Divide it between four bowls, topping with tofu, carrots, and a tablespoon of basil and peanuts.
4. Drizzle with sauce before serving.

Nutrition: Calories: 260; Fat: 8 g; Carbs: 25 g; Proteins: 22 g; Fiber: 12 g.

Ratatouille

Preparation Time: 15 minutes
Cooking Time: 1 hour and 15 minutes
Servings: 10
Ingredients:

- 2 tablespoons olive oil
- 2 eggplants, peeled & cubed
- 8 zucchinis, chopped
- 4 tomatoes, chopped
- ¼ cup basil, chopped
- 4 thyme sprigs
- 2 yellow onions, diced
- 3 cloves garlic, minced
- 3 bell peppers, chopped
- 1 bay leaf
- Sea salt to taste

Directions:

1. Salt your eggplant and leave it in a strainer.
2. Heat a teaspoon of oil in a Dutch oven, cooking your onions for ten minutes.
3. Season with salt.
4. Mix your peppers in, cooking for five more minutes. Place this mixture in a bowl.
5. Heat your oil and sauté zucchini, sprinkling with salt. Cook for five minutes, and place it in the same bowl.
6. Rinse your eggplant, squeezing the water out, and heat another two teaspoons of oil in your Dutch oven.
7. Cook your eggplant for ten minutes, placing it in your vegetable bowl.
8. Heat the remaining oil and cook your garlic. Add in your tomatoes, thyme sprigs and bay leaves to deglaze the bottom.
9. Toss your vegetables back in, and then bring it to a simmer.
10. Simmer for forty-five minutes, and make sure to stir. Discard your thyme and bay leaf. Mix in your basil and serve warm.

Nutrition: Calories: 230; Fat: 3 g; Carbs: 26 g; Proteins: 6 g; Fiber: 18 g.

Tomato Gazpacho

Preparation Time: 2 hours
Cooking Time: 0 minutes **Servings:** 6
Ingredients:

- 2 tablespoons + 1 teaspoon red wine vinegar, divided
- ½ teaspoon pepper
- 1 teaspoon sea salt
- 1 avocado
- ¼ cup basil, fresh and chopped
- 3 tablespoons + 2 teaspoons olive oil, divided
- 1 red bell pepper, sliced and seeded
- 1 cucumber, chunked
- 2 ½ lbs. large tomatoes, cored and chopped

Directions:

1. Place half of your cucumber, bell pepper, and ¼ cup of each tomato in a bowl, covering. Set it in the fried.
2. Puree your remaining tomatoes, cucumber and bell pepper with garlic, three tablespoons oil, two tablespoons of vinegar, sea salt and black pepper into a blender, blending until smooth. Transfer it to a bowl, and chill for 2 hours.
3. Chop the avocado, adding it to your chopped vegetables, adding your remaining oil, vinegar, salt, pepper and basil.
4. Ladle your tomato puree mixture into bowls, and serve with chopped vegetables as a salad.

Nutrition: Calories: 310; Fat: 9 g; Carbs: 28 g; Proteins: 8 g; Fiber: 10 g.

Simple Chili

Preparation Time: 10 minutes
Cooking Time: 15/25 minutes
Servings: 4
Ingredients:

- 1 onion, diced
- 1 teaspoon olive oil
- 3 cloves garlic, minced
- 28 ounces tomatoes, canned
- ¼ cup tomato paste
- 14 ounces kidney beans, canned, rinsed and dried
- 2-3 teaspoons chili powder
- ¼ cup cilantro, fresh (or parsley)
- ¼ teaspoon sea salt, fine

Directions:

1. Get out of a pot, and sauté your onion and garlic in your oil at the bottom. Cook for 5 minutes. Add in your tomato paste, tomatoes, beans, and chili powder.
2. Season with salt.
3. Allow it to simmer for ten to twenty minutes.
4. Garnish with cilantro or parsley to serve.

Nutrition: Calories: 330; Fat: 10 g; Carbs: 29 g; Proteins: 5 g; Fiber: 10 g.

Cauliflower Rice Tabbouleh

Preparation Time: 20 minutes
Servings: 4
Ingredients:

- 4 cups cauliflower rice
- 1 ½ cups cherry tomatoes, quartered
- 3-4 tablespoons olive oil
- 1 cup parsley, fresh & chopped
- 1 cup mint, fresh & chopped
- 1 cup snap peas, sliced thin
- 1 small cucumber, cut into ¼ inch pieces
- ¼ cup scallions, sliced thin
- 3-4 tablespoons lemon juice, fresh
- 1 teaspoon sea salt, fine
- ½ teaspoon black pepper

Directions:

1. Get out a bowl and combine your cauliflower rice, tomatoes, mint, parsley, cucumbers, scallions and snap peas together.
2. Toss until combined.
3. Add your olive oil and lemon juice before tossing again. Season with salt and pepper.

Nutrition: Calories: 340; Fat: 4 g; Carbs: 45 g; Proteins: 6 g; Fiber: 16 g.

Dijon Maple Burgers

Preparation Time: 10 minutes
Cooking Time: 50 minutes
Servings: 12
Ingredients:

- 1 red bell pepper
- 19 ounces can chickpeas, rinsed and drained
- 1 cup almonds, ground
- 2 teaspoons Dijon mustard
- 1 teaspoon oregano
- ½ teaspoon sage
- 1 cup spinach, fresh
- 1 - ½ cups rolled oats
- 1 clove garlic, pressed
- ½ lemon, juiced
- 2 teaspoons maple syrup, pure

Directions:

1. Start by heating your oven to 350° F, and then get out a baking sheet. Line it with parchment paper.
2. Cut your red pepper in half, and then take the seeds out. Place it on your baking sheet and roast in the oven while you prepare your other ingredients. Process your chickpeas, almonds, mustard and maple syrup together in a food processor.
3. Add in your lemon juice, oregano, sage, garlic and spinach, processing again.
4. Make sure it's combined, but don't puree it.
5. Once your red bell pepper is softened, which should roughly take ten minutes, add this to the processor as well. Add in your oats, mixing well.
6. Form twelve patties, cooking in the oven for a half-hour. They should be browned.

Nutrition: Calories: 420; Fat: 9 g; Carbs: 65 g; Proteins: 8 g; Fiber: 12 g.

Black Bean Burgers

Preparation Time: 25 minutes
Cooking Time: 10 minutes
Servings: 6
Ingredients:

- 1 onion, diced
- ½ cup corn nibs
- 2 cloves garlic, minced
- ½ teaspoon oregano, dried
- ½ cup flour
- 1 jalapeño pepper, small
- 2 cups black beans, mashed and canned
- ¼ cup breadcrumbs (vegan)

THE PLANT-BASED COOKBOOK FOR BEGINNERS

- 2 teaspoons parsley, minced
- ¼ teaspoon cumin
- 1 tablespoon olive oil
- 2 teaspoons chili powder
- ½ red pepper, diced
- Sea salt to taste

Directions:
1. Set your flour on a plate, and then get out your garlic, onion, peppers and oregano, throwing it in a pan. Cook over medium-high heat, and then cook until the onions are translucent. Place the peppers in, and sauté until tender. Cook for 2 minutes, and then set it to the side.
2. Use a potato masher to mash your black beans. Then stir in the vegetables, cumin, breadcrumbs, parsley, salt and chili powder. Divide it into six patties.
3. Coat each side, and then cook until it's fried on each side. It should take ten minutes. It should be cooked all the way through.

Nutrition: Calories: 320; Fat: 5 g; Carbs: 35 g; Proteins: 13 g; Fiber: 10 g.

Grilled Eggplant Steaks

Preparation Time: 35 minutes
Cooking Time: 20 minutes
Servings: 6
Ingredients:
- 4 Roma tomatoes, diced
- 8 ounces feta, diced
- 2 eggplants
- 1 tablespoon olive oil

- 1 cup parsley, chopped
- 1 cucumber, diced
- Sea salt and black pepper to taste

Directions:
1. Slice your eggplants into three thick steaks, and then drizzle with oil. Season it with salt and pepper, and then grill for four minutes per side in a pan.
2. Top with the remaining ingredients.

Nutrition: Calories: 90; Fat: 3 g; Carbs: 12 g; Proteins: 9 g; Fiber: 6 g.

Fried Pineapple Rice

Preparation Time: 10 minutes
Cooking Time: 15 minutes
Servings: 6
Ingredients:
- 2-3 cups brown rice, cooked & cooled
- 1 tablespoon sesame oil
- 2 tablespoons raisins (optional)
- 1 onion, small and chopped
- ½ -3/4 cup pineapple, chopped
- 1 tablespoon soy sauce (or braggs liquid amino)
- ½ teaspoon turmeric
- 1 tomato, chopped
- 1 teaspoon curry powder
- 2 tablespoons cilantro, fresh and chopped
- Sea salt and black pepper to taste

Directions:
1. Start by getting out a saucepan, and then add your sesame oil to the pan.
2. Sauté your onions until they turn translucent.
3. Add in your cooked rice, soy sauce, pineapple, curry powder and turmeric.
4. Mix well and cook for eight to ten minutes.
5. Serve with cilantro, and season with salt and pepper.

Nutrition: Calories: 300; Fat: 6 g; Carbs: 55 g; Proteins: 6 g; Fiber: 8 g.

CHAPTER 23:

GLUTEN-FREE RECIPES

Veggie Hummus Tortillas

Preparation Time: 10 minutes
Cooking Time: 0 minutes
Servings: 4
Ingredients:

- 3 whole-grain, spinach, flour, or gluten-free tortillas
- 3 large Swiss chard leaves
- ¾ cup hummus
- ¾ cup shredded carrots

Directions:

1. Lay 1 tortilla flat on a cutting board. Place 1 Swiss chard leaf over the tortilla. Spread ¼ cup of hummus over the Swiss chard. Spread ¼ cup of carrots over the hummus.
2. Starting at one end of the tortilla, roll tightly toward the opposite side.
3. Slice each roll-up into six pieces. Place in a single-serving storage container. Repeat with the remaining tortillas and filling and seal the lids.

Nutrition: Calories: 254; Fat: 8 g; Carbohydrates: 39 g; Proteins: 10 g.

Peach Mango Crumble (Pressure Cooker)

Preparation Time: 10 minutes
Cooking Time: 15 minutes
Servings: 4-6
Ingredients:

- 3 cups chopped fresh or frozen peaches
- 3 cups chopped fresh or frozen mangos
- 4 tablespoons unrefined sugar or pure maple syrup, divided
- 1 cup gluten-free rolled oats
- ½ cup shredded coconut, sweetened or unsweetened
- 2 tablespoons coconut oil or vegan margarine

Directions:

1. In a 6- to 7-inch round baking dish, toss together the peaches, mangos, and 2 tablespoons of sugar.
2. In a food processor, combine the oats, coconut, coconut oil, and remaining 2 tablespoons of sugar. Pulse until combined. (If you use maple syrup, you'll need less coconut oil. Start with just the syrup and add oil if the mixture isn't sticking together.) Sprinkle the oat mixture over the fruit mixture.

3. Cover the dish with aluminum foil. Put a trivet in the bottom of your electric pressure cooker's cooking pot and pour in a cup or two of water. Using a foil sling or silicone helper handles, lower the pan onto the trivet.
4. Close and lock the lid, and select High Pressure for 6 minutes.
5. Pressure Release. Once the cooking time is complete, quick release the pressure, unlock and remove the lid.
6. Let cool for a few minutes before carefully lifting out the dish with oven mitts or tongs. Scoop out portions to serve.

Nutrition: Calories: 321; Fat: 18 g; Proteins: 4 g; Carbohydrates: 32 g.

Maple Raisin Oatmeal Cookies

Preparation Time: 15 minutes
Cooking Time: 10 minutes
Servings: 36
Ingredients:

- 1 cup whole wheat flour
- 1 teaspoon ground cinnamon
- ½ teaspoon baking soda
- ½ teaspoon sea salt (optional)
- ½ teaspoon baking powder
- ¼ teaspoon ground nutmeg
- ½ cup pure maple syrup (optional)
- ½ cup organic virgin coconut oil, at room temperature (optional)
- 1/3 cup almond butter
- 1 teaspoon pure vanilla extract
- 1 vegan egg
- 1½ cups gluten-free rolled oats
- ¾ cup raisins

Directions:

1. Mix the flour, cinnamon, baking soda, salt (if desired), baking powder, and nutmeg in a medium mixing bowl.
2. In a stand mixer fitted with the paddle attachment, beat together the maple syrup (if desired), oil (if desired), almond butter, vanilla, egg, and egg yolk. Add the flour mixture, a little at a time, mixing after each addition until just incorporated. You'll need to scrape down the sides as needed. Fold in the oats and raisins and mix again. Place the dough in a refrigerator until firmed and chilled.

3. Preheat the oven to 350ºF (180ºC). Line 2 baking sheets with parchment paper.
4. Using a spoon or mini-ice cream scoop, drop about 2 tablespoons of the dough onto the parchment-lined baking sheets for each cookie, spacing them 2 inches apart. Flatten each a bit with the back of a spoon.
5. Bake for 10 to 12 minutes, or until the cookies are golden brown.
6. Transfer the baking sheets onto a wire rack to cool completely before serving.

Nutrition: Calories: 257; Fat: 14 g; Carbohydrates: 33 g; Proteins: 6 g.

Mint Chocolate Chip Sorbet

Preparation Time: 5 minutes
Cooking Time: 0 minutes
Servings: 3
Ingredients:

- 1 frozen banana
- 1 tablespoon almond butter, or peanut butter, or other nut or seed butter
- 2 tablespoons fresh mint, minced
- ¼ cup or less non-dairy milk (only if needed)
- 2 to 3 tablespoons non-dairy chocolate chips, or cocoa nibs
- 2 to 3 tablespoons goji berries (optional)

Directions:
1. Put the banana, almond butter, and mint in a food processor or blender and purée until smooth.
2. Add the non-dairy milk if needed to keep blending (but only if needed, as this will make the texture less solid). Pulse the chocolate chips and goji berries (if using) into the mix, so they're roughly chopped up.

Nutrition: Calories: 212; Total Fat: 10 g; Carbohydrates: 31 g; Proteins: 3 g.

Ginger Spice Brownies

Preparation Time: 5 minutes
Cooking Time: 35 minutes
Servings: 6/12
Ingredients:

- 1¾ cups whole-grain flour
- 1 teaspoon baking powder
- 1 teaspoon baking soda
- ½ teaspoon salt
- 1 tablespoon ground ginger
- ½ teaspoon ground cinnamon
- ½ teaspoon ground allspice
- 3 tablespoons unsweetened cocoa powder
- ½ cup vegan semisweet chocolate chips
- ½ cup chopped walnuts
- ¼ cup canola oil
- ½ cup dark molasses
- ½ cup water
- 1/3 cup light brown sugar
- 2 teaspoons grated fresh ginger

Directions:
1. Preheat the oven to 350° F. Grease an 8-inch square baking pan and set aside. In a large bowl, combine the flour, baking powder, baking soda, salt, ground ginger, cinnamon, allspice, and cocoa. Stir in the chocolate chips and walnuts and set aside.
2. In medium bowl, combine the oil, molasses, water, sugar, and fresh ginger, then mix well.
3. Pour the wet ingredients into the dry ingredients and mix well.
4. Scrape the dough into the prepared baking pan. The dough will be sticky, so wet your hands to press it evenly into the pan.
5. Bake until a toothpick inserted in the center comes out clean for 30-35 minutes.
6. Cool on a wire rack 30 minutes before cutting. Store in an airtight container.

Nutrition: Calories: 422; Total fat: 21 g; Carbohydrates: 58 g; Proteins: 4 g.

Cherry Vanilla Rice Pudding (Pressure Cooker)

Preparation Time: 5 minutes
Cooking Time: 30 minutes **Servings:** 6
Ingredients:

- 1 cup short-grain brown rice
- 1¾ cups nondairy milk, plus more as needed
- 1½ cups water
- 4 tablespoons unrefined sugar or pure maple syrup (use 2 tablespoons if you use a sweetened milk), plus more as needed
- 1 teaspoon vanilla extract (use ½ teaspoon if you use vanilla milk)
- Pinch salt
- ¼ cup dried cherries or ½ cup fresh or frozen pitted cherries

Directions:
1. In your electric pressure cooker's cooking pot, combine the rice, milk, water, sugar, vanilla, and salt.
2. Close and lock the lid and ensure the pressure valve is sealed, then select High Pressure and set the time for 30 minutes.
3. Once the cooking time is complete, let the pressure release naturally, about 20 minutes. Once all the pressure has been released, carefully unlock and remove the lid. Stir in the cherries and put the lid back on loosely for about 10 minutes. Serve, adding more milk or sugar, as desired.

Nutrition: Calories: 177; Proteins: 3 g; Carbohydrates: 52 g; Fat: 1 g.

Mango Coconut Cream Pie

Preparation Time: 20 minutes + 30 minutes Chilling
Cooking Time: 0 minutes **Servings:** 8
Ingredients:
Crust:

- ½ cup rolled oats
- 1 cup cashews
- 1 cup soft pitted dates

Filling:

- 1 cup canned coconut milk
- ½ cup water
- 2 large mangos, peeled and chopped, or about 2 cups frozen chunks
- ½ cup unsweetened shredded coconut

Directions:

1. Put all the crust ingredients in a food processor and pulse until it holds together. If you don't have a food processor, chop everything as finely as possible and use ½ cup cashew or almond butter in place of half the cashews. Press the mixture down firmly into an 8-inch pie or springform pan.
2. Put the all-filling ingredients in a blender and purée until smooth for about 1 minute. It should be very thick, so you may have to stop and stir until it's smooth.
3. Pour the filling into the crust, use a rubber spatula to smooth the top, and put the pie in the freezer until set. Once frozen, it should be set out for about 15 minutes to soften before serving.
4. Top with a batch of Coconut Whipped Cream scooped on top of the pie once it's set. Finish it off with a sprinkling of toasted shredded coconut.

Nutrition: Calories: 427; Fat: 28 g; Carbohydrates: 45 g; Proteins: 8 g.

Cauliflower Wings

Preparation Time: 10 minutes
Cooking Time: 40 minutes
Servings: 6
Ingredients:

- 1 cup oat milk
- ¾ cup gluten-free or whole-wheat flour
- 2 teaspoons garlic powder
- 2 teaspoons onion powder
- ½ teaspoon paprika
- ¼ teaspoon freshly ground black pepper
- 1 head cauliflower, cut into bite-size florets

Directions:

1. Preheat the oven to 425° F. Line a baking sheet with parchment paper.
2. In a large bowl, whisk together the milk, flour, garlic powder, onion powder, paprika, and pepper. Add the cauliflower florets, and mix until the florets are completely coated.
3. Place the coated florets on the baking sheet in an even layer, and bake for 40 minutes, or until golden brown

and crispy, turning once halfway through the cooking process. Serve.
Nutrition: Calories: 96; Total fat: 1 g; Carbohydrates: 20; Proteins: 3 g.

Sautee Cauliflower with Sesame Seeds

Preparation Time: 5 minutes
Cooking Time: 10 minutes
Servings: 4
Ingredients:

- 1 cup vegetable broth
- 1 ½ pound cauliflower florets
- 4 tablespoons olive oil
- 2 scallion stalks, chopped
- 4 garlic cloves, minced
- Sea salt and freshly ground black pepper, to taste
- 2 tablespoons sesame seeds, lightly toasted

Directions:

1. In a large saucepan, bring the vegetable broth to a boil; then, add in the cauliflower and cook for about 6 minutes or until fork-tender; reserve.
2. Then, heat the olive oil until sizzling; now, sauté the scallions and garlic for about 1 minute or until tender and aromatic.
3. Add in the reserved cauliflower, followed by salt and black pepper; continue to simmer for about 5 minutes or until heated through.
4. Garnish with toasted sesame seeds and serve immediately. Bon appétit!

Nutrition: Calories: 217; Total fat: 17 g; Carbohydrates: 13 g; Proteins: 7 g.

Smashed Carrots

Preparation Time: 5 minutes
Cooking Time: 20 minutes
Servings: 4
Ingredients:

- 1 ½ pounds carrots, trimmed
- 3 tablespoons vegan butter
- 1 cup scallions, sliced
- 1 tablespoon maple syrup
- 1/2 teaspoons garlic powder
- 1/2 teaspoons ground allspice
- Sea salt, to taste
- 1/2 cup soy sauce
- 2 tablespoons fresh cilantro, chopped

Directions:

1. Steam the carrots for about 15 minutes until they are very tender; drain well.
2. In a sauté pan, melt the butter until sizzling. Now, turn the heat down to maintain an insistent sizzle.
3. Next, cook the scallions until they've softened. Add in the maple syrup, garlic powder, ground allspice, salt and soy sauce for about 10 minutes or until they are caramelized.

4. Add the caramelized scallions to your food processor; add in the carrots and puree the ingredients until everything is well blended.
5. Serve garnished with fresh cilantro. Enjoy!

Nutrition: Calories: 270; Proteins: 4.5 g; Carbohydrates: 29 g; Fat: 15 g

Eggplant Parmesan
Preparation Time: 10 minutes
Cooking Time: 15 minutes
Servings: 1
Ingredients:
- ¼ cup nondairy milk
- ¼ cup bread crumbs or panko
- 2 tablespoons nutritional yeast (optional)
- ¼ teaspoon salt
- 4 (¼-inch-thick) eggplant slices, peeled if desired
- 1 tablespoon olive oil, plus more as needed
- 4 tablespoons Simple Homemade Tomato Sauce
- 4 teaspoons Parm Sprinkle

Directions:
1. Put the milk in a shallow bowl. In another shallow bowl, stir together the bread crumbs, nutritional yeast (if using), and salt.
2. Dip one eggplant slice in the milk, making sure both sides get moistened. Dip it into the bread crumbs, flipping to coat both sides.
3. Transfer to a plate and repeat to coat the remaining slices. Heat the olive oil in a large skillet over medium heat and add the breaded eggplant slices, making sure there is oil under each.
4. Cook for 5 to 7 minutes, until browned. Flip, adding more oil as needed. Top each slice with 1 tablespoon tomato sauce and 1 teaspoon Parm Sprinkle. Cook for 5 to 7 minutes more.

Nutrition: Calories: 460; Fat: 31 g; Carbohydrates: 31 g; Proteins: 23 g.

Vegetarian Curry
Preparation Time: 10 minutes
Cooking Time: 5 hours
Servings: 6
Ingredients:
- 5 potatoes, peeled and cubed
- ¼ cup curry powder
- 2 tablespoons flour
- 1 tablespoon chili powder
- ½ teaspoon red pepper flakes
- ½ teaspoon cayenne pepper
- 1 green bell pepper, chopped
- 1 red bell pepper, chopped
- 2 tablespoons onion soup mix
- 14 oz. coconut cream, unsweetened
- 3 cups vegetable broth
- 2 carrots, peeled and sliced
- 1 cup green peas

- ¼ cup chopped cilantro

Directions:
1. Take a 6-quarts slow cooker, grease it with a non-stick cooking spray and place the potatoes pieces in the bottom. Set in the rest of the ingredients except for peas, cilantro, and carrots. Stir properly and cover the top.
2. Plug in the slow cooker; adjust the cooking time to 4 hours, and let it cook on the low heat setting or until it cooks thoroughly.
3. When the cooking time is over, add the carrots to the curry and continue cooking for 30 minutes. Stir in the peas to cook for 30 more minutes or until the peas get tender.
4. Garnish it with cilantro and serve.

Nutrition: Calories: 369; Fat: 23 g; Carbohydrates: 39 g; Proteins: 7 g.

Miso Noodle Soup
Preparation Time: 5 minutes
Cooking Time: 15 minutes **Servings:** 4
Ingredients:
- 7 ounces soba noodles (use 100% buckwheat for gluten-free)
- 4 cups water
- 4 tablespoons miso
- 1 cup adzuki beans (cooked or canned), drained and rinsed
- 2 tablespoons fresh cilantro or basil, finely chopped
- 2 scallions, thinly sliced

Directions:
1. Bring a large pot of water to a boil, then add the soba noodles. Stir them occasionally; they'll take about 5 minutes to cook.
2. Meanwhile, prepare the rest of the soup by warming the water in a separate pot to just below boiling, then remove it from heat. Stir the miso into the water until it has dissolved. Once the soba noodles are cooked, drain them and rinse with hot water.
3. Add the cooked noodles, adzuki beans, cilantro, and scallions to the miso broth and serve.

Nutrition: Calories: 102; Proteins: 11 g; Carbohydrates: 18 g; Fat: 1 g.

Portobello Mushroom Stew
Preparation Time: 10 minutes
Cooking Time: 8 hours
Servings: 5
Ingredients:
- 8 cups vegetable broth
- 1 cup dried wild mushrooms
- 1 cup dried chickpeas
- 3 cups chopped potato
- 2 cups chopped carrots
- 1 cup corn kernels
- 2 cups diced white onions
- 1 tablespoon minced parsley

- 3 cups chopped zucchini
- 1 tablespoon minced rosemary
- 1 1/2 teaspoons ground black pepper
- 1 teaspoon dried sage
- 2/3 teaspoon salt
- 1 teaspoon dried oregano
- 3 tablespoons soy sauce
- 1 1/2 teaspoons liquid smoke
- 8 ounces tomato paste

Directions:
1. Switch on the slow cooker, add all the ingredients to it, and stir until mixed.
2. Shut the cooker with a lid and cook for 8 hours at a high heat setting until cooked.
3. Serve straight away.

Nutrition: Calories: 447; Fat: 36 g; Carbohydrates: 24 g; Proteins: 11 g.

Italian Wedding Soup

Preparation Time: 5 minutes
Cooking Time: 15 minutes **Servings:** 4
Ingredients:
- 1 teaspoon olive oil
- 2 carrots, peeled and chopped
- ½ onion, chopped
- 3 or 4 garlic cloves, minced, or ½ teaspoon garlic powder Salt
- 8 cups water or Vegetable Broth
- 1 cup orzo or pearl couscous
- 1 tablespoon dried herbs
- Freshly ground black pepper
- 1 recipe quinoa meatballs (from Meatball Subs recipe)
- 2 cups chopped greens, such as spinach, kale, or chard

Directions:
1. Heat the olive oil in a large soup pot over medium-high heat.
2. Add the carrots, onion, garlic (if using fresh), and a pinch of salt. Sauté for to 4 minutes, until softened.
3. Add the water, orzo, and dried herbs (plus the garlic powder, if using). Season to taste with salt and pepper, and bring the soup to a boil. Turn the heat to low and simmer until the orzo is soft, about 10 minutes.
4. Add the meatballs and greens, and stir until the greens are wilted. Taste and season with more salt and pepper as needed.

Nutrition: Calories: 168; Fat: 3 g; Carbohydrates: 30 g; Proteins: 9 g.

Mixed Bean Soup

Preparation Time: 20 minutes
Cooking Time: 45 minutes
Servings: 12

Ingredients:
- ¼ cup vegetable oil
- 1 large onion, chopped
- 1 large sweet potato, peeled and cubed
- 3 carrots, peeled and chopped
- 3 celery stalks, chopped
- 3 garlic cloves, minced
- 2 teaspoons dried thyme, crushed
- 1 (4-ounce) can green chilies
- 2 jalapeño peppers, chopped
- 1 tablespoon ground cumin
- 4 large tomatoes, chopped finely
- 2 (16-ounce) cans great northern beans, rinsed and drained
- 2 (15¼-ounce) cans red kidney beans, rinsed and drained
- 1 (15-ounce) can black beans, drained and rinsed
- 9 cups homemade vegetable broth
- 1 cup fresh cilantro, chopped

Directions:
1. In a Dutch oven, heat the oil over medium heat and sauté the onion, sweet potato, carrots, and celery for about 6–8 minutes.
2. Add the garlic, thyme, green chilies, jalapeño peppers, and cumin and sauté for about 1 minute.
3. Add in the tomatoes and cook for about 2–3 minutes.
4. Add the beans and broth and bring to a boil over medium-high heat.
5. Cover the pan with a lid and cook for about 25–30 minutes. Stir in the cilantro and remove from heat. Serve hot.

Nutrition: Calories: 563; Fat: 6.8 g; Carbohydrates: 90 g; Proteins: 32 g.

Barley and Chickpea Soup

Preparation Time: 15 minutes
Cooking Time: 1 hour 30 minutes
Servings: 2
Ingredients:
- 1 cup pearl barley
- 1 (15-ounce) can chickpeas, rinsed and drained
- 2 large carrots, peeled and chopped
- 1 zucchini, chopped
- 2 celery stalks, chopped
- 1 red onion, chopped
- 2 cups tomatoes, chopped
- 1 teaspoon dried parsley, crushed
- 1 teaspoon curry powder
- 1 teaspoon paprika
- 3 bay leaves
- Salt and ground black pepper, to taste
- 5 cups homemade vegetable broth
- 4 cups water
- ½ cup fresh cilantro, chopped

Directions:

1. In a large soup pan, add all the ingredients (except parsley) over high heat and bring to a boil. Lower the heat to medium-low and simmer, covered for about 1½ hours.
2. Remove from the heat and discard the bay leaves. Serve hot with the garnishing of cilantro.

Nutrition: Calories: 326; Fat: 5 g; Proteins: 17 g; Carbohydrates: 59 g.

Yellow Potato Soup

Preparation Time: 10 minutes
Cooking Time: 25 minutes **Servings:** 4
Ingredients:

- 3 cups cubed potatoes (any kind)
- 1 cup diced onion
- 1 cup chopped carrots
- ½ teaspoon chipotle chili powder
- ½ teaspoon ground cinnamon
- ½ teaspoon sea salt
- ½ teaspoon ground turmeric
- ¼ teaspoon cayenne pepper
- 2 cups diced Anjou pear
- ½ cup dried yellow split peas
- 4 cups vegetable broth
- ½ teaspoon freshly ground black pepper

Directions:

1. In a large saucepan, combine the potatoes, onion, carrots, chipotle powder, cinnamon, salt, turmeric, and cayenne and dry sauté over medium-high heat for 5 minutes.
2. Add the pear, split peas, and broth and bring to a boil. Lower the heat to medium-low, cover, and simmer until the split peas are tender, 15 to 20 minutes.
3. Serve garnished with black pepper.

Nutrition: Calories: 252; Fat: 1 g; Carbohydrates: 55 g; Proteins: 9 g.

Spicy Bean Stew

Preparation Time: 10 minutes
Cooking Time: 50 minutes **Servings:** 4
Ingredients:

- 7 ounces cooked black eye beans
- 14 ounces chopped tomatoes
- 2 medium carrots, peeled, diced
- 7 ounces cooked kidney beans
- 1 leek, diced
- ½ a chili, chopped
- 1 teaspoon minced garlic
- 1/3 teaspoon ground black pepper
- 2/3 teaspoon salt
- 1 teaspoon red chili powder
- 1 lemon, juiced
- 3 tablespoons white wine
- 1 tablespoon olive oil
- 1 2/3 cups vegetable stock

Directions:

1. Take a large saucepan, place it over medium-high heat, add oil and when hot. Add leeks and cook for 8 minutes or until softened. Then add carrots; continue cooking for 4 minutes. Stir in chili and garlic. Pour in the wine, and continue cooking.
2. Add tomatoes, stir in lemon juice, pour in the stock and bring the mixture to boil.
3. Switch heat to medium level and simmer for 35 minutes until stew has thickened. Add both beans and remaining ingredients, and cook for 5 minutes until hot. Serve straight away.

Nutrition: Calories: 114; Fat: 1.6 g; Carbohydrates: 19 g; Proteins: 6 g.

Winter Chili with Tofu

Preparation Time: 15 minutes
Cooking Time: 1 hour 40 minutes
Servings: 4
Ingredients:

- 3/4-pound cannellini beans, soaked overnight and drained
- 3 tablespoons olive oil
- 1 large onion, diced
- 1 cup turnip, chopped
- 1 carrot, chopped
- 1 bell pepper, sliced
- 1 sweet potato, chopped
- 3 cloves garlic, minced
- 2 ripe tomatoes, pureed
- 3 tablespoons tomato paste
- 2 cups vegetable broth
- 2 bay leaves
- 1 tablespoon red chili powder
- 1 tablespoon brown sugar
- Sea salt and cayenne pepper, to taste
- 12 ounces silken tofu, cubed

Directions:

1. Cover the soaked beans with a fresh change of cold water and bring to a boil for about 10 minutes. Turn the heat to a simmer and continue cooking for 50 to 55 minutes or until tender.
2. In a heavy-bottomed pot, heat the olive oil over medium flame.
1. Once hot, sauté the onion, turnip, carrot, bell pepper and sweet potato.
2. Sauté the garlic for about 1 minute or so.
3. Add tomatoes, tomato paste, vegetable broth, bay leaves, red chili powder, brown sugar, salt, cayenne pepper and cooked beans. Let it simmer, stirring periodically, for 25 to 30 minutes or until cooked through.
4. Serve garnished with silken tofu. Bon appétit!

Nutrition: Calories: 605 g; Fat: 20 g; Carbohydrates: 74 g; Proteins: 38 g.

Baked Blueberry and Chia Seed Oatmeal

Preparation Time: 10 minutes
Cooking Time: 40 minutes
Servings: 4
Ingredients:

- 2 cups unsweetened almond milk
- 2 tablespoons chia seeds
- 1½ cups gluten-free rolled oats
- 2 tablespoons water
- 2 tablespoons maple syrup
- ½ teaspoon vanilla extract
- 1 teaspoon ground cinnamon
- ¼ teaspoon sea salt (optional)
- 1 ripe banana, sliced
- 1 cup blueberries, divided
- ½ cup chopped walnuts

Directions:

1. Preheat the oven to 350º F (180º C).
2. Whisk together the almond milk and chia seeds in a small bowl.
3. Let the chia seeds absorb the milk for about 5 minutes.
4. Meanwhile, combine the oats, water, maple syrup, vanilla, cinnamon, and salt (if desired) in a medium bowl, and whisk well.
5. Stir in the chia seed mixture.
6. Spread out the banana slices on a baking dish in an even layer.
7. Scatter the top with half of the blueberries and pour over the oat mixture.
8. Place the remaining blueberries and walnuts on top of the oats.
9. Bake in the preheated oven for about 35 to 40 minutes, or until the top is golden brown.
10. Remove from the oven and cool for 5 minutes before serving.

Nutrition: Calories: 461; Fat: 22 g; Carbohydrates: 52 g; Proteins: 2 g.

Sweet Potato Oatmeal

Preparation Time: 10 minutes
Cooking Time: 20 minutes
Servings: 2-3
Ingredients:

- 1 large sweet potato, peeled and diced
- 1 cup unsweetened almond milk
- 1 cup rolled oats
- ½ cup date molasses
- ½ teaspoon ground ginger
- ½ teaspoon ground cinnamon
- ¼ teaspoon ground allspice
- ¼ teaspoon orange zest
- Pinch salt (optional)

Directions:

1. Put the diced sweet potatoes in a large pot of water and bring to a boil over high heat for about 10 minutes until softened.
2. Drain the sweet potato well and mash it with a potato masher or the back of a fork.
3. Transfer the mashed sweet potato to a small saucepan. Add the almond milk, oats, molasses, ginger, cinnamon, allspice, orange zest, and salt (if desired), and whisk well. Cook the mixture over medium heat for 10 to 12 minutes, stirring frequently, or until the oats are cooked through.
4. Divide the oats between two serving bowls and serve.

Nutrition: Calories: 400; Proteins: 9.2 g; Carbohydrates: 79.7 g; Fat: 5 g.

Pineapple and Mango Oatmeal

Preparation Time: 5 minutes
Cooking Time: 0 minutes
Servings: 2
Ingredients:

- 2 cups unsweetened almond milk
- 2 cups rolled oats
- ½ cup pineapple chunks, thawed if frozen
- ½ cup diced mango, thawed if frozen
- 1 banana, sliced
- 1 tablespoon chia seeds
- 1 tablespoon maple syrup

Directions:

1. Stir together the almond milk, oats, pineapple, mango, banana, chia seeds, and maple syrup in a large bowl until you see no clumps.
2. Cover and refrigerate to chill for at least 4 hours, preferably overnight.
3. Serve chilled with your favorite toppings.

Nutrition: Calories: 512; Fat: 22.1 g; Carbohydrates: 13.1 g; Proteins: 14.1 g.

Overnight Muesli

Preparation Time: 10 minutes
Cooking Time: 0 minutes
Servings: 4-6
Ingredients:

- 2 cups gluten-free rolled oats
- ¼ cup no-added-sugar apple juice
- 1¾ cups unsweetened coconut milk
- 1 tablespoon apple cider vinegar (optional)
- 1 apple, cored and chopped
- Dash ground cinnamon

Directions:

1. Mix together the oats, apple juice, coconut milk, and vinegar (if desired) in a large bowl and stir to combine.
2. Cover and refrigerate for at least 3 hours, preferably overnight.
3. When ready, stir in the chopped apple and serve sprinkled with the cinnamon.

Nutrition: Calories: 214; Fat: 4.2 g; Carbohydrates: 28.9 g; Proteins: 6.1 g.

Vanilla Steel-cut Oatmeal

Preparation Time: 5 minutes
Cooking Time: 40 minutes
Servings: 4
Ingredients:

- 4 cups water
- Pinch sea salt (optional)
- 1 cup steel-cut oats
- ¾ cup unsweetened almond milk
- 2 teaspoons pure vanilla extract

Directions:

1. Place the water and salt (if desired) into a large pot over high heat and bring to a boil.
2. Reduce the heat to low and stir in the oats. Cook for about 30 minutes until the oats are softened, stirring occasionally.
3. Add the milk and vanilla and stir well. Cook for about 10 minutes more until your desired consistency is reached.
4. Remove the cereal from the heat and serve warm.

Nutrition: Calories: 187; Fat: 0 g; Proteins: 9.2 g; Carbohydrates: 28.8 g.

Slow Cooker Butternut Squash Oatmeal

Preparation Time: 15 minutes
Cooking Time: 6-8 hours
Servings: 4
Ingredients:

- 1 cup steel-cut oats
- 3 cups water
- 2 cups cubed (½-inch pieces) peeled butternut squash
- ¼ cup unsweetened coconut milk
- 1 tablespoon chia seeds
- 1½ teaspoons ground ginger
- 2 teaspoons yellow (mellow) miso paste
- 1 tablespoon sesame seeds, toasted
- 1 tablespoon chopped scallion, green parts only

Directions:

1. Mix the oats, water, and butternut squash in a slow cooker.
2. Cover and cook on Low for 6 to 8 hours, or until the squash is tender when tested with a fork. Mash the cooked butternut squash with a potato masher or heavy spoon. Stir together the butternut squash and oats until well mixed.
3. Mix the milk, chia seeds, ginger, and miso paste in a small bowl and stir to combine. Add this mixture to the squash mixture and stir well.
4. Ladle the oatmeal into bowls and serve hot topped with sesame seeds and scallion.

Nutrition: Calories: 229; Fat: 4.9 g; Carbohydrates: 39.7 g; Proteins: 7.1 g.

Fruit Salad with Lemon Ginger Syrup

Preparation Time: 10 minutes + chilling time
Cooking Time: 25 minutes
Servings: 4
Ingredients:

- 1/2 cup fresh lemon juice
- 1/4 cup agave syrup
- 1 teaspoon fresh ginger, grated
- 1/2 teaspoons vanilla extract
- 1 banana, sliced
- 2 cups mixed berries
- 1 cup seedless grapes
- 2 cups apples, cored and diced

Directions:

1. Bring the lemon juice, agave syrup and ginger to a boil over medium-high heat. Then, turn the heat to medium-low and let it simmer for about 6 minutes until it has slightly thickened. Remove from the heat and stir in the vanilla extract. Allow it to cool.
2. Layer the fruits in serving bowls. Pour the cooled sauce over the fruit and serve it well chilled. Bon appétit!

Nutrition: Calories: 164; Total fat: 0.5 g; Carbohydrates: 42 g; Proteins: 4 g.

Banana Pancakes

Preparation Time: 5 minutes
Cooking Time: 15 minutes **Servings:** 4
Ingredients:

- 2 tablespoons ground flaxseeds
- 1/2 cup oat flour
- 1/2 cup coconut flour
- 1/2 cup instant oats
- 1 teaspoon baking powder
- 1/4 teaspoon kosher salt
- 1/4 teaspoon ground cardamom
- 1/4 teaspoon ground cinnamon
- 1/2 teaspoons coconut extract
- 1 cup banana
- 2 tablespoons coconut oil, at room temperature

Directions:

1. To make the "flax" egg, in a small mixing dish, whisk 2 tablespoons of the ground flaxseeds with 4 tablespoons of the water. Let it sit for at least 15 minutes.
2. In a mixing bowl, thoroughly combine the flour, oats, baking powder and spices. Add in the flax egg and mashed banana.
3. Mix until everything is well incorporated.
4. Heat 1/2 tablespoon of the coconut oil in a frying pan over medium-low flame. Spoon about 1/4 cup of the batter into the frying pan; fry your pancake for approximately 3 minutes per side. Repeat until you run out of batter. Serve with your favorite fixings, and enjoy!

Nutrition: Calories: 302; Proteins: 7.1 g; Carbohydrates: 37.2 g; Fat: 15 g.

Classic French Toast

Preparation Time: 5 minutes
Cooking Time: 15 minutes **Servings:** 2
Ingredients:

- 1 tablespoon ground flax seeds
- 1 cup coconut milk
- 1/2 teaspoons vanilla paste
- A pinch of sea salt
- A pinch of grated nutmeg
- 1/2 teaspoons ground cinnamon
- 1/4 teaspoon ground cloves
- 1 tablespoon agave syrup
- 4 slices bread

Directions:

1. In a mixing bowl, thoroughly combine the flax seeds, coconut milk, vanilla, salt, nutmeg, cinnamon, cloves and agave syrup.
2. Dredge each slice of bread into the milk mixture until well coated on all sides.
3. Preheat an electric griddle to medium heat and lightly oil it with a nonstick cooking spray.
4. Cook each slice of bread on the preheated griddle for about 3 minutes per side until golden brown.

Nutrition: Calories: 233; Fat: 6.5 g; Carbohydrates: 35.5 g; Proteins: 8.2 g.

Oatmeal Muffins

Preparation Time: 10 minutes
Cooking Time: 20 minutes **Servings:** 12
Ingredients:

- ½ cup of hot water
- ½ cup of raisins
- ¼ cup of ground flaxseed
- 2 cups of rolled oats
- ¼ teaspoon of sea salt
- ½ cup of walnuts
- ¼ teaspoon of baking soda
- 1 banana
- 2 tablespoons of cinnamon
- ¼ cup of maple syrup

Directions:

1. Whisk the flaxseed with water and allow the mixture to sit for about 5 minutes.
2. In a food processor, blend all the ingredients along with the flaxseed mix. Blend everything for 30 seconds, but do not create a smooth substance.
3. To create rough-textured cookies, you need a semi-coarse batter.
4. Put the batter in cupcake liners and place them in a muffin tin.
5. As this is an oil-free recipe, you will need cupcake liners. Bake everything for about 20 minutes at 350° F.
6. Enjoy the freshly-made cookies with a glass of warm milk.

Nutrition: Calories: 133; Fat: 2 g; Carbohydrates: 27 g; Proteins: 3 g.

Omelet with Chickpea Flour

Preparation Time: 10 minutes
Cooking Time: 20 minutes **Servings:** 1
Ingredients:

- ½ teaspoon, onion powder
- ¼ teaspoon, black pepper
- 1 cup, chickpea flour
- ½ teaspoon, garlic powder
- ½ teaspoon, baking soda
- ¼ teaspoon, white pepper
- 1/3 cup, nutritional yeast
- 3 finely chopped green onions
- 4 ounces, sautéed mushrooms

Directions:

1. In a small bowl, mix the onion powder, white pepper, chickpea flour, garlic powder, black and white pepper, baking soda, and nutritional yeast. Add 1 cup of water and create a smooth batter.
2. On medium heat, put a frying pan and add the batter just like the way you would cook pancakes.
3. On the batter, sprinkle some green onion and mushrooms. Flip the omelet and cook evenly on both sides.
4. Once both sides are cooked, serve the omelet with spinach, tomatoes, hot sauce, and salsa.

Nutrition: Calories: 150; Proteins: 10.2 g; Carbohydrates: 24.4 g; Fat: 1.9 g.

CHAPTER 24:

RECIPES FOR CHILDREN

Chickpea and Mango Wraps

Preparation Time: 15 minutes
Cooking time: 0 minutes
Servings: 3 wraps
Ingredients:

- 3 tablespoons tahini
- 1 tablespoon curry powder
- ¼ teaspoon sea salt (optional)
- Zest and juice of 1 lime
- 3 to 4 tablespoons water
- 1½ cups cooked chickpeas
- 1 cup diced mango
- ½ cup fresh cilantro, chopped
- 1 red bell pepper, deseeded and diced
- 3 large whole-wheat wraps
- 1½ cups shredded lettuce

Directions:

1. In a large bowl, stir together the tahini, curry powder, lime zest, lime juice and sea salt until smooth and creamy. Whisk in 3 to 4 tablespoons of water to help thin the mixture.
2. Include the cooked chickpeas, mango, cilantro and bell pepper to the bowl. Toss until well coated.
3. Organize the wrapping on a spotless work surface. Divide the chickpea and mango mixture among the wraps. Spread the shredded lettuce on top and roll up tightly.
4. Serve immediately.

Nutrition: Calories: 436; Fat: 17.9 g; Carbs: 8.9 g; Proteins: 15.2 g; Fiber: 12.1 g.

Tofu and Pineapple in Lettuce

Preparation Time: 2 hours 20 minutes
Cooking Time: 15 minutes
Servings: 4
Ingredients:

- ¼ cup low-sodium soy sauce
- 1 garlic clove, minced
- 2 tablespoons sesame oil (optional)
- 1 tablespoon coconut sugar (optional)
- one (14-oz./397g) set extra-firm tofu, exhausted, sliced into half-inch dices
- 1 small white onion, diced
- ½ pineapple, shed, cored, cut into cubes
- Salt and ground black pepper, to taste

- 4 large lettuce leaves
- 1 tablespoon roasted sesame seeds

Directions:

1. Mix the soy sauce, garlic, sesame oil, and coconut sugar in a bowl. Stir to mix well.
2. Include the tofu cubes to the container of the soy sauce mix, then squeeze to coat well. Wrap the bowl in plastic and refrigerate to marinate for at least 2 hours.
3. Pour the marinated tofu and marinade in a skillet and heat at moderate flame. Add the onion and pineapple cubes to the skillet and stir to mix well.
4. Scatter using salt and pepper and cook for fifteen mins or till the onions are slightly browned and the pineapple cubes are tender. Divide the lettuce leaves among four plates, then top the leaves with the tofu and pineapple mixture. Sprinkle with sesame seeds and serve immediately.

Nutrition: Calories: 259; Fat: 15.4 g; Carbs: 20.5 g; Proteins: 12.1 g; Fiber: 3.2 g.

Quinoa and Black Bean Lettuce Wraps

Preparation Time: 30 minutes
Cooking Time: 15 minutes
Servings: 6
Ingredients:

- 2 tablespoons avocado oil (optional)
- ¼ cup deseeded and chopped bell pepper
- ½ onion, chopped
- 2 tablespoons minced garlic
- 1 teaspoon salt (optional)
- 1 teaspoon pepper (optional)
- ½ cup cooked quinoa
- 1 cup cooked black beans
- ½ cup almond flour
- ½ teaspoon paprika
- ½ teaspoon red pepper flakes
- 6 large lettuce leaves

Directions:

1. Heat one tbsp of the avocado oil in a skillet at moderate-high flame.
2. Include the bell peppers, onions, garlic, salt, as well as pepper.
3. Fry for five mins or till the bell peppers are soft.

4. Turn off the temperature and let it to calm for ten mins, then put the vegetables inside mixing bowl. Include the quinoa, beans, flour.
5. Scatter using paprika and red pepper fragments. Pulse until thick and well combined.
6. Contour a saucepan with baking sheet, then form the mix into 6 patties using your hands and put on the baking pan.
7. Place the saucepan in the refrigerator for five mins to make the patties steady.
8. Heat the residual avocado oil in the skillet at high flame.
9. Include the patties and cook for six mins or till well browned on both ends. Toss the patties midway through.
10. Position the patties in the lettuce leaves and serve instantly.

Nutrition: Calories: 200; Fat: 10.6 g; Carbs: 40.5 g; Proteins: 9.5 g; Fiber: 8.2 g.

Rice and Bean Lettuce Burgers

Preparation Time: 1 hour 25 minutes
Cooking Time: 45 minutes
Servings: 8
Ingredients:

- 1 cup uncooked medium grain brown rice
- 2 cups water
- ½ cup grated carrots
- ¾ cup chopped red onion
- ½ cup raw sunflower seeds
- ¾ cup cooked pinto beans
- 5 cloves garlic, peeled
- 2 tablespoons oat flour
- 2 teaspoons arrowroot powder
- 2 tablespoons nutritional yeast
- ¼ cup chopped fresh basil
- 4 teaspoons ground cumin
- 4 teaspoons low-sodium soy sauce
- 2 tablespoons low-sodium tomato paste
- Salt and ground black pepper and one to two tbsps. water
- 8 large lettuce leaves, for serving

Directions:

1. Put the rice and water inside a pan. Bring to a boil over medium heat.
2. Decrease the heat to low and fester for fifteen additional mins or till the rice is tender. Transfer the rice to a large bowl. Allow the rice to cool and fluff with a fork.
3. Place the carrots, onions, sunflower seeds, beans, and garlic inside a mixing bowl and beat till well united and chunky. Pour the mixture over the rice.
4. Include the residual components, excluding for the lettuce, to the container of rice, then swirl to combine well. Shape the mixture into eight patties and arrange them on a parchment-lined baking pan. Refrigerate for an hour until firm.
5. Preheat the oven to 350° F (180°C).

6. Put the baking pan in the microwave and bake for thirty mins or till well browned on each and every corner. Flip the patties halfway through.
7. Reveal the lettuce leaves on 8 dishes, then top each leaf with a patty.
8. Wrap and serve.

Nutrition: Calories: 197; Fat: 5.9 g; Carbs: 30.5 g; Proteins: 7.4 g; Fiber: 4.7 g.

Bulgur and Pinto Bean Lettuce Wraps

Preparation Time: 30 minutes
Cooking Time: 10 minutes
Servings: 8
Ingredients:

- 1½ cups plus 2 tbsps water, divided
- Salt and ground black pepper, to taste
- 2/3 cup bulgur, rinsed
- ¾ cup walnuts
- ½ cup fresh basil leaves
- 2 garlic cloves, minced
- 1 big beet (9 oz./255g), shed and tattered
- 1 (15-oz./425g) can pinto beans, rinsed
- 1 (4-ounce / 113-g) jar carrot
- 1 tablespoon Dijon mustard
- 1½ cups panko bread crumbs
- 6 tablespoons avocado oil (optional)
- 8 large lettuce leaves

Directions:

1. Put one and a half cup of water into a pan and scatter with salt to taste. Bring to a boil, then turn off the heat. Pour the bulgur into the boiling water. Cover the lid and let sit for 15 minutes or until the bulgur is soft. Drain the bulgur and spread it on a baking pan to cool.
2. Meanwhile, add the walnuts, basil, garlic, and beet inside a mixing bowl. Pulse to mix well. Then add the beans, carrot, 2 tablespoons of water, Dijon mustard, salt (if desired) and pepper.
3. Pulse to combine well.
4. Put the mix into a big container and crinkle in the cooked bulgur and panko. Shape the mixture into eight patties.
5. Heat the avocado oil in the pan at moderate-high flame.
6. Place the patties in a pan and cook for eight mins or till well browned on either portions. Flip the patties halfway through. Work in batches to avoid overcrowding.
7. Reveal the lettuce leaves on 8 dishes, then top the leaves with the patties and wrap to serve.

Nutrition: Calories: 317; Fat: 17.2 g; Carbs: 33.9 g; Proteins: 8.9 g; Fiber: 6.5 g.

Cannellini Bean and Bell Pepper Burger

Preparation Time: 15 minutes
Cooking Time: 35 minutes
Servings: 6
Ingredients:

- ¾ cup quinoa
- 1½ cups water
- two (15-oz./425g) cans cannellini beans, washed and clear out
- ½ cup ground flaxseeds
- 1 cup walnuts, finely chopped
- 1 tablespoon ground cumin
- 3 tablespoons Italian seasoning
- 1 tablespoon minced garlic
- 2 tablespoons almond butter
- 1 teaspoon salt (optional)
- ½ teaspoon freshly ground black pepper
- 3 tablespoons Dijon mustard
- 1½ tablespoons avocado oil (optional)
- 4 to 5 large red bell peppers cut into thirds

Topping:

- 1 cucumber, sliced
- 2 to 3 tomatoes, sliced
- ½ small red onion, sliced

Directions:

1. In a saucepan, combine the quinoa and water. Bring to a boil over high heat, then cover and reduce heat to medium-low. Simmer for 20 minutes or until all the water has been absorbed. Set aside.
2. On a large cutting board, spread out the beans. Pat dry with paper towels. Then press down firmly with the beans between the paper towel and cutting board, using your knuckles to mash them. When you remove the paper towel, you should have a layer of semi-smashed beans. Using a chef's knife, chop the beans a little bit more, leaving a few larger chunks.
3. Transfer the mashed beans to a medium bowl. Add the cooked quinoa, flaxseeds, walnuts, cumin, Italian seasoning, garlic, almond butter, salt (if desired), pepper, and mustard. Mix until well combined.
4. Put your fingers in water to avoid the burger mix from piercing and form twelve burger patties.
5. In a nonstick skillet, heat ½ tbsp. olive oil at moderate flame. Once hot, add four patties. Cook for 3 minutes, then flip to the other side and cook for 3 minutes more.
6. To serve, slice bell peppers into thirds and sandwiching a burger patty among two portions of pepper.
7. Season with cut cucumber, tomatoes, and onion.

Nutrition: Calories: 304, Fat: 16.1 g; Carbs: 27.9 g; Proteins: 12.2 g; Fiber: 11.8 g.

Oil-Free Mushroom and Tofu Burritos

Preparation Time: 15 minutes
Cooking Time: 28 to 45 minutes
Servings: 4
Ingredients:

- One and a half cups shiitake mushrooms, stemmed and cut
- Two big leeks, white and light green shares, chopped
- 1 medium red bell pepper, diced
- 3 cloves garlic, minced
- 3 tablespoons nutritional yeast
- 2 tablespoons low-sodium soy sauce
- 2 teaspoons ground coriander
- 2 teaspoons turmeric
- 2 teaspoons ground cumin
- Black pepper, to taste
- 1 lb. (454g) lite strong tofu, pushed and smashed
- Half cup sliced cilantro
- 4 whole-wheat tortillas
- 1 cup salsa

Directions:

1. Preheat the oven to 350°F (180°C). Line a baking pan with parchment paper.
2. Include the mushrooms, leeks and red bell pepper to a saucepan at moderate-high flame. Sauté for 8 to 10 minutes, or until the vegetables are softened.
3. Add the garlic, nutritional yeast, soy sauce, coriander, turmeric, cumin and black pepper to the saucepan. Reduce the heat to medium-low. Sauté for 5 minutes. Stir in the tofu mash.
4. Spread the mixture in an even layer in the prepared pan. Bake for 25 to 30 minutes. Transfer the mixture to a large bowl and mix with the cilantro to combine well.
5. On a clean work surface lay the tortillas. Spoon the mixture into the tortillas and spread it all over. Drizzle the salsa over the filling. Roll up the tortillas tightly.

6. Serve immediately.

Nutrition: Calories: 411; Fat: 15.1 g; Carbs: 48.9 g; Proteins: 28.1 g; Fiber: 12.4 g.

Tempeh and Vegetable Wraps

Preparation Time: 10 minutes
Cooking Time: 16 minutes
Servings: 4
Ingredients:

- 1-pound (454 g) tempeh
- 1 cup water
- ¼ cup maple syrup (optional)
- 2 teaspoons extra-virgin olive oil (optional)
- 1 teaspoon low-sodium soy sauce
- 1 teaspoon ground cayenne pepper
- 1/8 Teaspoon liquid smoke
- Cooking spray (optional)

- 4 whole-wheat tortillas
- 2 large tomatoes cut into eight slices total
- 8 lettuce leaves
- ½ cup almond butter

Directions:
1. Heat the water in a pot over medium heat and bring to a boil. Put a steam basket in the pot and place the tempeh in the basket.
2. Cover and steam for 10 minutes. Transfer the tempeh to a plate and let rest for 5 minutes. Slice into 16 strips. Set aside.
3. Stir together the maple syrup (if desired), olive oil (if desired), soy sauce, cayenne pepper and liquid smoke in a small bowl.
4. Spritz a pan over medium-high heat with cooking spray.
5. Place the tempeh slices in the pan. Spread the sauce over the tempeh and cook for 6 minutes, flipping halfway through. Transfer the tempeh back to the plate.
6. On a clean work surface, lay the tortillas. Place 4 tempeh slices, 2 tomato slices, 2 lettuce leaves and 2 tablespoons of almond butter on each tortilla. Roll up tightly and serve.

Nutrition: Calories: 433; Fat: 22.8 g; Carbs: 40.9 g; Proteins: 23.2 g; Fiber: 3.1 g.

Sumptuous Black and Veggie Tacos

Preparation Time: 15 minutes
Cooking Time: 10 minutes
Servings: 4
Ingredients:
- 2 (15-ounce / 425-g) cans black beans, drained and rinsed
- ¼ cup ground flaxseeds
- 1 teaspoon paprika
- 1 teaspoon dried oregano
- 1 teaspoon ground cumin
- 1 teaspoon salt (optional)
- 1 teaspoon freshly ground black pepper
- 1 tablespoon coconut oil (optional)
- 4 (6-inch) corn tortillas
- 1 medium tomato, diced (about 7 ounces / 198 g in total)
- ¼ cup chopped cilantro
- ½ yellow onion, diced (about 3½ ounces / 99 g in total)
- 3 romaine lettuce leaves, sliced into thin ribbons
- 2 avocados, sliced
- 4 lime wedges

Directions:
1. Pour the black beans in a food processor, then pulse to mash the beans until chunky.
2. Sprinkle the flaxseeds, paprika, oregano, cumin, salt (if desired), and ground black pepper over the mashed beans, then pulse to mix thoroughly.
3. Heat the coconut oil (if desired) in a skillet over medium heat.
4. Add the bean mixture to a single layer in the skillet and level with a spatula. Cook for 2 minutes or until the bottom of the mixture starts to brown. Flip the mixture and cook for 2 minutes to brown the other side. Turn off the heat and allow it to cool.
5. Unfold the tortillas among four plates, then divide the cooked bean mixture, tomato, cilantro, onion, lettuce, and avocado over the tortillas. Squeeze the lime wedges over and serve immediately.

Nutrition: Calories: 578; Fat: 22.0 g; Carbs: 75.0 g; Proteins: 20.0 g; Fiber: 20.0 g.

Refried Bean Taquitos

Preparation Time: 5 minutes
Cooking Time: 21 to 22 minutes
Servings: 4
Ingredients:
- 2 cups pinto beans, cooked
- 1 teaspoon chili powder
- 1 teaspoon ground cumin
- ½ teaspoon garlic powder
- ½ teaspoon onion powder
- ¼ teaspoon red pepper flakes
- 12 corn tortillas

Directions:
1. Preheat the oven to 400°F (205°C). Line a baking pan with parchment paper.
2. In a blender, combine all the ingredients, except the tortillas, and blend until creamy and smooth.
3. Arrange the tortillas in the baking pan and bake for 1 to 2 minutes, or until softened and pliable.
4. Transfer the tortillas to a clean work surface. Spoon the mashed beans into the center of each tortilla and spread over. Roll up tightly and secure with toothpicks.
5. Arrange the stuffed tortillas in the baking pan and bake for 20 minutes, or until golden brown and crispy, flipping halfway through.
6. Let rest for 5 minutes before serving.

Nutrition: Calories: 285; Fat: 13.1 g; Carbs: 5.8 g; Proteins: 12.2 g; Fiber: 12.9 g.

Avocado and Dulse Pitas

Preparation Time: 15 minutes
Cooking Time: 10 minutes
Servings: 4
Ingredients:
- 2 teaspoons coconut oil (optional)
- ½ cup dulse
- ¼ teaspoon liquid smoke
- Salt and ground black pepper, to taste (optional)
- 2 avocados, sliced
- ¼ cup chopped cilantro
- 2 scallions, white and light green parts, sliced
- 2 tablespoons lime juice

- 4 (8-inch) whole wheat pitas, sliced in half
- 4 cups chopped romaine
- 4 plum tomatoes, sliced

Directions:
1. Heat the coconut oil (if desired) in a skillet over medium heat.
2. Add the dulse and drizzle with liquid smoke. Cook for 5 minutes or until crispy. Stir constantly. Turn off the heat and sprinkle with ground black pepper. Transfer on a plate and set aside.
3. Put the avocado, cilantro, and scallions in a food processor, then drizzle with lime juice and sprinkle with salt (if desired) and ground black pepper. Pulse to combine well and mash the avocado.
4. Toast the pita halves in the skillet for 4 minutes or until lightly browned on both sides. Set aside until cool enough to handle.
5. Stuff the pita halves with the avocado mixture, romaine, plum tomatoes, and crispy dulse. Serve immediately.

Nutrition: Calories: 434; Fat: 18.9 g; Carbs: 61.0 g; Proteins: 9.6 g; Fiber: 13.5 g.

Creamy Cauliflower Chipotle Spread

Preparation Time: 10 minutes
Cooking Time: 20 minutes
Servings: 1 cup
Ingredients:
- 2 chipotle peppers in adobo sauce
- 1½ cups cauliflower florets
- ½ cup low-sodium vegetable soup
- Sea salt and black pepper, to taste (optional)
- 3 shallots, minced
- 2 cloves garlic, minced
- ¼ cup dry white wine

Directions:
1. Cook the cauliflower in a steamer for 10 minutes or until soft.
2. Transfer the cauliflower to a food processor. Add the chipotle peppers, then pour in the vegetable soup and sprinkle with salt (if desired). Pulse to purée until creamy and smooth. Set aside.
3. Add the shallots in a skillet and sauté over medium heat for 5 minutes or until translucent.
4. Add the garlic and sauté for 1 more minute or until fragrant.
5. Pour the wine into the skillet and cook until the liquid is almost absorbed.
6. Reduce the heat to medium-low and pour in the puréed cauliflower and chipotle peppers. Cover and simmer for 5 minutes until it becomes thick. Stir occasionally.
7. Smear on the fillings of the tortillas or pitas to serve.

Nutrition: Calories: 235; Fat: 1.8 g; Carbs: 39.7 g; Proteins: 8.8 g; Fiber: 8.2 g.

Coriander Mushroom Wraps

Preparation Time: 10 minutes
Cooking Time: 5 minutes
Servings: 4
Ingredients:
- ½ cup Spicy Cilantro Pesto or Coriander Chutney
- 8 romaine lettuce leaves
- 2 cups cooked brown rice
- Batch Grilled Portobello Mushrooms, cut into ¾-inch-wide strips

Directions:
1. Spread one tablespoon of the pesto in the bottom of one of the lettuce leaves and top with ¼ cup of the rice and about half of a grilled mushroom.
2. Roll the lettuce leaf up around the filling. Repeat for the remaining lettuce leaves.

Nutrition: Calories: 115; Fat: 1.39 g; Carbs: 21.92 g; Proteins: 6.21 g.

Brown Rice Lettuce Wraps

Preparation Time: 10 minutes
Cooking Time: 5 minutes
Servings: 4
Ingredients:
- 1 batch Potato Samosa Filling
- 8 romaine lettuce leaves
- 3 cups cooked brown rice
- Coriander Chutney

Ingredients:
1. Place some of the samosa filling on the bottom of one of the lettuce leaves. Top with some brown rice and a spoonful of the coriander chutney.
2. Roll the leaf up around the filling. Repeat for the remaining lettuce leaves.

Nutrition: Calories: 284; Fat: 0.33 g; Carbs: 64.46 g; Proteins: 7.45 g.

Guacamole Lettuce Wraps

Preparation Time: 10 minutes
Cooking Time: 0 minutes
Servings: 6
Ingredients:
- 1 batch Black Beans and Rice
- 1 large head of romaine lettuce leaves separated
- 1 batch Not-So-Fat Guacamole

Directions:
1. Place some of the black beans and rice into the center of one of the lettuce leaves. Top with some of the guacamole.
2. Fold the leaf in from the sides and roll it up like a cigar.
3. Repeat for any remaining lettuce leaves until the beans and rice, and guacamole are used up.

Nutrition: Calories: 3586; Fat: 357.09 g; Carbs: 19.04 g; Proteins: 77.51 g.

Tomato Salad Lettuce Wraps

Preparation Time: 10 minutes
Cooking Time: 5 minutes
Servings: 4
Ingredients:

- 1½ cups Fava Bean Spread
- 8 romaine lettuce leaves
- 1 batch Tomato, Cucumber and Mint Salad

Directions:

1. Place some of the fava bean spread in the center of one of the lettuce leaves. Top with some of the tomato salad.
2. Fold the leaf in from the sides and roll it up like a cigar.
3. Repeat for the remaining lettuce leaves.

Nutrition: Calories: 789; Fat: 3.69 g; Carbs: 135.94 g; Proteins: 59.85 g.

Onion Mushroom Wraps

Preparation Time: 10 minutes
Cooking Time: 5 minutes **Servings:** 4
Ingredients:

- 1 tablespoon grated ginger
- 2 cloves garlic, peeled and minced
- Zest and juice of 1 lime
- 3 tablespoons low-sodium soy sauce
- 1 teaspoon crushed red pepper flakes
- 2 large shallots, diced small
- 1 pound Portobello mushrooms, stemmed and finely chopped
- ½ cup coarsely chopped cilantro
- 3 tablespoons finely chopped mint
- 4 green onions (white and green parts), thinly sliced
- 4 large romaine lettuce leaves or 8 small ones

Directions:

1. Combine the ginger, garlic, lime zest and juice, soy sauce, and crushed red pepper flakes in a small bowl and set aside.
2. Heat a large skillet over high heat. Add the shallots and mushrooms and stir-fry for 3 to 4 minutes.
3. Add water 1 to 2 tablespoons at a time to keep the vegetables from sticking to the pan.
4. Add the ginger mixture and cook for another minute. Add the cilantro, mint, and green onions and remove from the heat.
5. To serve, place some of the mushroom mixture on the bottom of one lettuce leaves and fold the lettuce over the filling. Repeat for the remaining lettuce leaves.

Nutrition: Calories: 3225; Fat: 62.15 g; Carbs: 541.15 g; Proteins: 206.58 g.

Lime Bean Artichoke Wraps

Preparation Time: 10 minutes
Cooking Time: 10 minutes
Servings: 2
Ingredients:

- Lime bean spread

- 1 cup cooked baby lime beans
- 14-oz. can artichoke hearts
- 2 tablespoons nutritional yeast
- 2 tablespoons parsley, chopped
- ½ teaspoon garlic, minced
- ½ teaspoon onion powder
- 2 teaspoons fresh lime juice
- 2 teaspoons white balsamic vinegar

Wraps:

- 2 gluten-free vegan wraps
- 1 cup raw broccoli, sliced lengthwise
- 2 whole hearts of palm, sliced lengthwise

Directions:

1. Blend lime beans with yeast, parsley, artichoke hearts, garlic, onion powder, lime juice and vinegar in a blender until smooth.
2. Spread the beans mixture on top of the wraps and top them with broccoli and hearts of palm.
3. Roll the wraps like a burrito and cut them in half.
4. Grill the wraps in the grill over high heat for 5 minutes per side.
5. Serve.

Serving Suggestion: Serve the wraps with roasted veggies on the side.
Variation Tip: Add chopped spinach to filling.
Nutrition: Calories: 324; Fat 1 g; Sodium: 236 mg; Carbs 42 g; Fiber 0.3 g; Sugar: 0.1 g; Proteins: 1 g.

Butternut Squash Lasagna

Preparation Time: 10 minutes
Cooking Time: 1 hour 40 minutes
Servings: 6
Ingredients:

- 2 tablespoons olive oil
- 2 pounds butternut squash, cubed
- ½ cup water
- 4 amaretti cookies, crumbled
- 8 ounces shiitake mushrooms, sliced
- ¼ cup butter
- ¼ cup whole-wheat flour
- 3½ cups almond milk
- ½ teaspoon ground nutmeg
- 1 cup fresh basil leaves
- 13 ounces DeLillo no-boil lasagna noodles
- 3 cups vegan cheese, shredded
- Salt and black pepper, to taste

Directions:

1. Preheat your oven to 375° F.
2. Sauté squash with black pepper, salt and oil in a skillet for 5 minutes.
3. Add water to the squash, cover and cook for about 20 minutes on medium heat.
4. Blend the squash with amaretti in a blender until smooth.
5. Sauté mushrooms with oil and ¼ teaspoons salt in a skillet for 10 minutes.

6. Mix butter with flour in a skillet for 1 minute.
7. Pour in milk, mix well until lump-free, then boil the mixture.
8. Stir in black pepper, nutmeg and ¼ teaspoons salt.
9. Mix well, then cook for about 5 minutes until the sauce thickens.
10. Add basil and blend well with a blender.
11. Grease a 13x9 -inch baking dish with butter.
12. Spread ¾ cup sauce in the baking dish.
13. Arrange the lasagna noodles at the bottom of this dish.
14. Top the noodles with 1/3 squash puree and add 1/3 mushroom on top.
15. Drizzle 1 cup vegan cheese on top.
16. Repeat all the layers and cover this dish with a foil sheet.
17. Bake the prepared lasagna for 40 minutes in the oven.
18. Remove the tin foil from the top and bake for another 15 minutes.
19. Serve warm.

Serving Suggestion: Serve the lasagna with mashed cauliflower.
Variation Tip: You can replace lasagna noodles with zucchini slices.
Nutrition: Calories: 438; Fat 7 g; Sodium: 316 mg; Carbs 34 g; Fiber 0.3 g; Sugar: 0.3 g; Proteins: 3 g.

Sweet Potato Penne Pasta

Preparation Time: 15 minutes
Cooking Time: 15 minutes **Servings:** 6
Ingredients:
Sauce:

- ½ cup cashews
- 1 roasted sweet potato, peeled
- 2/3 cup water
- 2 garlic cloves
- 1 chipotle pepper
- 1/8 teaspoon nutmeg
- ½ teaspoon sea salt
- Black pepper, to taste

Pasta:

- 3 cups of quinoa penne
- Mushrooms
- ½ tablespoon olive oil
- 1 cup baby bella mushrooms, sliced
- ¼ teaspoon garlic powder
- Salt and black pepper, to taste

Directions:
1. Soak cashews in 4 cups water in a bowl for 2 hours, then drain.
2. Blend cashews with black pepper, salt, nutmeg, chili pepper, garlic, water, and sweet potato in a blender until smooth.
3. Boil pasta in boiling water in a cooking pot as per the package's instructions.
4. Drain the pasta and transfer to the pot.

5. Sauté mushrooms with oil, black pepper, salt and garlic powder in a skillet for 5 minutes.
6. Add the sweet potato sauce and pasta, then mix well.
7. Garnish with sage.
8. Serve warm.

Serving Suggestion: Serve the pasta with roasted broccoli florets.
Variation Tip: Drizzle lemon juice on top before cooking.
Nutrition: Calories: 456; Fat 4 g; Sodium: 634 mg; Carbs 31 g; Fiber 1.4 g; Sugar: 1 g; Proteins: 3 g.

Roasted Butternut Squash Pasta

Preparation Time: 15 minutes
Cooking Time: 35 minutes **Servings:** 4
Ingredients:

- ½ tablespoon olive oil
- 4 cups butternut squash, cubed
- 2 garlic cloves, unpeeled
- Salt and black pepper, to taste
- 8 ounces brown rice pasta
- 2 tablespoons vegan cream cheese
- 1 cup almond milk
- ½ cup frozen peas, thawed

Directions:
1. Preheat your oven to 400° F.
2. Toss butternut squash with oil, black pepper and salt in a baking pan.
3. Add garlic and roast for 30 minutes.
4. Cook the pasta as per the package's instruction, then drain.
5. Peel the roasted garlic and add to a blender along with squash, salt, black pepper, almond milk and vegan cream cheese, then blend until smooth.
6. Add peas and squash sauce to the pasta and serve.

Serving Suggestion: Serve the pasta with crumbled tofu on top.
Variation Tip: Add garlic salt on top for more taste.
Nutrition: Calories: 449; Fat 31 g; Sodium: 723 mg; Carbs 32 g; Fiber 2.5 g; Sugar: 2 g; Proteins: 26 g.

Cashew Mac and Cheese

Preparation Time: 15 minutes
Cooking Time: 10 minutes
Servings: 4
Ingredients:

- 1½ cups raw cashews
- 2 garlic cloves
- ½ cup nutritional yeast
- 1¼ cups almond milk
- 1 jalapeño, chopped
- ¾ teaspoon ground turmeric
- ¾ teaspoon paprika
- ½ teaspoon onion powder
- 1 teaspoon Dijon mustard
- 1 teaspoon salt
- Black pepper, to taste
- 1-pound shell Conchiglie pasta

Directions:
1. Soak cashews in 4 cups water in a bowl for 2 hours, then drain.
2. Drain and blend the cashews with black pepper, salt, mustard, onion powder, paprika, turmeric, jalapeño, almond milk, yeast, and garlic in a blender until smooth.
3. Cook the noodles as per the package's instructions, then drain.
4. Mix the noodles with the cashews sauce in a bowl.
5. Garnish with black pepper.
6. Serve warm.

Serving Suggestion: Serve the mac and cheese with mashed sweet potatoes.
Variation Tip: Add a drizzle of taco seasoning on top.
Nutrition: Calories: 310; Fat 6 g; Sodium: 220 mg; Carbs 31 g; Fiber 2.4 g; Sugar: 1.2 g; Proteins: 12 g.

Taco Pasta with Sweet Corn

Preparation Time: 15 minutes
Cooking Time: 10 minutes
Servings: 6
Ingredients:
Pasta cheese sauce:
- ¾ cup cashews
- ¾ cup water
- 1 garlic clove
- 2 tablespoons lime juice
- 2½ teaspoons cumin
- 2 teaspoons chili powder
- 1 teaspoon dried oregano
- ½ teaspoon paprika
- 1/8 teaspoon cayenne pepper
- ¾ teaspoon salt

Pasta:
- 8 ounces large elbow noodles
- 1 (15-ounce) can black beans, rinsed
- 1¼ cups Birds Eye Sweet Corn, cooked ¾ cup chunky salsa

Preparation:
1. Soak cashews in 2 cups of water for 2 hours, then drain.
2. Blend cashews with paprika, oregano, chili powder, cumin, lime juice, garlic, and ½ cup of water.
3. Boil the pasta as per the package's instruction, then drain.
4. Return the pasta to a cooking pot, then add cashew sauce, corn, salsa and beans.
5. Mix well and garnish with all the toppings.
6. Serve warm.

Serving Suggestion: Serve the pasta with mashed cauliflower.
Variation Tip: Add hot sauce for a tangy taste.
Nutrition: Calories: 382; Fat 6 g; Sodium: 620 mg; Carbs 15 g; Fiber 2 g; Sugar: 1.2 g; Proteins: 12 g.

Vegetarian Lentil Loaf

Preparation Time: 15 minutes

Cooking Time: 1 hr. 23 minutes
Servings: 6
Ingredients:
- 1 cup dry green lentils
- 4 cups water
- 3 tablespoons flaxseed meal
- 1/3 cup water
- ½ tablespoon olive oil
- 4 garlic cloves, minced
- 1 small white or yellow onion, diced
- 1 red bell pepper, diced
- 1 carrot, diced
- 1 jalapeño, seeded and diced
- 2 teaspoons cumin
- 1 teaspoon chili powder
- ½ teaspoon paprika
- ½ teaspoon garlic powder
- ½ teaspoon onion powder
- ¼ teaspoon coriander
- ½ cup gluten free rolled oats
- ½ cup gluten free oat flour
- ½ cup fresh cilantro, chopped
- 1 teaspoon salt
- Black pepper, to taste

Glaze:
- ½ cup ketchup
- ½ teaspoon yellow mustard
- ½ teaspoon apple cider vinegar
- ¼ teaspoon chipotle chili powder

Directions:
1. Rinse and add lentils to a cooking pot with 4 cups of water.
2. Add a dash of salt and cook for 30 minutes on a simmer, then drain.
3. Mix 1/3 cup water and flaxseed meal in a bowl. Preheat your oven to 350° F.
4. Grease a loaf pan with cooking spray.
5. Sauté garlic, jalapeño, cilantro, carrot, bell pepper, onion with oil in a suitable skillet for 7 minutes. Stir in spices and cook for 30 seconds. Blend the 2 cups of cooked lentils in a blender until smooth.
6. Return the lentils to the cooking pot and add the veggies. Stir in the rest of the ingredients, then mix well. Prepare the glaze by mixing its ingredients in a bowl.
7. Brush the glaze over the meatloaf.
8. Spread the mixture in a meatloaf pan and bake for 45 minutes.
9. Allow it to cool, then slice. Serve warm.

Serving Suggestion: Serve the lentil loaf with roasted vegetables.
Variation Tip: Add corns to the lentil loaf.
Nutrition: Calories: 93; Fat 3 g; Sodium: 510 mg; Carbs 22 g; Fiber 3 g; Sugar: 4 g; Proteins: 4 g.

Black Bean Loaf with Avocado Sauce

Preparation Time: 15 minutes
Cooking Time: 42 minutes
Servings: 6
Ingredients:

- 3 tablespoons flaxseed meal
- ½ cup water - 1 teaspoon olive oil
- 1 small yellow onion
- 3 garlic cloves, minced
- 1 red bell pepper, finely diced
- 1 carrot, shredded
- 1 jalapeño, seeded and diced
- 2 teaspoons cumin
- 1 tablespoon chili powder
- 1 teaspoon dried oregano
- ¼ teaspoon cayenne pepper
- ¼ cup cilantro, diced
- 2 (15-ounce) cans black beans, rinsed
- ¾ cup sweet corn organic preferred
- ½ cup gluten-free oats
- ½ cup gluten-free oat flour
- Salt and black pepper, to taste

Sauce:

- 1/3 cup salsa Verde green salsa
- ½ avocado, mashed
- 2 tablespoons cilantro, chopped

Directions:

1. Preheat your oven to 350° F.
2. Layer a 9-inch loaf pan with cooking spray.
3. Mix ½ cup water with flaxseed meal in a bowl, then leave for 10 minutes.
4. Sauté garlic, jalapeño, carrots, bell pepper, and onion with 1 teaspoon oil in a skillet for 7 minutes. Blend beans with sautéed veggies, black pepper, salt and the rest of the ingredients, along with flaxseeds.
5. Spread this meatloaf mixture in the pan and bake for 35 minutes in the oven.
6. Allow the meatloaf to cool, then slice.
7. Mix salsa with cilantro and avocado in a bowl. Add this sauce over the meatloaf. Serve warm

Serving Suggestion: Serve the bean loaf with sautéed vegetables on the side.
Variation Tip: Add boiled peas to the bean loaf.
Nutrition: Calories: 378; Fat 3.8 g; Sodium: 620 mg; Carbs 33 g; Fiber 2.4 g; Sugar: 1.2 g; Proteins: 5.4 g.

Pineapple Tofu Kabobs

Preparation Time: 10 minutes
Cooking Time: 10 minutes
Servings: 4
Ingredients:

- 2 tablespoons tamari
- 1 teaspoon apple cider vinegar
- 2 tablespoons fresh pineapple juice
- 2 teaspoons ginger, grated

- 2 garlic cloves, minced
- ½ teaspoon ground turmeric
- 1 (14-ounce) package Nagoya extra firm tofu
- 2 cups fresh pineapple, cubed

Garnish:

- Fresh chopped cilantro
- Diced onion
- Hot sauce

Directions:

1. Pat dry the tofu block with a paper towel and cut it into cubes.
2. Mix tamari, turmeric, garlic, ginger, pineapple juice, and apple cider vinegar in a large bowl.
3. Toss in tofu cubes, then mix well and cover to marinate for 30 minutes.
4. Set a grill over medium-high heat and grease its grilling grates.
5. Thread tofu and pineapple on the skewers and grill the skewers for 5 minutes per side.
6. Garnish with hot sauce, green onion and cilantro.
7. Serve warm.

Serving Suggestion: Serve the tofu kebobs with mashed cauliflower.
Variation Tip: Brush the kebabs with sriracha sauce for seasoning.
Nutrition: Calories: 304; Fat 31 g; Sodium: 834 mg; Carbs 27 g; Fiber 0.2 g; Sugar: 0.3 g; Proteins: 4.6 g

Lentil Sloppy Joes with Spaghetti Squash

Preparation Time: 10 minutes
Cooking Time: 4 hours
Servings: 4
Ingredients:

- 1¼ cups uncooked green lentils, rinsed
- 1 white onion, diced
- 1 red pepper, diced
- 1 carrot, sliced
- 3 garlic cloves, minced
- 1½ tablespoons chili powder
- 1 teaspoon cumin
- ½ teaspoon onion powder
- ¼ teaspoon cayenne pepper
- 1 (15-ounce) can tomato sauce
- 1 (15-ounce) can diced tomatoes
- 1½ cups water
- 2 tablespoons organic ketchup
- 1 teaspoon yellow mustard
- 1 spaghetti squash, halved and seeded
- 1 teaspoon soy sauce
- Salt and black pepper, to taste

Directions:

1. Add all the ingredients except spaghetti squash to a slow cooker.
2. Mix well and place the spaghetti squash on top.

3. Cover and slow-cook on high for 4 hours on high heat.
4. Remove the squash from the top and shred the flesh.
5. Transfer the flesh to a serving plate and then top it with lentils mixture.
6. Garnish with cheese and serve warm.

Serving Suggestion: Serve the sloppy joe with some vegan cheese on top.
Variation Tip: Add cabbage coleslaw to the sloppy joe.
Nutrition: Calories: 341, Fat: 24 g; Sodium: 547 mg; Carbs: 24 g; Fiber: 1.2 g; Sugar: 1 g; Proteins: 10.3 g

Sesame-Orange Chickpea Stir-Fry

Preparation Time: 15 minutes
Cooking Time: 25 minutes
Servings: 6
Ingredients:
Sauce:

- ¾ cup orange juice
- 1 tablespoon honey
- 2 tablespoons soy sauce
- 1 teaspoon ginger, grated
- 1 tablespoon cornstarch organic
- Zest of 1 orange

Stir-fry:

- 1½ tablespoon toasted sesame oil
- 1 (15-ounce) can chickpeas, rinsed
- ½ red onion, chopped
- 3 garlic cloves, minced
- 1 large red bell pepper, sliced
- 8 ounces green beans, chopped
- Green onion, for garnish
- Toasted sesame seeds, for garnish
- Red pepper flakes
- Cooked Quinoa, for serving

Directions:
1. Mix orange zest, cornstarch, ginger, soy sauce, honey, and orange juice in a large bowl.
2. Set a suitable skillet with 1 tablespoon of sesame oil over medium-high heat.
3. Stir in chickpeas, then sauté for 5 minutes.
4. Mix well and transfer the chickpeas to a plate.
5. Sauté onion with ½ tablespoons of oil in a skillet over medium heat for 4 minutes.
6. Stir in bell pepper and garlic; then sauté for 3 minutes.
7. Add green beans and sauté for 4 minutes.
8. Pour in the prepared sauce. Mix and cook until the sauce thickens.
9. Add chickpeas and cook on low heat for 4 minutes.
10. Garnish with green onion, red pepper flakes and sesame seeds.
11. Serve warm.

Serving Suggestion: Serve the stir-fry with zucchini noodles or rice.
Variation Tip: Add peas to the stir-fry.
Nutrition: Calories: 318; Fat: 15.7 g; Sodium: 124 mg; Carbs: 31 g; Fiber: 0.1 g; Sugar: 0.3 g; Proteins: 4.9 g.

Sweet Potato Zoodles

Preparation Time: 15 minutes
Cooking Time: 21 minutes
Servings: 4
Ingredients:

- 1 teaspoon coconut oil
- 3 garlic cloves, minced
- 2 teaspoons fresh grated ginger
- 1 small white onion, diced
- 1 red pepper, diced
- 2 medium sweet potatoes, peeled and diced
- 1¼ teaspoon ground turmeric
- ½ teaspoon salt
- Black pepper, to taste
- 1 (15-ounce) can light coconut milk
- 2 tablespoons creamy peanut butter
- 2 medium zucchinis, spiralized

Directions:
1. Sauté ginger and garlic with oil in a suitable skillet for 30 seconds.
2. Stir in sweet potatoes cubes, onion and red pepper, then cook for 5 minutes.
3. Add turmeric, coconut milk, black pepper, salt and peanut butter, then cook to a boil.
4. Reduce heat, and cook for 15 minutes.
5. Add zucchini noodles, then mix well.
6. Garnish with green onion, cilantro and lime juice.
7. Serve warm.

Serving Suggestion: Serve the zoodles with tofu stir fry.
Variation Tip: Add vegan cheese on top of the zoodles.
Nutrition: Calories: 391; Fat: 2.2 g; Sodium: 276 mg; Carbs: 27 g; Fiber: 0.9 g; Sugar: 1.4 g; Proteins: 8.8 g.

Butternut Squash Chickpea Stew

Preparation Time: 15 minutes
Cooking Time: 21 minutes
Servings: 6
Ingredients:

- 1 tablespoon olive oil
- 1 medium white onion, chopped
- 6 garlic cloves, minced
- 2 teaspoons cumin
- 1 teaspoon cinnamon
- 1 teaspoon ground turmeric
- ¼ teaspoon cayenne pepper
- 1 (28-ounce) can crushed tomatoes
- 2½ cups vegetable broth
- 1 (15-ounce) can chickpeas, rinsed
- 4 cups butternut squash, cubed
- 1 cup green lentils, rinsed
- ½ teaspoon salt
- Black pepper, to taste
- Fresh juice of ½ lemon
- 1/3 cup cilantro, chopped

- Basil leaves, chopped

Directions:
1. Sauté garlic and onion with oil in a suitable pot over medium-high heat for 5 minutes.
2. Stir in cayenne, turmeric, cinnamon and cumin, then sauté for 30 seconds.
3. Add black pepper, salt, lentils. Butternut squash, chickpeas, broth and tomatoes.
4. Cook to a boil, reduce its heat, then cover and cook for 20 minutes.
5. Add basil, cilantro and lemon juice.
6. Serve warm.

Serving Suggestion: Serve the stew with roasted mushrooms.
Variation Tip: Add lemon zest on top for better taste.
Nutrition: Calories: 324; Fat: 5 g; Sodium: 432 mg; Carbs: 31 g; Fiber: 0.3 g; Sugar: 1 g; Proteins: 5.7 g.

Strawberry and Banana Smoothie

Preparation Time: 5 minutes
Cooking Time: 0 minutes
Servings: 1
Ingredients:

- 1 cup sliced banana, frozen
- 2 tablespoons chia seeds
- 2 cups strawberries, frozen
- 2 teaspoons honey
- ¼ teaspoon vanilla extract, unsweetened
- 6 ounces coconut yogurt
- 1 cup almond milk, unsweetened

Directions:
1. Place all the ingredients in a food processor or blender jar, and then cover it with the lid.
2. Pulse until smooth and then serve.

Nutrition: Calories: 114; Fat: 2.1 g; Proteins: 3.7 g; Carbs: 22.3 g; Fiber: 3.8 g.

Orange Smoothie

Preparation Time: 5 minutes
Cooking Time: 0 minutes **Servings:** 1
Ingredients:

- 1 cup slices of oranges
- ½ teaspoon grated ginger
- 1 cup of mango pieces
- 1 cup of coconut water
- 1 cup chopped strawberries
- 1 cup crushed ice

Directions:
1. Place all the ingredients in a food processor or blender jar, and then cover it with the lid.
2. Pulse until smooth and then serve.

Nutrition: Calories: 198.7; Fat: 1.2 g; Proteins: 6.1 g; Carbs: 34.3 g; Fiber: 0 g.

Pumpkin Chai Smoothie

Preparation Time: 5 minutes
Cooking Time: 0 minutes **Servings:** 1

Ingredients:

- 1 cup cooked pumpkin
- ¼ cup pecans
- 1 frozen banana
- ¼ teaspoon ground cinnamon
- ¼ teaspoon cardamom
- ¼ teaspoon ground nutmeg
- 2 teaspoons maple syrup
- 1 cup of water, cold
- ½ cup of ice cubes

Directions:
1. Place pecans in a small bowl, cover with water and then let them soak for 10 minutes. Drain the pecans, add them into a blender, and then add the remaining ingredients.
2. Pulse for 1 minute until smooth and then serve.

Nutrition: Calories: 157.5; Fat: 3.8 g; Proteins: 3; Carbs: 32.3 g; Fiber: 4.5 g.

Banana Shake

Preparation Time: 5 minutes
Cooking Time: 0 minutes
Servings: 1
Ingredients:

- 3 medium frozen bananas
- 1 tablespoon cocoa powder, unsweetened
- 1 teaspoon shredded coconut
- 1 tablespoon maple syrup
- 1 tablespoon peanut butter
- 1 teaspoon vanilla extract, unsweetened
- 2 cups of coconut water
- 1 cup of ice cubes

Directions:
1. Add banana in a food processor. Incorporate maple syrup and vanilla; pour in water, and add ice.
2. Pulse until smooth, and then pour half of the smoothie into a glass.
3. Add butter and cocoa powder into the blender. Pulse until smooth, and add to the smoothie glass. Sprinkle coconut over the smoothie and then serve.

Nutrition: Calories: 301; Fat: 9.3 g; Proteins: 6.8 g; Carbs: 49 g; Fiber: 1.9 g.

Green Honeydew Smoothie

Preparation Time: 5 minutes
Cooking Time: 15 minutes **Servings:** 4
Ingredients:

- 1 large banana
- 6 large leaves of basil
- ½ cup frozen pineapple
- 1 teaspoon lime juice
- 1 cup pieces of Honeydew melon
- 1 teaspoon green tea matcha powder
- ¼ cup almond milk, unsweetened

Directions:

1. Place all the ingredients in a food processor or blender jar, and then cover it with the lid.
2. Pulse until smooth and then serve.

Nutrition: Calories: 223.5; Fat: 2.7 g; Proteins: 20.1 g; Carbs: 32.7 g; Fiber: 5.2 g.

Summer Salsa

Preparation Time: 5 minutes
Cooking Time: 15 minutes **Servings:** 8
Ingredients:

- 1 cup cherry tomatoes chopped
- 1/4 cup chopped cilantro
- 2 tablespoons chopped red onion
- 1 teaspoon minced garlic
- 1 small jalapeno, seeded, chopped
- 1/2 of a lime, juiced
- 1/8 teaspoon salt
- 1 tablespoon olive oil

Directions:

1. Place all the ingredients in the jar of a food processor or blender except for cilantro. Then cover with its lid. Pulse until smooth, and then pulse in cilantro until evenly mixed. Tip the salsa into a bowl and then serve with vegetable sticks.

Nutrition: Calories: 51; Fat: 0.1 g; Proteins: 1.7 g; Carbs: 11.4 g; Fiber: 3.1 g.

Red Salsa

Preparation Time: 35 minutes
Cooking Time: 15 minutes
Servings: 8
Ingredients:

- 4 Roma tomatoes, halved
- ¼ cup chopped cilantro
- 1 jalapeno pepper, seeded, halved
- ½ of a medium white onion, peeled, cut into quarters
- 3 cloves of garlic, peeled
- ½ teaspoon salt
- 1 tablespoon brown sugar
- 1 teaspoon apple cider vinegar

Directions:

1. Switch on the oven, then set it to 425° F and let it preheat.
2. Meanwhile, take a baking sheet, line it with foil, and spread tomato, jalapeno pepper, onion, and garlic.
3. Bake the vegetables for 15 minutes until vegetables have cooked and begun to brown. Then let the vegetables cool for 3 minutes.
4. Transfer the roasted vegetables into a blender. Add the remaining ingredients and then pulse until smooth.
5. Tip the salsa into a medium bowl and chill it for 30 minutes before serving with vegetable sticks.

Nutrition: Calories: 240; Fat: 0 g; Proteins: 0 g; Carbs: 48 g; Fiber: 16 g.

Pinto Bean Dip

Preparation Time: 5 minutes
Cooking Time: 0 minutes
Servings: 4
Ingredients:

- 15 ounces canned pinto beans
- 1 jalapeno pepper
- 2 teaspoons ground cumin
- 3 tablespoons nutritional yeast
- 1/3 cup basil salsa

Directions:

1. Place all the ingredients in a food processor, cover with the lid and then pulse until smooth.
2. Tip the dip in a bowl and then serve with vegetable slices.

Nutrition: Calories: 360; Fat: 0 g; Proteins: 24 g; Carbs: 72 g; Fiber: 24 g.

Smoky Red Pepper Hummus

Preparation Time: 5 minutes
Cooking Time: 0 minutes
Servings: 4
Ingredients:

- 1/4 cup roasted red peppers
- 1 cup cooked chickpeas
- 1/8 teaspoon garlic powder
- 1/2 teaspoons salt
- 1/8 teaspoon ground black pepper
- 1/4 teaspoon ground cumin
- 1/4 teaspoon red chili powder
- 1 tablespoon tahini
- 2 tablespoons water

Directions:

1. Place all the ingredients in the jar of the food processor and then pulse until smooth.
2. Tip the hummus in a bowl and then serve with vegetable slices.

Nutrition: Calories: 489; Fat: 30 g; Proteins: 9 g; Carbs: 15 g; Fiber: 6 g.

Spinach Dip

Preparation Time: 20 minutes
Cooking Time: 5 minutes
Servings: 8
Ingredients:

- ¾ cup cashews
- ounces soft tofu
- 6 ounces of spinach leaves
- 1 medium white onion, peeled, diced
- 2 teaspoons minced garlic
- ½ teaspoon salt
- 3 tablespoons olive oil

Directions:

1. Place cashews in a bowl, cover with hot water and then let them soak for 15 minutes.
2. After 15 minutes, drain the cashews and then set them aside until required.
3. Take a medium skillet pan, add oil to it and then place the pan over medium heat.
4. Add onion, cook for 3 to 5 minutes until tender. Stir in garlic, and continue cooking for 30 seconds until fragrant.
5. Spoon the onion mixture into a blender. Add the remaining ingredients and then pulse until smooth.
6. Tip the dip into a bowl and then serve with chips.

Nutrition: Calories: 134.6; Fat: 8.6 g; Proteins: 10 g; Carbs: 6.3 g; Fiber: 1.4 g.

Tomatillo Salsa

Preparation Time: 5 minutes
Cooking Time: 20 minutes
Servings: 8
Ingredients:

- 5 medium tomatillos, chopped
- 3 cloves of garlic, peeled, chopped
- 3 Roma tomatoes, chopped
- 1 jalapeno, chopped
- ½ of a medium red onion, peeled, chopped
- 1 Anaheim chili
- 2 teaspoons salt
- 1 teaspoon ground cumin
- 1 lime, juiced
- ¼ cup cilantro leaves
- ¾ cup of water

Directions:

1. Take a medium pot, place it over medium heat, pour in water. Add onion, garlic, tomatoes, tomatillo, jalapeno, and Anaheim chili.
2. Sauté the vegetables for 15 minutes and remove the pot from heat. Add cilantro, cumin, and lime juice. Stir in salt.
3. Remove the pot from heat and then pulse by using an immersion blender until smooth.
4. Serve the salsa with chips.

Nutrition: Calories: 317.4; Fat: 0 g; Proteins: 16 g; Carbs: 64 g; Fiber: 16 g.

Arugula Pesto Couscous

Preparation Time: 10 minutes
Cooking Time: 20 minutes
Servings: 4
Ingredients:

- 8 ounces Israeli couscous
- 3 large tomatoes, chopped
- 3 cups arugula leaves
- ½ cup parsley leaves
- 6 cloves of garlic, peeled
- ½ cup walnuts
- ¾ teaspoon salt
- 1 cup and 1 tablespoon olive oil

- 2 cups vegetable broth

Directions:

1. Take a medium saucepan and place it over medium-high heat. Add 1 tablespoon oil and then let it heat.
2. Add couscous. Stir until mixed, and then cook for 4 minutes until fragrant and toasted.
3. Pour in the broth, stir until mixed and bring it to a boil. Switch heat to medium level and then simmer for 12 minutes until the couscous has been absorbed all the liquid and turn tender.
4. When done, remove the pan from heat. Fluff it with a fork, and then set it aside until required.
5. While couscous cooks, prepare the pesto. Place walnuts in a blender, add garlic and then pulse until nuts have broken.
6. Add arugula, parsley and salt. Pulse until well combined, and then blend in oil until smooth.
7. Transfer couscous to a salad bowl. Add tomatoes and the prepared pesto. Then toss until mixed.
8. Serve straight away.

Nutrition: Calories: 73; Fat: 4 g; Proteins: 2 g; Carbs: 8 g; Fiber: 2 g.

Oatmeal and Raisin Balls

Preparation Time: 40 minutes
Cooking Time: 0 minutes **Servings:** 4
Ingredients:

- 1 cup rolled oats
- ¼ cup raisins
- ½ cup peanut butter

Directions:

1. Place oats in a large bowl. Add raisins and peanut butter and then stir until well combined.
2. Shape the mixture into twelve balls, 1 tablespoon of mixture per ball, and then arrange the balls on a baking sheet.
3. Place the baking sheet into the freezer for 30 minutes until firm and then serve.

Nutrition: Calories: 135; Fat: 6 g; Proteins: 8 g; Carbs: 13 g; Fiber: 4 g.

Nacho Cheese

Preparation Time: 10 minutes
Cooking Time: 15 minutes
Servings: 4
Ingredients:

- 1 cup chopped carrots
- ½ teaspoon onion powder
- 2 cups peeled and chopped potatoes
- ½ teaspoon garlic powder
- 1 teaspoon salt
- ½ cup nutritional yeast
- 1 tablespoon lemon juice
- ¼ cup of salsa
- ½ cup of water

Directions:

1. Take a medium pot and place carrots and potato in it. Cover with water and then place the pot over medium-high heat.
2. Boil the vegetables for 10 minutes. Drain them and then transfer them into a blender.
3. Add the remaining ingredients and then pulse until smooth.
4. Tip the cheese into a bowl and then serve with vegetable slices.

Nutrition: Calories: 611.7; Fat: 17.2 g; Proteins: 32.1 g; Carbs: 62.1 g; Fiber: 12.1 g.

Pico de Gallo

Preparation Time: 5 minutes
Cooking Time: 0 minutes
Servings: 6
Ingredients:

- 1/2 of a medium red onion, peeled, chopped
- 2 cups diced tomato
- 1/2 cup chopped cilantro
- 1 jalapeno pepper, minced
- 1/8 teaspoon salt
- 1/4 teaspoon ground black pepper
- 1/2 of a lime, juiced
- 1 teaspoon olive oil

Directions:

1. Take a large bowl, place all the ingredients in it and then stir until well mixed.
2. Serve the Pico de Gallo with chips.

Nutrition: Calories: 790; Fat: 6.4 g; Proteins: 25.6 g; Carbs: 195.2 g; Fiber: 35.2 g.

Beet Balls

Preparation Time: 10 minutes
Cooking Time: 0 minutes
Servings: 6
Ingredients:

- 1/2 cup oats
- 1 medium beet, cooked
- 1/2 cup almond flour
- 1/3 cup shredded coconut and more for coating
- 3/4 cup Medjool dates, pitted
- 1 tablespoon cocoa powder
- 1/2 cup peanuts
- 1/4 cup chocolate chips, unsweetened

Directions:

1. Place cooked beet in a blender and then pulse until chopped into very small pieces.
2. Add the remaining ingredients and then pulse until the dough comes together.
3. Shape the dough into eighteen balls. Coat them in some more coconut and then serve.

Nutrition: Calories: 114.2; Fat: 2.4 g; Proteins: 5 g; Carbs: 19.6 g; Fiber: 4.9 g.

Cheesy Crackers

Preparation Time: 10 minutes
Cooking Time: 20 minutes
Servings: 3
Ingredients:

- 1 ¾ cups almond meal
- 3 tablespoons nutritional yeast
- ½ teaspoon and a pinch of sea salt
- 2 tablespoons lemon juice
- 1 tablespoon melted coconut oil
- 1 tablespoon ground flaxseed
- 2 (½) tablespoons water

Directions:

1. Switch on the oven, then set it to 350°F and let it preheat.
2. Meanwhile, take a medium bowl, place flaxseed in it, stir in water and then let the mixture rest for 5 minutes until thickened.
3. Place almond meal in a medium bowl, add sea salt and yeast, and then stir until mixed.
4. Add lemon juice and coconut oil into the flaxseed mixture and then whisk until mixed.
5. Pour the flaxseed mixture into the almond meal mixture, and then stir until the dough comes together.
6. Place a piece of wax paper on a clean working space. Place the dough on it, cover with another piece of wax paper, and then roll dough into a 1/8-inch-thick crust.
7. Cut the dough into a square shape. Sprinkle salt over the top and then bake for 15 to 20 minutes until done.
8. Serve straight away.

Nutrition: Calories: 30; Fat: 1 g; Proteins: 1 g; Carbs: 5 g; Fiber: 0 g.

Butterscotch Tart

Preparation Time: 50 minutes
Cooking Time: 20 minutes
Servings: 10
Ingredients:
Crust:

- ½ cup sugar
- ¼ cup coconut oil
- 1 teaspoon vanilla extract, pure
- ½ teaspoon sea salt
- 2 cups almond meal flour

Filling:

- 2/3 cup light brown sugar, packed
- 1 teaspoon kosher salt
- ½ cup coconut oil
- 2/3 cup coconut cream, canned
- Flaked sea salt, as needed
- 1 green apple, sliced

Directions:

1. Turn the oven to 375° F, and then get out a bowl. Prepare your crust ingredients by mixing everything until smooth. Spread this into a nine inches tart pan. Spread it as evenly as possible. Freeze for 10 minutes, and then bake for fifteen. It should be golden brown.

2. Prepare the filling by cooking it all in a saucepan for 25 minutes. It should thicken and allow it to cool. You will need to stir often to keep it from burning.
3. Add this to the tart, and then chill for two hours before serving.

Nutrition: Calories: 40; Fat: 1 g; Proteins: 3 g; Carbs: 5 g; Fiber: 2 g.

Easy Brownies

Preparation Time: 20 minutes
Cooking Time: 25 minutes
Servings: 12
Ingredients:

- 2 tablespoons coconut oil, melted
- ½ cup peanut butter, salted
- ¼ cup warm water
- 2 cups dates, pitted
- 1/3 cup dark chocolate chips
- 1/3 cup cocoa powder
- ½ cup raw walnuts, chopped

Directions:

1. Heat the oven to 350° F, and then get out a loaf pan. Place parchment paper in it, and then get out a food processor. Blend your dates until it's a fine mixture. Add in some hot water, and blend well until the mixture become a smooth batter.
2. Add in the coconut oil, cacao powder, and peanut butter. Blend more, and then fold in the chocolate and walnuts. Spread this into your loaf pan.
3. Bake for fifteen minutes, and then chill before serving.

Nutrition: Calories: 50; Fat: 5 g; Proteins: 4 g; Carbs: 6 g; Fiber: 0 g.

Avocado Blueberry Cheesecake

Preparation Time: 1 hour
Cooking Time: 1 hour 20 minutes
Servings: 8
Ingredients:
Crust:

- 1 cup rolled oats
- 1 cup walnuts
- 1 teaspoon lime zest
- 1 cup soft pitted dates

Filling:

- 2 tablespoons maple syrup
- 1 cup blueberries, frozen
- 2 avocados, peeled & pitted
- 2 tablespoons basil, fresh & minced fine
- 4 tablespoons lime juice

Directions:

1. Pulse all crust ingredients together in your food processor, and then press into a pie pan.
2. Blend all filling ingredients until smooth, and pour it into the crust.
3. Smooth out and freeze for two hours before serving.

Nutrition: Calories: 70; Fat: 4 g; Proteins: 4 g; Carbs: 8 g; Fiber: 3 g.

CHAPTER 25:

OTHER FOODS

Zucchini with Red Beans and Tomatoes

Preparation Time: 5 minutes
Cooking Time: 25 minutes
Servings: 2
Ingredients:

- ¼ cup Flavorful Vegetable Broth
- two zucchinis, shed, sliced sideways, and cut into half-moons
- 1 large ripe tomato, cut into wedges
- ½ cup canned kidney beans, drained
- 2 tablespoons tomato paste
- 1 teaspoon dried minced garlic
- 1 teaspoon dried minced onion
- ½ teaspoon ground turmeric
- 1 bay leaf (optional)
- ½ cup chopped scallions (optional)
- 1 tablespoon chopped fresh dill (optional)

Directions:

1. Place the chopped zucchini and vegetable stock in a medium-sized pan that has a cover for it. Cap the pan and cook the zucchini for ten mins at moderate flame till it has become mushy. During this time, flip the zucchini pieces either once twice to ensure that they all become roasted evenly.
2. After adding the tomatoes, kidney beans, and tomato paste in addition to the garlic, onion, and turmeric, thoroughly combine the ingredients. Cook the tomatoes for five to ten mins with the lid off, till they become extremely soft.
3. Just one or two mins before the end of the cooking time, include the bay leaf, if you utilize it.
4. Serve while still warm, garnished using chopped scallions and dill, if desired.

Cooking Tip: Do not stir often, just a few times to make sure the vegetables are cooked. If there isn't enough vegetable broth, add more as necessary until the vegetables are done.

Swap It: For more taste, add yellow squash or any other type of squash to this recipe. Use Italian parsley or cilantro instead of dill.

Flavor Boost: Add sliced mushrooms and diced red bell peppers to the zucchini and cook together. Add red pepper flakes or hot sauce for extra spice.

Nutrition: Calories: 123; Total Fat: 1 g; Sodium: 31 mg; Carbohydrates: 24 g; Fiber: 7 g; Proteins: 8 g.

Quinoa, Bean, and Olive Dip Wrap

Preparation Time: 10 minutes
Cooking Time: 30 minutes
Servings: Makes 3
Ingredients:

- ½ cup quinoa, uncooked
- 1¼ cups Flavorful Vegetable Broth
- 1 teaspoon dried minced onion
- 1 teaspoon dried minced garlic
- Pinch freshly ground black pepper
- ¼ cup chopped fresh cilantro
- 3 (8-inch) whole-grain tortillas
- one mug Kalamata Olives and White Bean Incline, separated
- 1 red bell pepper, seeded and thinly sliced

Directions:

1. The quinoa should be washed in a filter over running cold water, after which the filter should be shook to remove any remaining water. Mix the quinoa and the vegetable broth together in a pan of moderate size that is set at high temperature, and raise to a boil.
2. After adding the onion and garlic, close the pot and bring the temperature down to a low setting.
3. Maintain a low boil for fifteen to twenty mins, or till the stock is fully immersed. When it is ready, the quinoa ought to have a supple texture, as well as a germ ring ought to be evident running along the perimeter of each grain.
4. Blend in the ground black pepper and chopped cilantro, then withdraw the pan from the flame to allow it to cool.
5. On a plate, place one tortilla, a 1/3 of the Kalamata Olives and White Bean Dip, a 1/3 of the quinoa, and 3 pieces of bell pepper, and then top with the remaining tortilla.
6. Place the filling in the folded tortilla. Continue the procedure with the other tortillas and fillings, and then dig in!

Cooking Tip: Buy pre-washed quinoa to save time.

Swap It: Use dill or parsley instead of cilantro. Try other vegetables like cucumbers or radishes instead of bell pepper.

Nutrition: Calories: 345; Total Fat: 9 g; Sodium: 283 mg; Carbohydrates: 54 g; Fiber: 11 g; Proteins: 14 g.

Mason Jar Rice and Vegetables

Preparation Time: 15 minutes
Cooking Time: 15 minutes
Servings: 1
Ingredients:

- 1/3 cup Flavorful Brown Rice Pilaf
- 1/3 cup cannellini beans, drained
- ¼ cup diced Persian cucumbers
- ¼ cup diced fresh tomatoes
- ¼ cup chopped avocado
- ½ cup arugula
- Pinch onion powder
- Pinch garlic powder
- ½ tbsp freshly squeezed lemon juice
- Pinch freshly ground black pepper

Directions:

1. Arrange the following ingredients in the order listed in a big Glass jar that has a cover: rice, beans, cucumbers, tomatoes, avocado, and arugula. Place the lid on it and seal it.
2. In order to finish the dish, stir in the onion powder, garlic powder, and lemon juice.
3. Put the top back on and give it a light toss to evenly sprinkle all of the components. Sprinkle some pepper over the lettuce once it has been transferred to a container or dish.

Cooking Tip: To save time, use microwavable rice.
Swap It: Try different vegetables like radishes, red or yellow bell peppers, and broccoli. Also try balsamic vinegar instead of lemon juice. Choose different grains like bulgur wheat or farro. Swap arugula for spinach, lettuce, or mixed greens.
Flavor Boost: Season with fresh herbs like dill, cilantro, or parsley.
Nutrition: Calories: 221; Total Fat: 6 g; Sodium: 14 mg; Carbohydrates: 36 g; Fiber: 7 g; Proteins: 9 g.

Vegetable "Poke" Bowl

Preparation Time: 10 minutes
Cooking Time: 30 minutes
Servings: 1
Ingredients:

- ½ cup flavorful brown rice pilaf
- ½ cup mixed greens
- ¼ cup cooked edamame
- ¼ cup creamy chimichurri sauce
- ½ cup mango salsa
- ½ small avocado, peeled, pitted, and cut
- two shredded sheets of raw nori seaweed
- ¼ cup microgreens
- Sesame seeds (optional)

Directions:

1. Combine the rice pilaf, the mixed greens, the edamame, and the Creamy Chimichurri Sauce together in a medium-sized container. Combine thoroughly.
2. Add the Mango Salsa, sliced avocado, shredded nori sheets, and microgreens to the surface of the dish. Top using sesame seeds.

Cooking Tip: To save time, use microwavable rice. Try replacing the Mango Salsa with fresh diced mango.
Swap It: If there is a wasabi arugula at the store or at your local farmers' market, pick that up and give it a try instead of the mixed greens.
Flavor Boost: Add wasabi.
Nutrition: Calories: 450; Total Fat: 26 g; Sodium: 40 mg; Carbohydrates: 58 g; Fiber: 16 g; Proteins: 13 g.

Plant-Based Charcuterie Board

Preparation Time: 20 minutes
Cooking Time: 0 minutes
Servings: 1
Ingredients:

- 13 unsalted almonds, toasted
- ¼ cup sliced fresh strawberries
- 10 grapes
- ½ apple, cored and sliced into wedges
- 3 baby carrots
- 1 celery stalk, cut into 3-inch-long pieces
- 1 tablespoon peanut butter
- 5 whole-grain crackers
- 3 low-sodium olives
- ½ cup Chickpea Hummus with Roasted Bell Peppers
- ¼ cup Smoked Cashew Cheese Spread (optional) Fresh dill, for garnish

Directions:

1. On a serving tray, set out the almonds, strawberries, grapes, apples, carrots, celery, peanut butter, crackers, and olives.
2. Place the hummus in a small bowl in the middle of the tray. In a second bowl, place the cashew cheese spread.
3. Garnish with fresh dill.

Swap It: Use any unsalted nuts, but keep in mind that different nuts have different amounts of calories. The goal is to keep the serving at 100 calories. If preferred, skip the olives and hummus and serve the Kalamata Olives and White Bean Dip. Instead of peanut butter, substitute almond butter.
Nutrition: Calories: 676; Total Fat: 24 g; Sodium: 377 mg; Carbohydrates: 92 g; Fiber: 22 g; Proteins: 23 g.

Red Bell Pepper Stuffed with Edamame and Avocado

Preparation Time: 15 minutes
Cooking Time: 20 minutes
Servings: 1
Ingredients:

- ½ cup shelled edamame
- 1 small avocado, peeled and pitted
- 1 tablespoon freshly squeezed lemon juice
- ½ teaspoon garlic powder
- ½ teaspoon onion powder
- 1 teaspoon ginger powder
- Pinch freshly ground black pepper
- Red pepper flakes (optional)
- 1 red bell pepper, seeded and halved
- 1 tablespoon diced scallions
- 2 tablespoons finely chopped cilantro
- 1 tomato, diced
- 2 tablespoons microgreens (optional)
- 2 tsps. everything but the Bagel and Salt Mix

Directions:

1. In a medium bowl, combine the edamame, avocado, lemon juice, garlic powder, onion powder, ginger powder, black pepper (if using), and red pepper flakes to taste (if using).
2. Mash all the ingredients together with a potato masher or fork until the mixture reaches a chunky consistency.
3. In each half of the bell pepper, spoon the edamame mixture; then sprinkle on the scallions, cilantro, and tomatoes, and top with the microgreens (if using).
4. Top with everything but the bagel and salt mix; then serve.

Cooking Tip: If using frozen edamame, defrost it in cold water for 2 to 3 minutes; then drain the water and dry the beans.

Swap It: Instead of lemon juice, try freshly squeezed lime juice. Instead of Everything but the Bagel and Salt Mix, use toasted peanuts or pepitas. Instead of microgreens, use alfalfa.

Nutrition: Per Servings: Calories: 490; Total Fat: 34 g; Sodium: 33 mg; Carbohydrates: 40 g; Fiber: 22 g; Proteins: 15 g.

Cheesy Polenta with Kale, Butternut Squash, and Pepitas

Preparation Time: 10 minutes
Cooking Time: 30 minutes
Servings: 3
Ingredients:

- 2 cups cubed butternut squash
- ½ tablespoon ground cinnamon
- 2/3 cup canned coconut milk
- 2 cups Flavorful Vegetable Broth
- 2/3 cup shredded kale
- 2/3 cup polenta
- 2 tablespoons nutritional yeast (optional)
- 3 tablespoons pepitas

Directions:

1. Preheat the oven to 425° F.
2. Place the butternut squash in a single layer on a baking sheet covered with nonstick foil or parchment paper. Sprinkle the cinnamon on the squash. If the squash

is too dry, lightly sprinkle it with water so the cinnamon will stick better. Bake for 25 to 30 minutes until the squash is tender, turning once halfway through.
3. Meanwhile, in a medium pot, combine the coconut milk and vegetable broth and bring to a boil.
4. Add the kale, polenta, and nutritional yeast (if using). Reduce the heat to low and cook for 3 to 5 minutes, stirring with a whisk or fork to prevent clumping.
5. Serve 1 cup of the polenta mixture with ¾ cup of roasted squash.
6. Sprinkle with 1 tablespoon of the pepitas.
7. Store extra polenta and squash in separate airtight containers in the refrigerator for up to 3 days. Top with the pepitas only when ready to serve.

Cooking Tip: When reheating polenta, add extra water or plant-based milk to ensure it stays creamy.

Swap It: Add yams or sweet potatoes to the butternut squash, or use them in place of the butternut squash. Also, try swapping pepitas for pine nuts.

Flavor Boost: Drizzle the butternut squash with maple syrup before roasting it.

Nutrition: Calories: 239; Total Fat: 15 g; Sodium: 97 mg; Carbohydrates: 26 g; Fiber: 4 g; Proteins: 5 g.

Buddha Bowl with Root Vegetables

Preparation Time: 15 minutes
Cooking Time: 35 minutes
Servings: 1
Ingredients:

- ½ cup cubed beets
- ½ cup cubed carrots
- ½ cup cubed yams
- Pinch garlic powder
- Pinch onion powder
- Pinch freshly ground black pepper
- ½ cup Flavorful Brown Rice Pilaf
- ½ cup mixed greens
- ¼ cup Sweet Peanut Butter Dip in Sauce
- 1 tablespoon sunflower seeds
- ¼ cup Smoked Cashew Cheese Spread

Directions:

1. Preheat the oven to 425° F.
2. Place the beets, carrots, and yams in a single layer on a baking sheet shielded with nonstick foil or baking paper. Sprinkle with garlic powder, onion powder, and pepper. Bake for 25 to 35 minutes until the vegetables are tender, turning once halfway through.
3. Warm the Flavorful Brown Rice Pilaf in the microwave. In a serving bowl, combine the warmed rice pilaf, roasted vegetables, and mixed greens. Top with the peanut butter sauce, then sprinkle with the sunflower seeds. Add the cashew cheese spread (if using).

Swap It: Sweet potatoes are wonderful in this dish in addition to the other root vegetables, as are purple or yellow carrots. You can swap the rice pilaf for quinoa or farro.

Flavor Boost: Roasted bell peppers also work well in this dish.

Nutrition: Calories: 449; Total Fat: 19 g; Sodium: 122 mg; Carbohydrates: 70 g; Fiber: 10 g; Proteins: 15 g.

Vega Burger Patties with Black Beans and Edamame

Preparation Time: 15 minutes
Cooking Time: 15 minutes
Servings: Makes 8
Ingredients:

- one (15-oz.) can black beans, shattered and washed
- ¾ cup shelled edamame
- 2/3 cup minced yellow onion
- 3 garlic cloves, minced
- ½ cup bread crumbs
- ¾ cup rolled oats, uncooked
- 3 tablespoons Dijon mustard
- 1 teaspoon ground ginger
- Pinch red pepper flakes
- Pinch freshly ground black pepper
- 1/3 cup Flavorful Vegetable Broth

Directions:

1. Combine the black beans and edamame in a large bowl and mash with a potato masher or fork.
2. Add the onion, garlic, bread crumbs, rolled oats, Dijon mustard, ginger, red pepper flakes, and pepper. Combine well.
3. Scoop out about 1/3 cup of the mixture and form a patty. Repeat to make 8 patties.
4. In a large pan, heat the Flavorful Vegetable Broth over medium heat.
5. Add patties and cook for 5 to 7 minutes per side. Add more broth if it evaporates too quickly.
6. Serve the patties hot with a side dish or salad.

Cooking Tip: If the mixture is too dry and the patties are not holding together, add water or liquid from the drained black beans. Patties can be refrigerated for 1 to 2 hours before cooking.
Flavor Boost: Top with spicy mustard.
Nutrition: Calories: 109; Total Fat: 2 g; Sodium: 91 mg; Carbohydrates: 18 g; Fiber: 4 g; Proteins: 6 g.

Barley Bowl with Cranberries and Walnuts

Preparation Time: 5 minutes
Cooking Time: 30 minutes
Servings: 4
Ingredients:

- 1 cup pearl barley, uncooked
- 3 cups water
- ¼ cup poppy seeds
- ½ cup dried cranberries
- ½ cup chopped walnuts, toasted

Directions:

1. In a medium pot, combine the barley and water and bring to a boil.

2. Reduce the heat to medium and cook until the barley is tender, 25 to 30 mins. Once done, drain off any excess water and let cool. While the barley is cooking, place the poppy seeds and dried cranberries in a small bowl and soak them in hot water for 5 to 10 minutes; then drain the water and let cool.
3. In a large bowl, combine the cooked barley, cranberries, poppy seeds, and walnuts. Mix well, cover, and refrigerate for 30 minutes to 1 hour before serving cold.

Swap It: Dried cranberries can be substituted with dried cherries or raisins. Pecans, almonds, sunflower seeds, and pumpkin seeds may be used instead of walnuts or combinations. Try this recipe with farro instead of pearl barley.
Cooking Tip: The nuts can be finely chopped and lightly toasted in an oven, or a sauté pan or skillet for up to 5 minutes or until they develop a pleasant smell. To save time, purchase pre-cooked grains.
Nutrition: Calories: 341; Total Fat: 14 g; Sodium: 12 mg; Carbohydrates: 50 g; Fiber: 11 g; Proteins: 9 g.

Sweet Pineapple Brown Rice

Preparation Time: 15 minutes
Cooking Time: 10 minutes
Servings: 4
Ingredients:

- ½ cup canned coconut milk
- 2 garlic cloves, minced
- 1½ cups chopped fresh pineapple
- 1 large red bell pepper, seeded and diced
- ¾ cup chopped scallions
- ½ cup chopped unsalted cashews
- 2 cups Flavorful Brown Rice Pilaf
- 1 cup chopped fresh cilantro
- 1 small lime, quartered

Directions:

1. In a large pot, bring the coconut milk to a low boil over medium heat.
2. Stir in the garlic.
3. Add the pineapple, bell pepper, scallions, cashews, and rice pilaf. Mix well and cook for 5 to 7 minutes.
4. Reduce the heat to low, add the cilantro, and stir for 3 minutes more.
5. Serve hot with lime wedges.

Flavor Boost: Consider adding a teaspoon of chili sauce, or serve with a spoonful of Spicy Tomato and Pepper Sauce.
Nutrition: Calories: 330; Total Fat: 15 g; Sodium: 20 mg; Carbohydrates: 44 g; Fiber: 4 g; Proteins: 8 g.

Vegan Chili

Preparation Time: 5 minutes
Cooking Time: 25 minutes
Servings: 4
Ingredients:

- 1 cup Flavorful Vegetable Broth
- 1 (28-ounce) can crushed tomatoes

- 1 medium sweet onion, diced
- 1 medium carrot, thinly sliced
- One (15-oz.) can black beans, wearied and washed
- One (15-oz.) can chickpeas, wearied and washed
- 1 cup frozen corn
- 3 garlic cloves, minced
- 1 cup chopped low-sodium olives
- 1 teaspoon mild chili powder
- 2 teaspoons ground cumin
- 1 tablespoon smoked paprika
- Dash cayenne pepper (optional)
- 2 tablespoons maple syrup (optional)
- ½ cup chopped fresh chives

Directions:

1. In a large pot, combine the vegetable broth and tomatoes with their juices. Bring to a low boil over medium heat.
2. Add the onions and carrots and cook for about 15 minutes on medium-low heat.
3. Add the black beans, chickpeas, corn, garlic, and olives (if using).
4. Top with chili powder, cumin, smoked paprika, cayenne pepper, and maple syrup. Cover with a lid and simmer 5 minutes more.
5. Top with the new chives and serve warm.

Swap It: Use scallions or fresh cilantro instead of chives. Feel free to try a different variety of beans with this recipe. If using canned corn instead of frozen, make sure it has no added salt.

Flavor Boost: For extra spice and flavor, stir in 1 tablespoon of Spicy Tomato and Pepper Sauce per serving and add a slice of lemon.

Nutrition: Calories: 307; Total Fat: 3 g; Sodium: 67 mg; Carbohydrates: 59 g; Fiber: 18 g; Proteins: 16 g.

Fully Loaded Sweet Potatoes

Preparation Time: 10 minutes
Cooking Time: 25 minutes
Servings: 2
Ingredients:

- 2 large sweet potatoes
- 4 tbsps. spicy tomato and pepper sauce
- 4 tablespoons creamy chimichurri sauce
- 2 tbsps. kalamata olives and white bean dip
- 4 tablespoons chopped scallions
- 2 tbsps. all but the bagel and salt mix

Directions:

1. Preheat the oven to 425° F.
2. Poke the potatoes with a fork all over; then fully cover in foil. Bake for 25 minutes or until the potatoes are easily pierced with a fork.
3. Remove the potatoes from the oven and let cool. Remove the foil and slice each potato lengthwise to open it slightly.
4. Lightly mash the inside of each potato with a fork. Top each potato with 2 tablespoons of spicy tomato and pepper sauce, 2 tablespoons of creamy chimichurri sauce, 1 tablespoon of kalamata olives

and white bean dip, 2 tablespoons of chopped scallions, and 1 tablespoon of everything but the bagel and salt mix (if using).

Cooking Tip: Place both potatoes in a casserole baking dish and cover with a lid or a sheet of foil instead of wrapping each potato individually.

Swap It: Top with sliced avocado instead of the Creamy Chimichurri Sauce.

Nutrition: Calories: 187; Total Fat: 5 g; Sodium: 103 mg; Carbohydrates: 34 g; Fiber: 7 g; Proteins: 4 g.

Dried Tomatoes

Preparation Time: 5 minutes
Cooking Time: 15 minutes
Servings: 2
Ingredients:

- 4 cups water
- 1½ cups whole-wheat rigatoni, uncooked
- ½ cup sun-dried tomatoes, julienned
- 1 cup fresh or frozen broccoli florets
- 6 black pitted low-sodium olives, diced
- ¼ cup thinly sliced fresh basil leaves
- ¼ cup pine nuts, toasted
- ¼ cup Creamy Chimichurri Sauce

Directions:

1. In a big pot, raise the water to a boil. Add the pasta, stir, and cook on medium heat for 10 minutes.
2. Add the tomatoes and broccoli. Cover with a lid and bring back to a boil. Reduce the heat to medium-low and cook for 3 minutes more.
3. Drain the liquid.
4. In a large bowl, combine the cooked pasta and vegetables with the olives, basil (if using), and pine nuts.
5. Dress with the Creamy Chimichurri Sauce and serve warm or cold. Leftover pasta can be stored in an airtight container in the refrigerator for up to 3 days.

Nutrition: Calories: 430; Total Fat: 19 g; Sodium: 217 mg; Carbohydrates: 58 g; Fiber: 11 g; Proteins: 15 g.

Chickpea Masala

Preparation Time: 10 minutes
Cooking Time: 15 minutes
Servings: 4
Ingredients:

- ¼ cup canned coconut milk
- ½ medium sweet onion, chopped
- one moderate jalapeño pepper, seeded, ribs detached, and chopped
- 2 garlic cloves, minced
- 1 tablespoon minced fresh ginger
- 1 (15-ounce) can crushed tomatoes
- one (15-oz.) can chickpeas, washed and wearied
- 1 teaspoon ground cinnamon
- 1 teaspoon ground coriander
- 1 teaspoon ground turmeric

- ½ teaspoon ground cloves
- ½ teaspoon ground cumin

Directions:

1. In a small pot, add the coconut milk, onion, jalapeño pepper, garlic, and ginger. Cook on moderate flame for two mins.
2. Include the tomatoes using their juices, the chickpeas, cinnamon, coriander, turmeric, cloves, and cumin. Reduce the heat to low and cook for 10 minutes more.
3. Serve warm.

Flavor Boost: Add a touch of freshly squeezed lemon juice and a pinch of fresh chopped cilantro. For extra spice, add chilis or ¼ teaspoon of cayenne pepper while cooking.

Nutrition: Calories: 149; Total Fat: 5 g; Sodium: 138 mg; Carbohydrates: 23 g; Fiber: 7 g; Proteins: 6 g.

Sweet Potato and Peanut Stew

Preparation Time: 10 minutes
Cooking Time: 20 minutes
Servings: 4
Ingredients:

- 1 cup canned coconut milk
- 1 cup Flavorful Vegetable Broth
- 1 medium sweet onion, diced
- 2 cloves garlic, minced
- 2 moderate sweet potatoes, shed and cut into quarter inch cubes
- ¼ cup peanut butter
- 1 teaspoon yellow curry
- 1 teaspoon mild chili powder
- ½ cup chopped peanuts, toasted
- 2 cups chopped kale
- 1 cup chopped cilantro
- 1 cup chopped scallions
- Dash cayenne pepper (optional)

Directions:

1. In a medium pot, combine the coconut milk and Flavorful Vegetable Broth. Add the onion, garlic, sweet potatoes, peanut butter, yellow curry, and chili powder. Cook on medium heat for 15 minutes, stirring occasionally.
2. Stir in the peanuts and kale and continue cooking for 3 to 5 minutes more.
3. Top individual portions with the cilantro, scallions, and cayenne pepper.
4. Serve warm.

Cooking Tip: Feel free to add up to 1 extra cup of the Flavorful Vegetable Broth if the preference is for a thinner stew.

Swap It: Use turmeric instead of yellow curry.

Flavor Boost: Stir in 1 tablespoon of Spicy Tomato and Pepper Sauce while cooking.

Nutrition: Calories: 408; Total Fat: 30 g; Sodium: 83 mg; Carbohydrates: 43 g; Fiber: 6 g; Proteins: 12 g.

Cabbage and Mushroom Ragout

Preparation Time: 10 minutes
Cooking Time: 15 minutes
Servings: 3
Ingredients:

- 1 cup flavorful vegetable broth
- 2 cups shredded fresh cabbage
- 10 Baby Bella mushrooms, sliced
- 1 cup diced onion
- ½ cup shredded carrots
- 1 cup crushed tomatoes
- 2 teaspoons mild chili powder
- 2 bay leaves (optional)

Directions:

1. Mix the vegetable broth, cabbage, mushrooms, onions, carrots, tomatoes with their juices, chili powder, and bay leaves in a medium saucepan. Cover with a lid and bring to a boil over medium heat.
2. Decrease the heat and cook on moderate-low for ten mins more.
3. Eliminate the bay leaves prior to serving, and serve hot or cold.

Flavor Boost: Top with chopped fresh parsley when serving.

Nutrition: Calories: 106; Total Fat: 1 g; Sodium: 240 mg; Carbohydrates: 23 g; Fiber: 7 g; Proteins: 6 g.

Plantain Boats

Preparation Time: 5 minutes
Cooking Time: 20 minutes
Servings: 2
Ingredients:

- 2 ripe plantains, halved
- 2 tablespoons freshly squeezed lime juice
- 1 teaspoon chili powder
- 1 cup flavorful brown rice pilaf
- ½ cup mango salsa

Directions:

1. Preheat the oven to 425° F.
2. Line the bottom of a casserole dish using foil. Coat the plantain halves with lime juice and sprinkle with chili powder.
3. Put the seasoned plantain halves in the set dish, cut-side up.
4. Lid the dish with foil and bake for twenty mins or till the plantains are lenient and caring.
5. Remove the dish from the oven. Carefully transfer the cooked plantains onto a serving plate, and top each with ¼ cup of rice pilaf and a spoonful of Mango Salsa.
6. Serve warm. Store the unused portion for a leftover meal.

Swap It: Use Chipotle Relish instead of Mango Salsa.

Flavor Boost: Drizzle with hot sauce for extra spice.

Nutrition: Calories: 118; Total Fat: 1 g; Sodium: 8 mg; Carbohydrates: 25 g; Fiber: 1 g; Proteins: 3 g.

Black Bean Dip

Preparation Time: 1 hour and 30 minutes
Cooking Time: 1 hour
Servings: 10
Ingredients:

- Two (15-oz.) cans black beans, washed and shattered
- 1 jalapeno pepper, seeded and minced
- ½ red bell pepper, seeded and diced
- ½ yellow bell pepper, seeded and diced
- ½ small red onion, diced
- 1 cup fresh cilantro, finely chopped
- Zest of 1 lime
- Juice of 1 lime
- 1 10-ounce can Rotel, drained
- ½ teaspoon Kosher salt
- ¼ teaspoon ground black pepper

Directions:

1. Inside a big container, mix the garlic, green onions, beans, jalapeno, red and yellow bell pepper, onion, cilantro, and stir together.
2. Include the lime zest and juice, Rotel, salt and pepper, and stir. Adjust seasoning to your own taste.
3. Store at a low temperature for at least one hr., prior to serving, so the flavors have time to mix. Serve with wheat tortilla slices that have been crisped in the oven or with wheat or sesame crackers.

Nutrition: Proteins: 658g; Fat: 136 g; Carbohydrates: 235.4 g.

Cannellini Bean Cashew Dip

Preparation Time: 1 hour
Cooking Time: 1 hour
Servings: 8
Ingredients:

- One (15-oz.) can cannellini beans, washed and wearied
- ½ cup raw cashews
- 1 clove garlic, smashed
- 2 tablespoons diced, red bell pepper
- ½ teaspoon sea salt
- ¼ teaspoon cayenne pepper
- 4 teaspoons lemon juice
- 2 tablespoons water
- Dill sprigs or weed for garnish

Directions:

1. Put the beans, cashews, garlic and bell pepper in the mixing bowl and beat numerous times to disrupt it.
2. Include the salt, cayenne, lemon juice and water, and develop till homogenous.
3. Fix inside a container, seal and chill it for approximately an hr. prior to serving.

4. Relish using fresh dill and serve using vegetables, crackers or pita chips.

Nutrition: Proteins:13g; Fat: 18g; Carbohydrates: 78g.

Green Beans Gremolata

Preparation Time: 15 minutes
Cooking Time: 5 minutes
Servings: 6
Ingredients:

- 1-pound fresh green beans
- 3 garlic cloves, minced
- Zest of 2 oranges
- 3 tablespoons minced fresh parsley
- 2 tablespoons pine nuts
- 3 tablespoons olive oil
- Sea salt to taste
- Freshly ground black pepper to taste

Directions:

1. Boil water at high flame. Cook green beans for three mins. Drain and rinse with cold water to stop the cooking.
2. Blend garlic, orange zest, and parsley.
3. In a big fry pan at moderate-high flame, toast the pine nuts in the dry, hot saucepan for three mins. Remove from the pan and set aside.
4. Cook olive oil in the same pan until it shimmers. Add the beans and cook, stirring frequently, until heated for about 2 minutes.
5. Take the pan away from the heat and add the parsley mixture and pine nuts. Season with salt and pepper. Serve immediately.

Nutrition: Calories: 98; Fiber: 2 g; Proteins: 3 g.

Cinnamon Apple Chips with Dip

Preparation Time: 3 hours and 30 minutes
Cooking Time: 3 hours
Servings: 2
Ingredients:

- 1 cup raw cashews
- 2 apples, thinly sliced
- 1 lemon
- 1½ cups water, divided
- Cinnamon plus more to dust the chips
- Another medium cored apple quartered
- 1 tablespoon honey or agave
- 1 teaspoon cinnamon
- ¼ teaspoon sea salt

Directions:

1. Put the cashews within a container of warm water, shallow enough to seal them, and let them dry during night time.
2. Preheat the oven to 200º F. Line two baking sheets with parchment paper.
3. Juice the lemon into a large glass bowl and add two cups of water. Place the sliced apples in the water as you cut them, and when done, swish them around and drain.

4. Spread the apple slices across the baking sheet in a single layer and sprinkle with a little cinnamon. Bake for 90 minutes.
5. Remove the slices from the oven and flip each of them over. Put them back in the oven and bake for another 90 minutes, or until they are crisp. Remember, they will get crisper as they cool.
6. While the apple slices are cooking. Drain the cashews and put them in a blender, along with the quartered apple, the honey, a teaspoon of cinnamon and a half cup of the remaining water. Process until thick and creamy. I like to refrigerate my dip for about an hour to chill before serving alongside the room temperature apple slices.

Nutrition: Proteins:113g;Fat:11.45g; Carbohydrates: 66.6 g.

Crunchy Asparagus Spears

Preparation Time: 25 minutes
Cooking Time: 25 minutes
Servings: 4
Ingredients:

- 1 bunch asparagus spears (12 spears)
- ¼ cup nutritional yeast
- 2 tablespoons hemp seeds
- 1 teaspoon garlic powder
- ¼ teaspoon paprika
- 1/8 teaspoon ground pepper
- ¼ cup whole-wheat breadcrumbs
- Juice of ½ lemon

Directions:

1. Preheat the oven to 350° F. Line a baking sheet with parchment paper.
2. Wash the asparagus, snapping off the white part at the bottom. Save it for making vegetable stock."
3. Mix the nutritional yeast, hemp seed, garlic powder, paprika, pepper and breadcrumbs.
4. Put asparagus spears on the baking papers giving them a slight room and scatter with the mix within the container.
5. Bake for up to 25 minutes, until crispy.
6. Serve with lemon juice if desired.

Nutrition: Proteins: 91g;Fat: 84g; Carbohydrates: 125 g.

Cucumber Bites with Chive and Sunflower Seeds

Preparation Time: 5 minutes
Cooking Time: 5 minutes
Servings: 2
Ingredients:

- 1 cup raw sunflower seed
- ½ teaspoon salt
- ½ cup chopped fresh chives
- 1 clove garlic, chopped
- 2 tablespoons red onion, minced
- 2 tablespoons lemon juice
- ½ cup water (might need more or less)

- 4 large cucumbers

Directions:

1. Put the sunflower seeds and salt in the mixing bowl and progress to a fine powder. It will take at least ten secs.
2. Include the chives, garlic, onion, lemon juice and water. Process until creamy, scraping down the sides frequently. The mixture should be very creamy; if not, add a little more water.
3. Cut the cucumbers into 1 ½-inch coin-like bits.
4. Distribute a spoonful of the sunflower mix on the surface and set it on a dish.
5. Scatter extra sliced chives on the surface and refrigerate till ready to serve.

Nutrition: Proteins: 130 g; Fat: 621 g; Carbohydrates: 231 g.

Garlicky Kale Chips

Preparation Time: 1 hour and 30 minutes
Cooking Time: 1 hour
Servings: 2
Ingredients:

- 4 cloves garlic
- 1 cup olive oil
- 8 to 10 cups fresh kale, chopped
- 1 tablespoon of garlic-flavored olive oil
- ½ teaspoon garlic salt
- ½ teaspoon pepper
- 1 pinch red pepper flakes (optional)

Directions:

1. Peel and crush the garlic clove and place it in a small jar with a lid. Pour the olive oil over the top. Cover tightly and shake. This will keep in the refrigerator for several days. When you're ready to use it, strain out the garlic and retain the oil.
2. Preheat the oven to 175° F.
3. Spread out the kale on a baking sheet and drizzle with olive oil. Sprinkle with garlic salt, pepper and red pepper flakes.
4. Bake for an hour. Remove from the oven and let the chips cool.
5. Store in an airtight container. If you don't plan to eat them right away.

Nutrition: Proteins: 54 g; Fat: 22.02 g; Carbohydrates: 249 g.

Hummus-stuffed Baby Potatoes

Preparation Time: 30 minutes
Cooking Time: 30 minutes
Servings: 2
Ingredients:

- 12 small red potatoes, walnut-sized or slightly larger Hummus
- 2 green onions, thinly sliced
- ¼ teaspoon paprika, for garnish

Directions:

1. Put two to three inches of water in a saucepan. Set a steamer inside and bring the water to a boil.
2. Place the whole potatoes in the steamer basket and steam for about 20 minutes or until soft. "Keep the pan from boiling dry by adding additional hot water as needed."
3. Dump the potatoes into a colander and run cold water over them until they can be handled.
4. Cut each potato open and scoop out most of the pulp. leaving the skin and a thin layer of potato intact.
5. Mix the hummus with most green onions and spoon a little into the area where the potato has been scooped out.
6. Scatter each occupied potato half with paprika and serve.

Nutrition: Proteins: 233 g; Fat: 53 g; Carbohydrates: 283.8 g.

Homemade Trail Mix

Preparation Time: 20 minutes
Cooking Time: 20 minutes
Servings: 2
Ingredients:

- ½ cup uncooked old-fashioned oatmeal
- ½ cup chopped dates
- 2 cups whole-grain cereal
- ¼ cup raisins
- ¼ cup almonds
- ¼ cup walnuts

Directions:

1. Mix all the ingredients in a large bowl.
2. Put in an airtight bowl until ready to use.

Nutrition: Proteins: 69 g; Fat: 142 g; Carbohydrates: 582 g.

Nut Butter Maple Dip

Preparation Time: 1 hour
Cooking Time: 1 hour
Servings: 3
Ingredients:

- ½ tablespoon ground flaxseed
- 1 teaspoon ground cinnamon
- ½ tablespoon maple syrup
- 2 tablespoons cashew milk
- ¾ cups crunchy, sour peanut butter

Directions:

1. Consider a container. Then, combine the flaxseed, cinnamon, maple syrup, cashew milk and peanut butter.
2. Use a fork to mix everything in. I stir it like I'm scrambling eggs. The mixture should be creamy. If it's too runny, add a little more peanut butter; if it's too thick, add a little more cashew milk.
3. Chill for about an hour, cover and serve.

Nutrition: Proteins: 202 g; Fat: 639 g; Carbohydrates: 357 g.

Oven-Baked Sesame Fries

Preparation Time: 30 minutes
Cooking Time: 30 minutes
Servings: 4
Ingredients:

- one-lbs Yukon Gold potatoes, skins on and sliced into pieces
- 2 tablespoons sesame seeds
- 1 tablespoon potato starch
- 1 tablespoon sesame oil
- Salt to taste
- Black pepper to taste

Directions:

1. Preheat the oven to 425° F. Then, cover a baking sheet or two with parchment paper.
2. Slice the potatoes and put them in a big bowl.
3. Include the sesame seeds, potato starch, sesame oil, salt as well as pepper.
4. Throw with your hands and ensure that all the wedges are covered. Add more sesame seeds or oil if needed.
5. Blowout the potato wedges on the parchment paper with some room among every wedge.
6. Bake for fifteen mins. Flip the wedges over, and return them to the oven for 10 to 15 more minutes until they look golden and crispy.

Nutrition: Proteins: 60 g; Fat: 209 g; Carbohydrates: 602 g.

Pumpkin Orange Spice Hummus

Preparation Time: 30 minutes
Cooking Time: 30 minutes
Servings: 3
Ingredients:

- 1 cup canned, sour pumpkin puree
- 1 16-oz. can garbanzo beans, washed and wearied
- 1 tablespoon apple cider vinegar
- 1 tablespoon maple syrup
- ¼ cup tahini
- 1 tablespoon fresh orange juice
- ½ tsp orange zest and extra zest for relish
- 1/8 teaspoon ground cinnamon
- 1/8 teaspoon ground ginger
- 1/8 teaspoon ground nutmeg
- ¼ teaspoon salt

Directions:

1. Pour the pumpkin puree and garbanzo beans into a food processor and pulse to break up. Add the vinegar, syrup, tahini, orange juice and orange zest; pulse a few times. Add the cinnamon, ginger, nutmeg and salt and process until smooth and creamy. Serve in a bowl sprinkled with more orange zest with wheat crackers alongside.

Nutrition: Proteins: 148 g; Fat: 379 g; Carbohydrates: 635 g.

Quick English Muffin Mexican Pizzas

Preparation Time: 30 minutes
Cooking Time: 15 minutes
Servings: 6
Ingredients:

- 2 whole-wheat English muffins parted
- 1/3 cup tomato salsa
- ¼ cup refried beans
- 1 small jalapeno, seeded and sliced
- ¼ cup onion, sliced
- 2 tbsps. diced plum or cherry tomato
- 1/3 cup vegan cheese shreds

Directions:

1. Preheat the oven to 400° F. Cover a baking sheet with foil. The foil makes the crust crispier.
2. Distinct the English muffin and binge it on some salsa and refried beans.
3. Put a few of the jalapenos and onions on the surface and scatter the cheese generally.
4. Put on the baking sheet and bake for ten to fifteen mins or till brown. You can turn on the broiler for a minute or two to melt the cheese.

Nutrition: Proteins: 92 g; Fat: 146 g; Carbohydrates: 328 g.

Quinoa Trail Mix Cups

Preparation Time: 30 minutes
Cooking Time: 30 minutes
Servings: 16
Ingredients:

- 2 tablespoons ground flaxseed
- 1/3 cup unsweetened soy milk
- 1 cup old-fashioned rolled oats
- 1 cup cooked and cooled quinoa
- ¼ cup brown sugar
- 1 teaspoon ground cinnamon
- ¼ teaspoon salt
- ¼ cup pumpkin or sunflower seeds
- ¼ cup shredded coconut
- ½ cup almonds
- ½ cup raisins or dried cherries

Directions:

1. Stir the flaxseed and milk inside a small container. Set aside for 10 minutes so the seed can absorb the milk.
2. Heat the microwave to 350-degree Fahrenheit. Also, coat a muffin tin with coconut oil.
3. In a big container, combine the oats, quinoa, brown sugar, cinnamon, salt, pumpkin seeds, coconut, almonds as well as raisins.
4. Mix in the flaxseed and milk mix and stir continuously.
5. Put two heaping tsps of the trail mix combination in every muffin cup.
6. Once finished, damp your fingers and press down on every muffin cup to compress the trail mix.
7. Bake for 12 minutes.

8. Cool entirely before eliminating and each little cup will fall out. Store in an airtight container.

Nutrition: Proteins: 108 g; Fat: 330 g; Carbohydrates: 665 g.

Homemade Granola

Preparation Time: 5 minutes
Cooking Time: 1 hour and 15 minutes
Servings: 7
Ingredients:

- 5 cups rolled oats
- 1 cup almonds, slivered
- ¾ cup coconut, shredded
- ¾ tsp salt
- ¼ cup coconut oil
- ½ cup maple syrup

Directions:

1. Preheat oven to 250° F.
2. Mix all ingredients in a large bowl.
3. Bake at 250° F for one hr. and fifteen mins, mixing every twenty to twenty-five mins.
4. Let cool in pans, and serve.

Nutrition: Calories: 240; Fat: 9 g; Carbs: 32 g; Proteins: 14 g; Fiber: 5 g.

Country Breakfast Cereal

Preparation Time: 5 minutes
Cooking Time: 40 minutes
Servings: 6
Ingredients:

- 1 cup brown rice, uncooked
- ½ cup raisins, seedless
- 1 teaspoon cinnamon, ground
- ¼ tablespoon butter
- 2 ¼ cups water
- Honey, to taste
- Nuts, toasted

Directions:

1. Mix rice, butter, raisins, and cinnamon in a pan. Add 2 ¼ cups water. Bring to boil.
2. Simmer enclosed for forty mins until rice is soft.
3. Fluff using fork. Add honey and nuts to taste.

Nutrition: Calories: 210; Fat: 4 g; Carbs: 34 g; Proteins: 9 g; Fiber: 6 g.

Oatmeal Fruit Shake

Preparation Time: 6 minutes
Cooking Time: 0 minutes
Servings: 2
Ingredients:

- 1 cup oatmeal, already prepared, cooled
- 1 apple, cored, roughly chopped
- 1 banana, halved
- 1 cup baby spinach
- 2 cups coconut water
- 2 cups ice, cubed
- ½ tsp ground cinnamon

- 1 teaspoon pure vanilla extract

Directions:
1. Add all ingredients to a blender.
2. Mix low to high for few mins till flat.

Nutrition: Calories: 270; Fat: 2 g; Carbs: 45 g; Proteins: 8 g; Fiber: 5 g.

Amaranth Banana Breakfast Porridge

Preparation Time: 10 minutes
Cooking Time: 25 minutes
Servings: 8
Ingredients:

- 2 cups amaranth
- 2 cinnamon sticks
- 4 bananas, diced
- 2 tablespoons chopped pecans
- 4 cups water

Directions:
1. Mix the amaranth, water, and cinnamon sticks, and banana within a pan.
2. Seal and let it simmer for almost twenty-five mins.
3. Eradicate from high temperature and remove the cinnamon. Place into bowls, and top with pecans.

Nutrition: Calories: 210; Fat: 5 g; Carbs: 38 g; Proteins: 10 g; Fiber: 6 g.

Breakfast Quinoa with Figs and Honey

Preparation Time: 5 minutes
Cooking Time: 15 minutes
Servings: 4
Ingredients:

- 2 cups water
- 1 cup white quinoa
- 1 cup dried figs, sliced
- 1 cup walnuts, chopped
- 1 cup almond milk
- ½ teaspoon cinnamon, ground
- ¼ teaspoon cloves, ground
- Honey to taste

Directions:
1. Rinse quinoa under cool water.
2. Mix it with water, cinnamon, and cloves. Raise to a boil.
3. Simmer covered for 10-15 minutes.
4. Include dried figs, nuts, and milk. Relish with honey.
5. Serve.

Nutrition: Calories: 310; Fat: 12 g; Carbs: 45 g; Proteins: 11 g; Fiber: 10 g.

Maple Walnut Teff Porridge

Preparation Time: 5 minutes
Cooking Time: 20 minutes

Servings: 2
Ingredients:

- 1 ½ cups water
- 1 cup teff, whole grain
- ½ cup coconut milk
- ½ tablespoon cardamom, ground
- ¼ cup walnuts, chopped
- 1 tablespoon sea salt
- 1 tablespoon maple syrup

Directions:
1. Mix the water and coconut oil in a moderate pan. Bring to boil, then stir in the teff.
2. Include the cardamom, and simmer exposed for fifteen-twenty mins.
3. Include in the maple syrup and walnuts. Serve.

Nutrition: Calories: 310; Fat: 12 g; Carbs: 22 g; Proteins: 10 g; Fiber: 8 g.

PB & J Overnight Oatmeal

Preparation Time: 25 minutes + 6 hours
Cooking Time: 20 minutes
Servings: 4
Ingredients:

- 1½ cups blueberries, frozen
- 4 tablespoons chia seeds, divided
- 2 cups rolled oats
- 3 cups almond milk
- 4 pitted dates
- 2 tablespoons peanut butter

Directions:
1. Oven the blueberries in one tbsp water for two-three mins.
2. Mix in two tbsp chia seed to the blueberries. Refrigerate for 20 minutes.
3. Put half cup oats and half tbsp chia seeds into four jars.
4. Mix milk, dates, and peanut butter. Put it into the jars.
5. Include blueberry chia jam to the jars. Chill for six-eight hrs.

Nutrition: Calories: 290; Fat: 10 g; Carbs: 35 g; Proteins: 13 g; Fiber: 10 g.

Southwest Tofu Scramble

Preparation Time: 10 minutes
Cooking Time: 15 minutes
Servings: 6
Ingredients:

- 1 package firm tofu, crumbled
- 1-2 teaspoons ground cumin
- ½ cups nutritional yeast
- 2 teaspoons tamari
- 2 teaspoons extra-virgin olive oil

- 1 zucchini, diced
- 1 bell pepper, diced
- 1 onion, diced

Directions:

1. Mix the first four ingredients with a fork.

2. In a heavy skillet, combine the zucchini, pepper, shallot, and olive oil. Sauté for 5 minutes.

3. Mix in tofu and cook for further ten mins. Serve.

Nutrition: Calories: 190; Fat: 8 g; Carbs: 15 g; Proteins: 12 g; Fiber: 8 g.

CHAPTER 26:

MEASUREMENT CONVERSION TABLE

VOLUME EQUIVALENTS(DRY)

US STANDARD	METRIC (APPROXIMATE)
1/8 teaspoon	0.5 mL
1/4 teaspoon	1 mL
1/2 teaspoon	2 mL
3/4 teaspoon	4 mL
1 teaspoon	5 mL
1 tablespoon	15 mL
1/4 cup	59 mL
1/2 cup	118 mL
3/4 cup	177 mL
1 cup	235 mL
2 cups	475 mL
3 cups	700 mL
4 cups	1 L

VOLUME EQUIVALENTS(LIQUID)

US STANDARD	US STANDARD (OUNCES)	METRIC (APPROXIMATE)
2 tablespoons	1 fl.oz.	30 mL
1/4 cup	2 fl.oz.	60 mL
1/2 cup	4 fl.oz.	120 mL
1 cup	8 fl.oz.	240 mL
1 1/2 cup	12 fl.oz.	355 mL
2 cups or 1 pint	16 fl.oz.	475 mL
4 cups or 1 quart	32 fl.oz.	1 L
1 gallon	128 fl.oz.	4 L

TEMPERATURES EQUIVALENTS

FAHRENHEIT(F)	CELSIUS(C) (APPROXIMATE)
225 °F	107 °C
250 °F	120 °C
275 °F	135 °C
300 °F	150 °C
325 °F	160 °C
350 °F	180 °C
375 °F	190 °C
400 °F	205 °C
425 °F	220 °C
450 °F	235 °C
475 °F	245 °C
500 °F	260 °C

WEIGHT EQUIVALENTS

US STANDARD	METRIC (APPROXIMATE)
1 ounce	28 g
2 ounces	57 g
5 ounces	142 g
10 ounces	284 g
15 ounces	425 g
16 ounces (1 pound)	455 g
1.5 pounds	680 g
2 pounds	907 g

CHAPTER 27: 30-Day Meal Plan

Days	Breakfast	Lunch	Snacks	Dinner
1	Berry Cobbler	Mango Chutney Wraps	Strawberry Watermelon Ice Pops	Spicy Homemade Tortilla Chips
2	Cauliflower Oatmeal	Mediterranean Chickpeas with Vegetables	Zucchini Chips	Grilled Eggplant Roll - Ups
3	Pumpkin Oatmeal	Broccoli and Rice Stir Fry	Roasted Chickpeas	Stuffed Artichokes
4	Quinoa and Rice Stuffed Peppers (Oven-Baked)	Quinoa Crunch Salad	Almond, Date Energy Bites	Tomato and Basil Bruschetta
5	Banana Malt Bread	Eggplant Parmesan	Sweet Potato Bites	Sprout Wraps
6	Buckwheat Crepes	Miso Noodle Soup	Buffalo Cauliflower Dip	Grilled Eggplant Steaks
7	Protein Bars	Cauliflower Carrot Soup	Sweet 'N' Spicy Crunchy Snack Mix	Brown Rice with Vegetables and Tofu
8	Corn Muffins	Chickpea Tagine with Pickled Raisins	Nuts and Seeds Squares	Spinach and Mushroom Soup
9	Hummus Carrot Sandwich	Black Beans with Crumbled Tofu	Tamari Almonds	Country Cornbread with Spinach
10	Avocado Miso Chickpeas Toast	Black Bean and Corn Salad with Cilantro Dressing	Italian Tomato Snack	Cauliflower Rice Tabbouleh
11	Berry Compote Pancakes	Mango Coconut Cream Pie	Eggplant Sticks	Corn and Okra Casserole
12	Chickpeas with Harissa	Tomato Gazpacho	Cauliflower Spinach Rice	Easy Millet Nuggets
13	Eggplant Sandwich	Pasta Pomodoro with Olives and White Beans	Pineapple, Peach, and Mango Salsa	Dijon Maple Burgers
14	Corn with Tofu	Three-Bean Cassoulet	Banana Bulgur Bars	Sweet Coconut Pilaf
15	Zucchini Oatmeal	Coconut Curry Lentils	Seed Bars	Cauliflower Steaks

16	Hemp Breakfast Cookies	Mediterranean Chickpea Casserole	Chocolate Almond Bars	Ratatouille
17	Chocolate Zucchini Bread	Beluga Lentils with Lacinato Kale	Strawberry Avocado Toast	Grilled Eggplant Steaks
18	Corn Griddle Cakes with Tofu Mayonnaise	Veggie Hummus Tortillas	Carrot Energy Balls	Tofu Poke
19	Banana Vegan Bread	Black-Eyed Peas with Spinach	Basil, Zucchini Noodles	Black Bean Burgers
20	Almond Plum Oats Overnight	Black Bean and Pepper Tacos	Sweet Potato Hummus	Lima Bean Casserole
21	High Protein Toast	Coconut Tofu Curry	Spinach-Artichoke Dip	Baked Potatoes & Asparagus & Pine Nuts
22	French Toast	Broccoli Salad	Spicy Nuts and Seeds Snack Mix	Adzuki Beans and Vegetable Bowl
23	Chickpeas Spread Sourdough Toast	Greek Salad Skewers	Eggplant Caponata Bruschetta	Savory Sweet Potatoes
24	Overnight Oats	Fast Navy Beans and Rice Bowls	Creamy Southwestern Salsa Bean Dip	Stuffed Artichokes
25	Quinoa Black Beans Breakfast Salad	Cannellini Bean Soup with Kale	Rosemary and Lemon Zest Popcorn	Vegetable Tacos
26	Broccoli Oatmeal	Black Beans with Lime	Hummus	Avocado Chickpea Lettuce Cups
27	Southwest Breakfast Bowl	Avocado-Potato Salad	Chocolate Protein Bites	Fried Pineapple Rice
28	Savory Breakfast Salad	Vegetarian Curry	White Bean Tzatziki Dip	Barbecue Northern Bean Bake
29	Peanut Butter Muffins	Nettle Soup with Rice	Rosemary – Onion Jam	Chickpeas with Lemon and Spinach
30	Healthy Cereal Bars	Lettuce Bean Burritos	Spiced and Herbs Nuts	Black Bean Taquitos

CONCLUSION

A plant-based diet typically includes fewer animal products than an omnivorous diet. This means you'll consume more plants than animal-based foods (i.e., meats). This helps reduce the risk of diseases caused by meat consumption and promotes a more environmentally sustainable way of eating.

Plant-based diets also typically exclude foods that come from animals, such as eggs, dairy products and honey and it is a popular nutritional choice among many famous individuals.

The most common reason people adopt vegetarian diets is due to ethical or religious reasons. A plant-based diet is sometimes seen as a more ethical choice as it doesn't involve killing animals. It's important to exercise caution and not to make the mistake of blindly following what you think is good advice.

Depending on your health condition or your general energy level, consuming foods high in carbohydrates and fats may not be favorable for your health. Therefore, it's important to adjust your eating habits accordingly.

Whether you're a vegetarian, vegan, or just exploring the world of plant-based cooking for the first time, we hope this selection of plant-based cookbooks has helped you find a few new favorite recipes.

RECIPE INDEX

Manufactured by Amazon.ca
Bolton, ON